Our Sisters' Keepers

STUDIES IN AMERICAN LITERARY REALISM AND NATURALISM

Our Sisters' Keepers

Nineteenth-Century Benevolence Literature by American Women

Edited by

Jill Bergman and Debra Bernardi

The University of Alabama Press
Tuscaloosa

The University of Alabama Press
Tuscaloosa, Alabama 35487-0380

Manufactured in the United States of America

Typeface: Minion

∞

The paper on which this book is printed meets the minimum requirements of American National Standard for Information Sciences—Permanence of Paper for Printed Library Materials, ANSI Z39.48-1984.

Library of Congress Cataloging-in-Publication Data

Our sisters' keepers : nineteenth-century benevolence literature by American women / edited by Jill Bergman and Debra Bernardi.
p. cm. — (Studies in American literary realism and naturalism)
Includes bibliographical references and index.
ISBN 0-8173-1467-9 (cloth : alk. paper) — ISBN 0-8173-5193-0 (pbk. : alk. paper)
1. American literature—19th century—History and criticism. 2. Benevolence in literature. 3. Literature and society—United States—History—19th century. 4. Women and literature—United States—History—19th century. 5. American literature—Women authors—History and criticism. 6. Charity in literature. 7. Poverty in literature. 8. Poor in literature.
I. Bergman, Jill, 1963- II. Bernardi, Debra, 1954- III. Series.
PS169.B54O94 2005
810.9'3556—dc22

2004029736

"I am my sister's keeper!" should be the hearty response of every man and woman of the race.

—Anna Julia Cooper
Voice from the South

Contents

Preface

While this book deals with connections between nineteenth-century women, the idea of this project derived from a connection established between two twenty-first-century women. Finding ourselves in Montana after completing our respective Midwest graduate school experiences, we stumbled upon each other by accident and discovered, to our amazement, that we were "scholarly sisters": with similar training, similar interests, and similar attitudes toward our field of nineteenth-century American women writers.

The result of this discovery was a panel on "Theories of Poverty Relief by Late-Nineteenth-Century Fiction Writers," which we organized for a conference held by the Society for the Study of American Women Writers (SSAWW), in San Antonio in February 2001. Two of our contributors, Karen Tracey and Monika Elbert, were also on that panel, and the idea for this book was born. The collaboration process has been somewhat surprising and highly enjoyable. We found our different strengths complemented each other's, and while most of our writing has been done separately, drafting and redrafting each other's prose, on occasion we wrote side by side at one computer, grappling for the right words.

In addition, then, to each other, there are a number of people whom we would like to acknowledge who have helped this project come to fruition. We would like to mention our early mentors who inspired our approaches to nineteenth-century women writers: for Jill, Nina Baym; for Debra, Dale Bauer and Jeffrey Steele. We would also like to thank the various people who encouraged us on this particular project, and who graciously answered our emails when we needed advice along the way: these include Sharon Harris, Nellie McKay, Frances Foster, Rochelle Johnson, Karen Offen, Lisa Long, and members of the SSAWW listserv. Our work in general owes a great deal to SSAWW, not just because it sponsored that first conference, but because it is an organization that continues to foster inspiring connections between scholars of women's writing across variances of region, institution, rank, and status. Indeed, a good portion of the contributors in this volume are active members of SSAWW. Our thanks also to the staff and readers of The University of Alabama Press for their fine suggestions.

We would also like to extend our gratitude to those who supported us on a daily basis at home in Montana. Jill would like especially to mention her colleagues in English and Women's Studies who have encouraged her in this project. Debra would like to thank John Thomas, reference librarian at the Corette Library at Carroll College, whose help finding materials through interlibrary loan was crucial to her research. She would also like to acknowledge the members of her writing group, Lauri Fahlberg, Charlotte Jones, Annette Moran, and Rebecca Stanfel, who encouraged this work from its inception and are always ready with good advice for finding time to write as well as time to relax.

Finally, we would also like to thank our family and friends for their support of this project and, more important, their support of us. Jill would like to thank Brady and Emma for their love, encouragement, and humor. Debra would like to thank Jerry Foley, for encouraging her to work when all she wanted to do was talk about relationships. And thanks to her parents, Norma Bernardi and Remo Bernardi, and her friends Nancy Meyers, Rocco Marinaccio, and Kay Satre, for always affirming her work and life.

Our Sisters' Keepers

Introduction

Benevolence Literature by American Women

Debra Bernardi and Jill Bergman

This collection of essays examines the ways American women thought and wrote about their role in poverty relief throughout the nineteenth century. Bringing together essays on topics that range from the seamstress figure of the 1830s to the immigrants involved with Jane Addams's Hull-House, this volume explores women writers' theories of benevolence and their consistent engagement with helping the poor. Taken as a group these texts investigate similar themes and tensions, emerging as a genre we call benevolence literature.

In this study, we have found that the writers of benevolence literature have done nothing less than re-envision the American individual. In the face of an ethos of individualism and self-reliance, nineteenth-century women writers saw the value of and need for connection with others. Hence, they imagined the self as a dynamic entity that seeks a balance between selfish and selfless pursuits, between concerns with the individual self and with the self that is created in relation to another. When we account for women's writings on benevolence, the entire concept of the nineteenth-century American individual becomes a complex negotiation between the responsibilities toward oneself and toward others.

The Mixed Legacy of Poverty Relief in the United States

American culture has long had a conflicted relationship with helping the poor. On the one hand, influenced by England's relief policy, the nation from its inception acknowledged the social needs of the impoverished. As Robert Bremner notes in his often-quoted history, *American Philanthropy*, "almost every effort at colonization had, or claimed to have, a philanthropic motivation: there were natives to be converted to Christianity, poor men to be provided with land and work, and a wilderness to be supplied with the institutions of civilization. It is not too much to say that many Europeans regarded the American continent mainly as a vastly expanded field for the exercise of benevolence" (7). John Winthrop's "A Model of Christian Charity" (1630) discusses the benevolent nature of the colonial experiment. According to Winthrop, the Puritans were attempting to establish God's "City upon a Hill," nurturing "Bond[s] of brotherly affection" (108). He writes specifically about the duties of helping the poor: "There is a tyme when a christian must sell all and give to the poore as they did in Apostles times. There is a tyme when a christian (though they give not all yet) must give beyond theire ability. . . . Lastly when there is noe other meanes whereby our Christian brother may be relieved in his distresse, wee must help him beyond our ability" (110).

Winthrop's philanthropic ideas persisted. For instance, eighty years later, Cotton Mather reminded colonists of the importance of benevolence. In *Bonifacius, An Essay upon the Good* (1710), he urges "*neighbors*" to "stand *related unto* one another" (125). In Mather's words, "the *poor* people that lie *wounded*, must have *wine* and *oil* poured into their *wounds*" (125). Mather encourages an active philanthropy: "Sirs, would it be too much for you, at least *once a week*, to think, 'What neighbor is reduced into a pinching and painful poverty?' . . . First, you will *pity* them. . . . But this is not all. . . . You may do well to *visit them*. . . . And lastly[, g]ive them all *assistances* that may answer their *occasions:* assist them with *advice;* assist them with *address* to others for them. And if it be needful, bestow your Alms upon them" (126). Mather's words serve as a precursor to the humanitarian impulse of the Great Awakening, which fostered humane attitudes and popularized philanthropy during the third and fourth decades of the eighteenth century (Bremner 20–21). And as Walter Trattner notes in his history of social welfare in the United States, *From Poor Law to Welfare State,* the Declaration of Independence, with its emphasis on reason and human equality, naturally drew attention to the need to improve the common person's lot (41).

However, in the face of this discourse of benevolence, American culture was highly conflicted about the place of the poor in society. Even Winthrop, for all his talk about the need to help the unfortunate, acknowledged that there was a natural, divinely ordained hierarchy, which kept the rich and the poor separate. "In all times," Winthrop wrote, "some must be rich some poore, some highe and eminent in power and dignitie; others meane and in subjection. . . . All men being thus (by divine providence) rancked into two sortes, riche and poore" (108). Winthrop might recommend benevolence, but embedded in his thinking is the idea that those at the bottom of society are somehow meant to be inferior and thereby live their appropriate role in life.

From the beginnings of the republic, colonists held a certain suspicion of the poor and desired to distinguish between those who deserved aid and those who did not. In some cases, deserving was simply a matter of membership in the community. In his study on *The Discovery of the Asylum,* David Rothman shows how colonists attempted to define the worthy poor. In New York in 1683, "An Act for . . . Maintaining the Poor and Preventing Vagabonds" articulated the need to help the indigent resident but not the dependent outsider (20). Trattner similarly notes that the establishment of residency requirements for public assistance began in the Plymouth Colony (21). But worthiness could also be defined in terms of one's character or perceived morality. While Mather encouraged aid to the poor, he was concerned that some did not deserve aid. In a popular 1698 sermon he expressed fears that benevolence could increase idleness among the undeserving poor (Bremner 15). Mather wrote, "For those who indulge themselves in idleness, the express command of God unto us is that we should let them starve" (qtd. in Trattner 23). And, as Karen Tracey points out in this volume, charity often held "contradictory goals: to provide charity to the needy, yet to deter needy people from asking for charity" (Tracey 26).

Whether "worthy" or not, the number of people needing assistance steadily increased, and by the nineteenth century the need to address social responsibilities toward poverty was pressing. Michael Katz gives a history of poverty and poverty relief in his study, *In the Shadow of the Poorhouse: A Social History of Welfare in America.* He notes that "in the early decades of the nineteenth-century, state and local officials everywhere claimed pauperism was rising at an alarming rate" (16). Among the reasons Katz supplies for this growth of poverty in the century is the reorganization of work around a wage labor system where people worked for others in mainly industrial jobs that were frequently poor paying, unsteady, unhealthy, and seasonal (4–10). And in *City of Women,* Christine Stansell has pointed out that "wealth from investments in trade and manufacturing ventures supported the emergence of an urban bourgeoisie; the expansion of capitalist labor arrangements brought into being a class of largely impoverished wageworkers" (xi). Further, she explains that while in the eighteenth century poverty tended to be seen as a result of one's inability to work—and was thus associated with the very old, the very young, or the disabled—by the nineteenth century poverty often occurred in tandem with work, resulting now from poor wages and a lack of available employment (4–5).

Like most moments of social significance, nineteenth-century industrialization and its accompanying urbanization, poverty, and crime inspired an outpouring of literary response. Whitney Womack notes in her study here that, during the nineteenth century, British literature grappled with issues of poverty in the industrial reform novel, thriving in Great Britain from the 1830s on. To quote Womack: "British industrial reform novels . . . sought to give a human face to the suffering of industrial workers and expose the injustices of industrial capitalism and laissez-faire policies" (107). On the other side of the Atlantic, too, literary minds in the United States turned to issues of benevolence, although their approach differed from that of the British in many cases. As Bremner notes, there is something about philanthropy that seems to go against the democratic grain (2). Influenced, perhaps, by images of that exemplary American, Ben Franklin, walking down the streets of Philadelphia with a roll under each arm, and by Spencerian notions of "survival of the fittest," Americans early developed their love affair with independence and the "self-made man." Earlier beliefs that poverty came to those who deserved it and therefore charity encouraged idleness and improvidence continued to inform theories of benevolence in the nineteenth century, and the best-known American renaissance writers frequently used the American democratic ideals of individualism and self-reliance to attack the concept of benevolence. In a famous passage in "Self-Reliance" (1841), Ralph Waldo Emerson sums up his suspicion of aid to the poor, suggesting that benevolence undermines the individualism, the very "manhood," of the giver:

> Then again, do not tell me, as a good man did to-day, of my obligation to put all poor men in good situations. Are they *my* poor? I tell thee, thou foolish philanthropist, that I grudge the dollar, the dime, the cent I give to such men as do not belong to me and to whom I do not belong. . . . your miscellaneous popular charities; the education at college of fools; the building of meeting-houses to the vain end to which many now stand; alms to sots, and the thousand-fold Relief Societies;—though I confess with shame that I sometimes succumb and give the dollar, it is a wicked dollar, which by and by I shall have the manhood to withhold. (152)

As Monika Elbert notes in her essay printed in this volume, Emerson goes on to say in his essay "Gifts" that giving does not just undermine the "manhood" of the giver, but of the receiver as well, whose independence is "invaded" when others give to him (*sic*).

Henry David Thoreau similarly sees the poor as well able to care for themselves. He claims in *Walden* (1854) that the poor are poor only because they refuse to live simply. Confronted with the poor family at Baker Farm, he asserts that their poverty is due to their desires for tea, coffee, butter, milk, and fresh meat (all of which Thoreau does without). According to Thoreau, if the family would only keep their life simpler, not only would they have their needs met, but they also would have to work little and could enjoy life more. "If he and his family would live simply," Thoreau writes, "they might all go a-huckleberrying in the summer" (134).

So skeptical were American romance writers of philanthropic endeavors that Nathaniel Hawthorne uses *The Blithedale Romance* (1852) to mock a philanthropist in the character of Hollingsworth, whose obsession with philanthropy (in his case, benevolence toward needy criminals in particular) keeps him from genuine kindness toward other individuals. As Hawthorne's narrator, Coverdale, acknowledges, Hollingsworth "had a closer friend than ever you could be. And this friend was the cold, spectral monster which he had himself conjured up, and on which he was wasting all the warmth of his heart. . . . It was his philanthropic theory" (55). Further, in the case of philanthropists like Hollingsworth, Coverdale fears that "godlike benevolence has been debased into all-devouring egotism" (71). There is some question of the reliability of Hawthorne's narrator—and therefore, perhaps, of his perceptions of Hollingsworth. But Hawthorne's philanthropist is decidedly problematic, befriending only those who will support his plans, egotistically denying that there might be any other way than his to aid those in need, generally using people for what they do for his benevolent designs. As the character Zenobia charges, he is "nothing but self, self, self" (218), the philanthropist ironically more selfish than any other characters in the tale. Hawthorne may not object to all practices of benevolence, but much of this romance acts as a cautionary tale against philanthropists.[1] Similarly, as Susan Ryan has shown in her essay "Misgivings," Herman Melville, too, expressed suspicion of benevolence in much of his writing, focusing on the possibilities for deception and invoking the distinction between the worthy and unworthy poor.

Given the suspicion of charity shared by many male American writers, how did women writers address issues of poverty relief? This is just the question that *Our Sisters' Keepers* addresses. The essays printed here reveal that nineteenth-century women writers approached issues of benevolence differently from many of their male counterparts: women writers repeatedly understand the need for community members to help the impoverished, and promote such action in their writing.

Women's Relation to Benevolence

That women's writing attested to the importance of helping others (as we shall see) should come as no surprise given women's practical response to the need for poverty relief in nineteenth-century America. The first female benevolent societies began to appear in the 1790s (Scott 11), and women continued to be involved in philanthropy throughout the century. Like their philanthropic ancestors, these female charitable societies sought to identify the deserving poor in order to ensure that their aid was used wisely. As Mary Bosworth Treudley states, most female societies limited aid to women of "fair character" (138). Relief was only given after a visit in the home and then usually only in the form of necessities.

Women's attention to the poor grew, in part, out of their understanding of their role as women. In her influential study *Women and the Work of Benevolence,* Lori Ginzberg traces the way benevolent work naturally sprung from nineteenth-century ideologies of womanhood, which gave women moral responsibilities in American society. As Ginzberg puts it, "With the advent of voluntary associations in the late eighteenth century and, especially, of the Second Great Awakening in the 1820s, writers demanded with increasing conviction that women assume a unique responsibility to disseminate Christian virtues and counter the materialism and greed of the nineteenth-century male" (14). Women's assumed moral superiority positioned them as the "natural" practitioners of benevolence, particularly since antebellum poverty relief was often connected to religious practice (Sáez 164) and went hand-in-hand with inculcating morality (Ginzberg 1–2). A natural extension of the influence attributed to women under the sentimental values of nineteenth-century womanhood, moral superiority gave women not only the justification but also the responsibility to help those in need. Since, as Ginzberg has argued, morality became conflated with femininity, women's sense of themselves as women was inextricable from their responsibility and ability to help others.

Even in the latter half of the nineteenth century, as philanthropy's focus became less religious and more secular (or, as Gregory Eiselein has argued, philanthropy turned from "moral suasion" to discipline and control), charity work was often articulated in terms of women's role as the nation's "civic stewards." Kathleen McCarthy, in her study on philanthropy in Chicago, *Noblesse Oblige,* notes that women had a "civilizing" mission in the home that was later projected onto the "larger society" (17). According to McCarthy, women were understood to be fit for benevolent work "not by formal training, but by the instinctive, biological prerogatives of motherhood" (17).

Implicit in and crucial to this idea was the tendency to define women relationally. This construction prompted women to think not in terms of self actualization or individualism as a primary goal—as the Transcendentalists touted—but in terms of connection to and responsibility for others. Anne Firor Scott has speculated that as outsiders to the nation's economic growth, women may have had greater awareness of the effects of this growth under the urban-industrial revolution. "Socialized to believe in their own compassionate instincts, living as close as they often did to the daily requirements of child raising and household management, they seem to have been more likely to empathize with people whose lives were a struggle against heavy odds" (4). Scott emphasizes the relational thinking of women who perceive their similarity to those in need. Likewise, women writers might have been more sensitive to the vulnerability of poverty precisely because of their vulnerable social positions as women. With property laws placing most economic control in the hands of the husband and father, women's financial well-being rested almost entirely on their husbands' or fathers' financial prowess. A woman in need due to her husband's gambling debts or business failure may have struck middle-class women as a very real possibility for themselves and prompted their sympathetic responses.

Nevertheless, in what may have appeared to the romantics as paradoxical, these relationally oriented women also sought self-improvement and education, and found benevolent organizations a fruitful site for such personal development. Benevolent activity and organizing gave women the opportunity to function in the public sphere while upholding the expectations of nineteenth-century womanhood. Because the goal of benevolence comported with traditionally feminine traits—nurturance, motherhood, and care—charitable work, as well as writing about issues of charity, registered as acceptable for women. Indeed, benevolent activity was one of the few professions available to women, not only allowing them to work but also granting them a voice in the public sphere. On a practical level, as Scott has pointed out, women who organized for the purposes of charitable work "learned how to conduct business, carry on meetings, speak in public, manage money" (2). Writing on the antebellum era, Susan Ryan notes that "benevolence offered [women] a means of participating in civic life without challenging the era's strictures against their more overt involvement in the political sphere (by voting, holding office, or speaking in public to mixed audiences)" (*Grammar* 7). And McCarthy notes that reformers "managed to excel in a variety of enterprises beyond their allotted domestic sphere. . . .

[These women] found enhanced mobility, a suitable arena in which to test their executive capabilities, an outlet for their religious zeal, and a healthy share of public approbation" (21, 24). Robyn Muncy similarly maintains that those who aided the poor professionally, such as social workers, were "freer in their attempts to reconcile professional ideals with values from female culture, which produced uniquely female ways of being professional" (xiv). Even for the nonprofessional, the domestic and moral nature of charity work allowed women to exercise a pronounced influence over the public sphere largely because the work was associated with the private sphere. In his study on Jane Addams, included here, James Salazar argues that women's interest in a "social ethic" is a product of the restrictive gender roles women writers must negotiate; in benevolent work, women can step out of their assigned roles and have "contact with the moral experiences of the many" (qtd. in Salazar 266). However, as Jill Conway notes, while benevolent activists such as Jane Addams wielded national power and influence, this did not change the prevailing perception that philanthropic women were acting as part of their traditional domestic, moral roles (166). In other words, the ideals dictated by an otherwise limiting domestic ideology gave women their ticket to work in the broader public sphere.

As the essays in this collection demonstrate, the possibilities afforded to women through the work of benevolence were also available to women who wrote about benevolence. Certainly, in their capacity as writers, the women discussed in these essays could take a public position on the political issue of poverty while retaining their femininity. Their writing about and involvement in benevolent activity, then, enabled them to uphold ideologies of womanhood that called them to think and behave relationally while simultaneously pursuing self-actualization through their work (Scott 2). The common thread running through all of these essays: In the face of the individualist rhetoric of their period, these writers sought to establish an individualism that could still care for others. This feminine self looked out for others, but the writers addressed here underscored the struggles in this process, including their need to maintain their individuality. Our title suggests this tension: to be our "sisters' keepers" is to be connected to the needy (as "sisters") and to be separate from and somewhat superior to them (powerful over them as "keepers"). In considering what it means to be "our sisters' (and, in a few cases, our brothers') keepers," nineteenth-century women writers broke from the ideas of individualism touted by the romantic literary elite, who saw little need for philanthropy in a society where "men" (*sic*) could and should take care of themselves. Instead, women writers defined the American individual as a complex negotiation between selfish and selfless interests.

But the significance of benevolence literature by women is more than this. The process of negotiating between the self-reliant and the selfless citizen frequently resulted in struggle. The need to help the poor competed with the need for women to maintain their individuality on multiple fronts. Our contributors reveal that as women writers explored aiding the poor, their struggles to maintain individuality manifested over such issues as privacy, class boundaries, gender, age, and sexuality. Wanting to help the needy—as James Salazar puts it, to see the world in terms of the implied subject "we"—does not negate the needs of the implied subject "I." It is this constant tension between "I" and "we" that becomes apparent in benevolence literature by women.

The Genre of Benevolence Literature

We believe that the texts discussed below gain in significance when brought together as a genre. As Lisa Long puts it in her discussion of reform literature, "While individually [the various texts under consideration here] have failed to compel significant critical attention, the intertextual conversation . . . carried on reveals a more complicated notion of reform fiction than is allowed under current understandings of the genre" (262). We also believe that it is the intertextual conversation carried out by benevolence literature (also part of the genre of reform literature that Long describes) that highlights the significance of the genre. When apprehended together, the various examples of benevolence literature written by women demonstrate that nineteenth-century American women were engaged with redefining the very notion of American identity.

Relatively little work has been done in treating this body of benevolence texts as a genre. In fact, in our research for this volume, we have been surprised at literary scholarship's relative silence on American women's benevolent work, given the attention to the subject by historians such as Lori Ginzberg, Anne Firor Scott, Christine Stansell, Robyn Muncy—already cited here—and others. In literary scholarship, the study of benevolence has received relatively little notice. Susan Ryan points out that benevolence "has been subsumed (and obscured) within the more familiar category of sentimentalism" (*Grammar* 5), and surely this is true of the intersection between benevolence and gender. The literary studies on benevolence that do exist focus on issues other than gender. A 1997 special issue of *American Transcendental Quarterly* on the "Discourse of Philanthropy in Nineteenth-Century America" brings together essays on Elizabeth Stuart Phelps, Jacob Riis, Nathaniel Hawthorne, and Gerrit Smith that look at the power dynamics of benevolence and that focus especially on class. Gregory Eiselein's 1996 study—*Literature and Humanitarian Reform in the Civil War Era*—has been highly informative for our thinking. Keith Gandal's *The Virtues of the Vicious* (1997) looks specifically at the representation of the slums in the work of Jacob Riis and Stephen Crane, a choice of authors he explains, intriguingly, by the "masculine nature of the turn-of-the-century interest in the slums" (7). And Susan Ryan's recent book, *The Grammar of Good Intentions,* examines rhetorics of benevolence as a means of defining categories of race. While these book-length studies include analyses of the work of several women writers, none of them foregrounds an investigation of the role of gender in benevolence literature.

Two important essays—by Deborah Carlin and Lisa A. Long—study benevolence literature through the lens of gender. As part of a collection of essays on "the (other) American traditions," Deborah Carlin's article, "'What Methods Have Brought Blessing': Discourses of Reform in Philanthropic Literature," identifies a tradition that she calls "a literature of philanthropy," written by women of the late nineteenth century. Narrowed to literature that focuses primarily on "largely cosmetic" reforms (210), this genre "stresses good will, generosity, and monetary contributions as the agencies of social welfare, rather than advocating any specific social plan of improvement, restoration, radicalization, or transformation of existing economic apportionments as the foundation of more far-reaching reforms" (204). Women's philanthropic literature, as Carlin conceives it, emphasizes the powerlessness of women defined by their domestic capacities. Carlin discovers that, in this literature, charitable action becomes a means of rescue for the middle-class heroine from a life restricted by gender constraints. More, she discovers that while the novels claim to set out to "institute reforms," they end up offering no solutions.

Like Carlin's, Long's essay is part of a collection that seeks to categorize nineteenth-century women's writings.[2] Her essay, "The Postbellum Reform Writings of Rebecca Harding Davis and Elizabeth Stuart Phelps," describes the general critical neglect of these two writers, attributing it to established generic categories into which their work does not easily fit. Where Carlin drew the parameters of the genre narrowly, Long's conception of reform fiction is broad: reform in her configuration is a trope that functions symbolically to facilitate the search for—the re-forming of—the self. As she puts it, "reform writers were compelled by explorations of subjectivity, a recognition of the inherently fragmented nature of human existence, and the insufficiency of traditional belief systems" (277). For Long, reform literature sought to theorize the individual. In contrast to the tendency to see women writers as thinking communally and proposing community-oriented solutions to problems, she argues that "reform is not a communal project . . . but an individual journey" (269).

We locate our conception of benevolence somewhere between Carlin's narrowly conceived definition and Long's broadly defined genre. As they describe the boundaries of reform literature, both Carlin and Long gesture toward what we propose here: in thinking and writing about their relationships with and responsibilities to others, American women contemplated their place in the nation and the role of the self in the national narrative. As both critics suggest, women writers of benevolence literature were struggling with defining an individual self. But, as the essays in this volume reveal, the individual, while marked by issues of class, race, gender, and age, was also located in relationship to others, and specifically in relationship to the poor.

Of course, women's place in the national narrative raises the question of identity. Who were these writers and how did they think of themselves? How did their identity inform their approach to questions of selfhood, relationality, and individualism? Of the writers taken up here—such well-known writers as Catharine Sedgwick, Rebecca Harding Davis, Elizabeth Stuart Phelps, Harriet Prescott Spofford, Mary Wilkins Freeman, Sarah Orne Jewett, Frances E. W. Harper, and Jane

Addams, along with authors less well known such as Sue M. D. Fry, Mrs. M. J. Herbert, Mrs. H. M. Field, Lizzie Lynn, and Hannah Lee—the majority are white and middle class. And as we seek to define the genre of "benevolence literature," this fact seems telling. Class issues have been of great interest to scholars working on some of the writers under consideration here. For example, some scholars have observed that philanthropic texts penned by middle-class white writers seek to pass on the values of mainstream, middle-class white Protestant culture to the poorer classes.[3] Carlin, in her article on philanthropic literature, argues that in these texts, "much emphasis was placed on how middle-class women could transport their 'civilizing' notions of domesticity into the unacculturated and, significantly, largely immigrant, slums" (210). Other scholars have noted that by teaching the values of the dominant culture, writers of benevolence literature reinscribe that culture's dominance, thus defining and fixing the other of the poorer class, and thereby solidifying their own middle-class identity. These scholars have focused on this phenomenon in their treatment of the surveillance and social control enacted through literature about the working classes.[4]

Such critical approaches focus primarily on the individuality of the writers—their tendency to see charitable labor as self-defining and self-serving, much as Hawthorne had seen Hollingsworth. And certainly this is a valid and important aspect of these texts. However, as we examine the ways women writers grapple with tension between relationality and individualism, and the complexity of analysis in the essays collected here, we are struck by what Carlin has referred to as the dual nature of what we are calling benevolence literature. As she argues, "women's philanthropic novels embody progressivism and conservatism simultaneously" (205). Indeed, what comes through in reading these chapters together is the sense that the nineteenth-century writers struggled to define the benevolent self. Sometimes anxious about their class position and the effect of raising up the poor to their own class status, these women writers also register distinct emotional engagement with their stories and with the recipients of charity or other benevolent attention. Several of the chapters here focus on the ways writers have found to build community and to celebrate relationality without finding in that connection a threat to self.

This complexity does not only occur in work by middle-class white women, although they are certainly the majority in this collection and in the writing population of the nineteenth century. And indeed, the topic of benevolence was especially important to white middle-class women, many of whom found the intersection of public work with domestic values to offer meaning and empowerment in their otherwise curtailed range of influence and activity (as described above). For the most part, African American women seem not to have written explicitly on issues of poverty relief; often using their writing to debunk prevalent stereotypes, they typically downplayed poverty in favor of portraying successful members of the black middle class. However, African American women, in small numbers also wrote in this genre, as Terry Novak's essay on Frances Harper demonstrates. The anonymous author of the story "Stray Leaves" (taken up in Lori Merish's essay) writes from the perspective of a working-class woman rather than the usual middle-class position, and may have been working class herself. With these examples, we find marginalized women writing within the genre of benevolence literature, appropriating the thematic content familiar to contemporary readers, and using it to negotiate their own identity and relationship to the nation in which they find themselves marginalized.

The essays in *Our Sisters' Keepers* explore variously the ways women negotiate a benevolent self. In the first part, "The Genre of Benevolence," we begin with four essays, each of which introduces a series of stories concerned with a specific aspect of poverty and charitable effort. Karen Tracey focuses her chapter on a group of "Stories of the Poorhouse," the poorhouse being a prominent image of poverty in nineteenth-century America. She identifies the almshouse as an apt vehicle for negotiating between what she terms the panoptic gaze and the sentimental gaze. Throughout these stories, Tracey argues, run competing disciplinary and sentimental styles of representing the poor. Lori Merish examines another icon of poverty in her essay, "Representing the 'Deserving Poor': The 'Sentimental Seamstress' and the Feminization of Poverty in Antebellum America." She argues that as a figure representative of the "deserving poor," the seamstress became a vehicle for feminizing economic dependency. While women are, for the most part, objects of representation in the seamstress stories, Merish offers one example of this genre, "Stray Leaves," in which the pen is taken up by the seamstress herself. Mary Templin finds similar acts of self-representation and self-empowerment in the panic fiction inspired by the economic panic of 1837. In "'Dedicated to Works of Beneficence': Charity as Model for a Domesticated Economy in Antebellum Women's Panic Fiction," Templin argues that women used these stories to demonstrate their economic savvy and to propose a broadly defined benevolence: a revised economic system in which benevolence is a way of life. We conclude this first part with an essay that situates benevolence literature in a wider literary context. Whitney Womack, in "Reforming Women's Reform Literature: Rebecca Harding Davis's Rewriting of the Industrial Novel," reads Davis's *Margret Howth* as a response to the well-established tradition of the British industrial reform novel.

In the second part of *Our Sisters' Keepers*, "Negotiating the Female American Self through Benevolence," contributors attempt to sort out the intentions and effects of the benevolence portrayed in, and enacted by, the works under consideration. As we have seen, scholars have documented the ambivalence felt for the term benevolence and the suspicion that often accompanies it. "No well-intended act . . . was utterly free from harmful consequences" (Ryan, *Grammar* 11). The writers in these essays examine the ways benevolence literature weighs the needs of doing for others—that is, the needs of the relational self—against the needs of the individual.

The first two essays in this section read the literature under consideration against discourses of nineteenth-century poverty relief that often undermined individual autonomy. Debra Bernardi's essay, "'The Right to Be Let Alone': Mary Wilkins Freeman and the Right to a 'Private Share,'" demonstrates how Freeman attempted to redefine benevolent acts with respect to nineteenth-century issues of privacy. Bernardi argues that Freeman's stories assert the rights of all individuals—even those who need charity—to have a "private share" of space in which to live the way they choose. In "Women's Charity vs. Scientific Philanthropy in Sarah Orne Jewett," Monika Elbert argues that Jewett transposes the charity Emerson and others objected to into a reciprocal and mutually uplifting act through the image of the gift. In Jewett, the tension between the individual and relational self is negotiated through the act of gift giving, an act, Elbert argues, that "takes on profound significance in the Jewett woman's quest for self-respect and self-reliance" (158).

The next two essays sound the possibilities of a benevolent community. In "'Oh the Poor Women!': Elizabeth Stuart Phelps's Motherly Benevolence," Jill Bergman examines the implications of Phelps's brand of philanthropy for the individual defined by class distinctions. Bergman argues that while Phelps's vision of society as an interconnected family holds promise as a socialist and feminist vision, ultimately her use of the trope of motherhood solidifies individuals' middle-class boundaries by maintaining the superiority of motherly reformers over their needy "children." Terry Novak's essay, "Frances Harper's Poverty Relief Mission in the African American Community," offers a less conflicted vision of communal aid. In her reading of *Iola Leroy,* Novak discusses Harper's belief that it was the duty of individual African Americans to help their less-fortunate sisters, unified as they all were by the oppression of the post-reconstruction United States.

The final two essays in this collection focus on the philanthropic work and writings of Jane Addams. Sarah Chinn's piece, "'To Reveal the Humble Immigrant Parents to Their Own Children': Immigrant Women, Their Daughters, and the Hull-House Labor Museum," explores individuality in terms of ethnicity, age, and generational identity. While respecting the identity markers of immigrants, Addams also attempted to establish harmony between ethnicities and between immigrant parents and their children. In this essay the Hull-House Labor Museum becomes a text that is part of the genre of benevolence literature. The final essay, "Character's Conduct: The Democratic Habits of Jane Addams's 'Charitable Effort,'" by James Salazar, examines the conflict between the self-reliant individual and the relational self that undergirds all the essays in this volume. By looking at discussions of the development of "character" in the late nineteenth and early twentieth centuries, Salazar argues that benevolence, which presumably marked women's "character," frequently stood in opposition to the self-reliant qualities that marked the possessor of "true character." For Salazar, Addams wrote as a critic of the individualist ethic of the Gilded Age.

In sum, the essays in this collection reveal the extent to which the rhetorical nineteenth-century self was complicated by female benevolence. A sustained focus on this genre allows us to re-envision the nineteenth-century American subject as a "we," specifically encompassing the tension between the individual "I" and the relational self. These essays illustrate the extent to which women writers attempted to embrace the romantic individual, while continually engaging the needs of their poorer sisters—that is, becoming their "sisters' keepers." The result is a genre that needs to be accounted for in any conception of nineteenth-century American identity.

Notes

1. In "Hawthorne's Reconceptualization of Transcendentalist Charity," Monika Elbert has argued that, in spite of his mixed history with "charity and the concomitant feeling of forced gratitude and subservience" (218) and thus its undermining of independence, Hawthorne saw value in charitable acts as redemptive in some cases, bringing the recipient back into relation with the community.

2. *The Cambridge Companion to Nineteenth-Century American Women's Writing,* edited by Dale Bauer and Philip Gould, includes essays on the captivity narrative, the sentimental novel, the spiritual novel, the narrative of citizenship, and such.

3. See, for example, Wendy B. Sharer, "'Going into Society' or 'Bringing Society In'?: Rhetoric and Problematic Philanthropy in *The Silent Partner*"; Amy Schrager Lang, "The Syntax of Class in Elizabeth Stuart Phelps's *The Silent Partner*"; and Laura Wexler, *Tender Violence: Domestic Visions in an Age of U.S. Imperialism.* Similarly, Lori Ginzberg makes the point in her historical study that benevolence was a vehicle for the emergence of middle-class identity (7).

4. See Susan M. Ryan, "'Rough Ways and Rough Work': Jacob Riis, Social Reform, and the Rhetoric of Benevolent Violence," and Reginald Twigg, "The Performative Dimension of Surveillance: Jacob Riis's *How the Other Half Lives.*"

Works Cited

Bremner, Robert. *American Philanthropy.* Chicago: U of Chicago P, 1960.

Carlin, Deborah. "'What Methods Have Brought Blessing': Discourses of Reform in Philanthropic Literature." *The (Other) American Traditions: Nineteenth-Century Women Writers.* Ed. Joyce W. Warren. New Brunswick: Rutgers UP, 1993. 203–25.

Conway, Jill. "Women Reformers and American Culture, 1870–1930." *Journal of Social History* 5.2 (Winter 1971–72): 164–77.

Eiselein, Gregory. *Literature and Humanitarian Reform in the Civil War Era.* Bloomington: Indiana UP, 1996.

Elbert, Monika. "Hawthorne's Reconceptualization of Transcendentalist Charity." *American Transcendental Quarterly* 11.3 (September 1997): 213–32.

Emerson, Ralph Waldo. "Self-Reliance." 1841. *Ralph Waldo Emerson: Selected Essays, Lectures, and Poems.* Ed. Robert D. Richardson, Jr. New York: Bantam, 1990. 148–71.

Gandal, Keith. *The Virtues of the Vicious: Jacob Riis, Stephen Crane, and the Spectacle of the Slum.* New York: Oxford UP, 1997.

Ginzberg, Lori D. *Women and the Work of Benevolence: Morality, Politics, and Class in the Nineteenth-Century United States.* New Haven: Yale UP, 1990.

Hawthorne, Nathaniel. *The Blithedale Romance.* 1852. New York: Penguin, 1986.

Katz, Michael B. *In the Shadow of the Poorhouse: A Social History of Welfare in America.* New York: Basic Books, 1986.

Lang, Amy Schrager. "The Syntax of Class in Elizabeth Stuart Phelps's *The Silent Partner.*" *Rethinking Class: Literary Studies and Social Formations.* Ed. Wai Chee Dimock and Michael T. Gilmore. New York: Columbia UP, 1994. 267–85.

Long, Lisa A. "The Postbellum Reform Writings of Rebecca Harding Davis and Elizabeth Stuart Phelps." *The Cambridge Companion to Nineteenth-Century American Women's Writing.* Ed. Dale M. Bauer and Philip Gould. Cambridge: Cambridge UP, 2001. 262–83.

Mather, Cotton. *Bonifacius, An Essay upon the Good.* 1710. *The Harper American Literature.* Ed. Donald McQuade et al. New York: Harper and Row, 1987. 119–26.

McCarthy, Kathleen D. *Noblesse Oblige: Charity and Cultural Philanthropy in Chicago, 1849–1929.* Chicago: U of Chicago P, 1982.

Muncy, Robyn. *Creating a Female Dominion in American Reform, 1890–1935.* New York: Oxford UP, 1991.

Rothman, David J. *The Discovery of the Asylum: Social Order and Disorder in the New Republic.* Boston: Little, Brown. 1971.

Ryan, Susan M. *The Grammar of Good Intentions: Race and the Antebellum Culture of Benevolence.* Ithaca: Cornell UP, 2003.

———. "Misgivings: Melville, Race, and the Ambiguities of Benevolence." *American Literary History* 12.4 (Winter 2000): 685–712.

———. "'Rough Ways and Rough Work': Jacob Riis, Social Reform, and the Rhetoric of Benevolent Violence." *American Transcendental Quarterly* 11.3 (September 1997): 191–212.

Sáez, Barbara J. "The Discourse of Philanthropy in Nineteenth-Century America." *American Transcendental Quarterly* 11.3 (September 1997): 163–70.

Scott, Anne Firor. *Natural Allies: Women's Associations in American History.* Urbana: U of Illinois P, 1993.

Sharer, Wendy B. "'Going into Society' or 'Bringing Society In'?: Rhetoric and Problematic Philanthropy in *The Silent Partner.*" *American Transcendental Quarterly* 11.3 (September 1997): 171–90.

Stansell, Christine. *City of Women: Sex and Class in New York, 1789–1860.* New York: Alfred A. Knopf, 1986.

Thoreau, Henry David. *Walden, Or, Life in the Woods.* 1854. New York: Dover, 1995.

Trattner, Walter I. *From Poor Law to Welfare State: A History of Social Welfare in America.* Fifth Edition. New York: The Free Press, 1994.

Treudley, Mary Bosworth. "The 'Benevolent Fair': A Study of Charitable Organization among American Women in the First Third of the Nineteenth Century." *Compassion and Responsibility: Readings in the History of Social Welfare Policy in the United States.* Ed. Frank R. Breul and Steven J. Diner. Chicago: U of Chicago P, 1980. 132–45.

Twigg, Reginald. "The Performative Dimension of Surveillance: Jacob Riis's *How the Other Half Lives.*" *Text and Performance Quarterly* 12 (1992): 305–28.

Wexler, Laura. *Tender Violence: Domestic Visions in an Age of U.S. Imperialism.* Chapel Hill: U of North Carolina P, 2000.

Winthrop, John. *A Modell of Christian Charity.* 1630. *Early American Writing.* Ed. Giles Gunn. New York, Penguin, 1994. 108–12.

PART I
The Genre of Benevolence

1

Stories of the Poorhouse

Karen Tracey

Nineteenth-century poorhouses sheltered and confined people who could not support themselves and had nowhere else to live: orphaned infants, abandoned children, deserted wives, alcoholics, persons disabled by disease or accident, destitute widows, the mentally incompetent, the mentally ill, and the elderly infirm. Poorhouses could provide short-term refuge for the able-bodied unemployed; however, the helpless frequently became long-term, even life-long, residents. The permanent helplessness of many poorhouse paupers posed a problem to charitable workers, who as a rule tried to help the poor become self-supporting. As demonstrated by Debra Bernardi's chapter in this volume on "The Right to Be Let Alone," charity often took the form of "Friendly Visits" that were aimed at helping the poor adopt the values and behaviors of the more genteel classes. This disciplinary goal meant that Friendly Visitors were also judgmental observers intent on manipulating the lives of the poor. As James Salazar points out, "the Friendly Visit was a means of scrutinizing and assessing the poor" (268). The patronizing gaze of charity finds its way into imaginative literature; as Deborah Carlin notes, "Much of the literature written about poverty after the Civil War is rooted in a middle-class perspective and is essentially spectatorial in nature" (205). Poorhouse stories almost always feature a gaze, yet they demonstrate how gazes may operate either to draw people together or to manifest the power of one over another. Stories told about poorhouses become sites where writers struggle with theories of poverty and practices of benevolence.

Women writers of poorhouse literature often participated in the genteel perspective on class difference, charity, and pauperism, but as the century progressed they became more likely to question, cross, or even re-conceive the divide between the paupers and the privileged. Two powerful cultural paradigms, both with their roots in the eighteenth century, helped shape how charity was conceived and administered and therefore how poorhouse stories were written in the second half of the nineteenth century. One paradigm derives from the ethos of sentimentalism, and the other may be called panoptic, after Jeremy Bentham's architectural device for controlling social deviants.

Poorhouses, while not literally designed like Jeremy Bentham's Panopticon, had much in common with that structure, which Bentham celebrated in 1787 as "a new mode of obtaining power of mind over mind" (39) for any institution, from prisons to madhouses to schools to poorhouses, in which "persons of any description are meant to be kept under inspection." Bentham levels the distinctions between institutions of "different and even opposite" (40) purposes, because the common goal is to control people. Michel Foucault argues that while Bentham's Panopticon was a specific architectural design, it "must be understood as a generalizable model of functioning; a way of defining power relations in terms of the everyday life of men" (205). The primary goal of the Panopticon is "to induce in the inmate a state of conscious and permanent visibility that assures the automatic functioning of power" (201). Separating the object of the gaze from the gazer guaranteed this functioning, Foucault explains, because the inmate "is seen, but he does not see; he is the object of information, never a subject in communication" (200).

Because poorhouses were owned and operated by town or county authorities and funded through private charity and/or taxation, the people living there were vulnerable to being scrutinized at any time by keepers, town selectmen, and visitors. Therefore, poorhouses indeed worked rather like panopticons: people classified as disruptive or dangerous were confined within a space where they could be observed at the will of those in power over them. This panoptic gaze helps enforce the disciplinary function of poorhouses, and thus provides one paradigm for interpreting literature that represents poorhouses. The panoptic structure and the objectifying gaze on which it is predicated are generally associated with patriarchal power and a masculine worldview, but such a gaze may operate in women's writing as well when writers identify with hegemonic power rather than with the oppressed.

Sentimentalism is a second cultural paradigm that provides a critical tool for thinking through the history and the literature of poorhouses. Joanne Dobson defines sentimentalism as "a complex imaginative phenomenon comprised . . . of feeling constellating around and valorizing a distinctive set of emotional priorities and a specific moral vision. . . . Sentimental imagination at its core manifests an irresistible impulse toward human connection" (170). June Howard traces sentimentalism to Enlightenment philosophers who derived "benevolence and, ultimately, morality in general from human faculties that dispose us to sympathize with others." This "notion of 'sentiment' . . . coordinates complex recognitions of the power of bodily sensations (including emotions), the possibilities of feeling distant from or connected with other human beings, and benevolence as a defining human virtue" (70). Whereas sentimentalism may have originated with male philosophers and writers, as the nineteenth century progressed it came to be understood as a feminine mode of thinking and writing. Howard writes that "as subjective and social life are remapped into their modern configurations, emotion is correlated with the private as opposed to the public, and with the feminine as opposed to the masculine" (72–73).

Gazing plays a pivotal role in both the sentimental and the panoptic paradigms, but while the panoptic gaze is always predicated on a power differential, a sentimental gaze is not necessarily objectifying. In her discussion of the eighteenth-century origins of sentimentalism, Dianne Price Herndl explains that sentimental responses are predicated on sight, and she explores a gaze "rooted in sympathy and pity, a sentimental gaze" that she contrasts to gazes that "function only in terms of desire or control" (260). A sentimental gaze may work to help one person identify with another, thus promoting human connectedness rather than detachment. Yet a sentimental gaze does not necessarily signify a progressive text; rather, a story that uses sentimental tropes may be ideologically conservative, or it may advocate empathy for progressive or even for radical ends. As Herndl suggests, we should "rethink sentimentalism more as a textual strategy than as a coherent generic or ideological distinction" (260). In stories of the poorhouse, sentimentalism sometimes functions to reinforce and sometimes to undermine panoptic discipline.

When women's writings about poorhouses are interpreted through panoptic and sentimental paradigms, an intriguing literary history emerges. Some writers, such as those publishing in the religious periodical the *Ladies' Repository,* reinforce disciplinary worldviews. Others, including Harriet Prescott Spofford, Mary E. Wilkins, and Annie E. P. Searing, offer sentimental domestic alternatives to the public charity of the almshouse. And two authors, Mary Mapes Dodge and Corinna Aldrich Hopkinson, present characters troubled by the presumption of the middle-class gaze upon the poor. Finally, as the century draws to a close, Flora Haines Loughead, the anonymous "A Working Girl," and Eva Anstruther actively interrogate panopticism and the presumptions of superiority and innate difference on which it is based. These late-century authors openly criticize systemic causes of pauperism, demonstrating how the inequities inherent in American culture might actually be rooted in exploitation of the poorer classes. In acknowledging causes of pauperism outside of individual misbehavior, their stories undermine and then entirely discard a panoptic understanding of poorhouses, using a sentimental style blended with realistic representation to identify ever more closely with the disadvantaged, and finally to offer new metaphors, imagined through reciprocal sentimental gazes, for telling poorhouse stories.

The contradictory impulses to sympathize and to discipline that are indexed in poorhouse stories derive from tensions inherent in charity efforts. Michael B. Katz, author of *In the Shadow of the Poorhouse: A Social History of Welfare in America,* demonstrates how the communities that operated poorhouses were preoccupied with separating the worthy from the unworthy poor. Towns and counties wanted to help the "worthy poor," but not to provide free room and board to able-bodied vagrants. They believed that doing so would not only waste the money of responsible citizens but also foster and increase the class of dependents. Thus poorhouses as they developed had contradictory goals: to provide charity to the needy, yet to deter needy people from asking for charity. Some poorhouses, beneficently run and not over-crowded, seemed to provide decent relief. But most of them were more successful, too successful really, at meeting the second goal: deterring people from seeking help. Many almshouses were so dirty, so noisy, so crowded, so cold, or so hot; the quality and quantity of food was so poor, the degradation and humiliation of living there was so intense, that few people actually *went* to the poorhouse. Instead, they were *taken* there, by families who refused or were unable to care for them, or by town authorities who decided they were a nuisance or a menace.

To bring the generalizations Katz provides into focus with specific historical circumstances, consider a conscientiously detailed 1851 report by Thomas R. Hazard on the poor and insane in Rhode Island. Hazard furnishes snapshots of widely varied public relief efforts in more than thirty locales, and the catalog of human woe that emerges demonstrates panoptic discipline at work: individuals are classified according to the cause of their poverty, with emphasis on their perceived moral character. For example, the Coventry poorhouse contained sixteen people: the only man and several of the women were intemperate, while the rest of the women had permanent physical and/or mental disabilities: "palsy" ("always confined to bed or chair"—for twenty-seven years) "deaf and dumb," "idiotic and blind," and "insane" (51). The 136 people in the Dexter Asylum in Providence included fifty-one women, forty-one men, twenty-eight boys, and sixteen girls. Many adult residents are labeled with faults—variously characterized as "immorality," "intemperate," "unprincipled," "bad character," and "dishonest"—while many others are described as having intractable problems: "Blind," "Insane," "Palsy and friendless," "Feeble and friendless," "old age and lame," "imbecility of mind," "broken back," and "deaf, dumb and deformed" (25–28). The poorhouse records contain abundant evidence of the inadequacy of the disciplinary approach to charity, because behavioral changes could not possibly make these helpless individuals self-supporting. But in spite of this futility, the records illustrate panopticism at work: individuals are classified according to their moral status, and, whenever possible, blamed for their own misery.

Demonstrating how complex the interactions between panoptic and sentimental impulses could be, Hazard juxtaposes these catalogues with occasional narratives that humanize rather than objectify individual inmates. In these stories, the observer's gaze, at first operating in the service of the institution, impulsively sympathizes with a sufferer. While reporting on the Coventry poorhouse, Hazard compares the poorhouse overseer to an animal trainer and a mentally ill woman to his wild beast:

> An insane woman who had been recently removed by the town from the Butler Hospital, was ordered from her filthy lair, (where she was confined by the corner of a bedstead being pushed against the door.) in a tone of voice such as keepers of wild beasts use in colloquy with Tigers. At the stern summons, she came forth and stood silent and motionless, to be gazed at—a caricature of dispair [*sic*] clothed in filth and rags. No sign, look or token, indicated that she noticed ought that was said, until at her keeper's bidding, she quietly retired to her den. (50)

Hazard is appalled at the harsh treatment of the resident and by her numb obedience. Yet Hazard's purpose is to study poorhouse residents, and the keeper yells at the woman so that "she came forth . . . to be gazed at" for the visitor's benefit. Hazard's awkward sense of complicity in the very ills he is working to relieve has parallels in later poorhouse stories by women.[1]

One periodical that illustrates how writers could employ a sentimental gaze in the service of a disciplinary view of charity was the *Ladies' Repository: A Monthly Periodical, Devoted to literature, arts, and religion,* published by the Methodist Episcopal Church. The covenant of church membership creates something of a doctrinal panopticon in which members observe each other's lives in order to administer reproof and discipline. According to an 1860 *Guide-Book in the Administration of the Discipline of the Methodist Episcopal Church,* church doctrine included belief in the innate depravity of human beings and in heaven and hell. Members promised to accept the oversight of others, and to "watch mutually over [one another] for their Christian improvement" (28). Thus, poverty and charity are viewed through a Protestant framework that categorizes people as "redeemed" or "unredeemed," and that advocates the discipline of others as important Christian work. Thus, in the *Ladies' Repository* a disciplinary view of charity is underwritten by divine sanction.

Poorhouse literature published in the *Ladies' Repository* deploys sentimental tropes while participating in panoptic discipline, in effect mapping a church panopticon onto the poorhouse panopticon. The sentimental passages create a one-way gaze from the privileged subject to the unfortunate object. The viewer pities the pauper who is the object of her gaze, but protected by religious assurance, she does not imagine herself in a similar position, or reach out to form a bond, or invite a responsive gaze.

This perspective is demonstrated in the May 1873 issue of the *Ladies' Repository*, in which Mrs. Sue M. D. Fry publishes a laudatory account of her visit to the large charity complex in Philadelphia, an almshouse "inhabited by more than four thousand poor, with accommodations for full five thousand" (352). Fry and her friend visit the "Magdalen's hospital" for "deserted and dishonored women," the children's quarters, the "little dormitories" of the elderly ladies, and the department of the insane, where they observe the inmates' ball. Fry presents herself and her friend as compassionate visitors who gaze sympathetically on the miserable residents, but the urge to decisively distinguish between the righteous and the unredeemed effectively seals her sentimental impulses within a panoptic perspective. At first Fry feels drawn to the gaze of the "fallen" girls and women: "Some were very young, almost children—somebody's daughter; perhaps an only one. The souls that looked out at those eyes!—homeless, friendless, abandoned souls." But, instead of meeting their gaze, Fry remains behind her panoptic divide, effectively separating herself, and by implication her readers, from these objects of pity: "all [have] found that the 'wages of sin is death,' few [have] learned that 'the gift of God is eternal life through Jesus Christ our Lord' " (352). As for the children, Fry notes that they appeal "even more strongly to womanly heart and sympathy," but then reflects that those who survive the "disease, hunger, and cold" are apt to live futile lives: "the survivors, if girls, may early sell virtue for bread; if girls or boys, may only know Satan to do his bidding. [I knew that] many of them would swell the tide of wicked ones already thronging our streets, up every garret and down every cellar." Fry concludes that "alms-houses and jails and prisons . . . stand as gloomy monuments of the sins and sufferings of mankind" (353). Sin both leads to and derives from destitution.

The church panopticon reappears in the *Ladies' Repository* short fiction. "Bread upon the Waters" and "Poor-House Jan" feature simple plots with straightforward religious morals. "Bread upon the Waters" teaches that right living may protect one from destitution, while "Poor-House Jan" rationalizes that even if worthy people become destitute, they may secure happiness in the afterlife.

"Bread upon the Waters" begins with a common social problem. Historian Katz discusses how elderly people "often found themselves completely destitute," with no financial resources and no children "able or willing to care for them" (9).[2] Jacob and Susan Manfred are in precisely this situation: they have lost their money, their children, and their health, and now wait in despair to be taken to the almshouse. But the couple is rescued by a man who in his youth was saved from a "house of correction" by Jacob. Both benefactor and worthy poor are marked by sentimental tropes, as an "earnest gaze" bonds Jacob with the younger man, while his wife raises "her streaming eyes to heaven" (468–69). "Bread upon the Waters" teaches that good Christians will be protected from destitution, implying that poorhouse inmates must fall into a different class. Fry's perspective that pauperism correlates with moral inadequacy is indirectly reinforced in this story.

"Poor-House Jan," by Miss M. J. Herbert, also suggests that sentiment marks both worthy poor and the truly benevolent, but she critiques a false sentimental gaze. Herbert narrates the pathetic fate of a baby who is left on the doorstep of the "wealthy and worldly Mrs. Hayes." Mrs. Hayes at first prides herself on her "sympathy for homeless children," which is conventionally demonstrated by her tears: "Positively, when I visited the asylum last Fall, I couldn't keep from crying at the sight of those motherless little ones." But her sympathetic feelings do not survive the sight of the baby's deformity: she immediately abandons her plans to shower him with love and wealth the moment she discovers "between the fair dimpled shoulders a large bony protuberance" (248). The disabled child is reared in the poorhouse, where he is mercilessly abused: "It was pitiful to see the poor crooked back bowed still more under the weight of great loads of wood . . . pitiful to see the muscles of the thin arms strained to their utmost tension by heavy pails of water. But it was far more pitiful to see, if there had been any human eye to see it . . . the heavier burdens that were daily and hourly laid upon the suffering, shrinking soul of the sensitive child" (249). Herbert directly solicits the reader to rise above Mrs. Hayes by manifesting a genuine sentimental gaze. For writers and readers of the *Ladies' Repository*, genuine sentimentalism helps distinguish between worthy and unworthy poor, and between benevolence and hypocrisy.

While the *Ladies' Repository* demonstrates how a sentimental gaze may reinforce disciplinary assumptions, other writers offered sentimental-domestic alternatives to public poorhouses. In each of four stories, published during the final three decades of the nineteenth century, individuals are rescued from the poorhouse by women whose own home is incomplete. In "Miss Moggaridge's Provider," "A Queer Mistake," "A Gentle Ghost," and "Mandy's Baby," a sympathetic gaze helps to create a strong sentimental connection, and a privileged character rescues a helpless individual from the poorhouse.

Harriet Prescott Spofford's "Miss Moggaridge's Provider," published in the *Atlantic Monthly* in 1871, sketches Ann Moggaridge's rashly unselfish acts of charity and her friend Miss Keturah's frustrated reactions. Keturah defends a disciplinary view of charity that was shared by Miss Moggaridge's strict clergyman father and by the town as a whole, while Ann offers charity wherever it is needed, regardless of the "worthiness" of the recipient and of the consequences to herself. Ann's years of unstinting generosity bring her to the threshold of the poorhouse, at which point Keturah relents and takes Ann into her own home.

In Spofford's story, the panoptic concept of charity enables most of the characters to justify their repeated refusals to help those in need, because they can always find a way to blame people for their miseries. Keturah in particular resists a sentimental gaze, instead keeping "one eye on the community and one on her old pastor" (18). Ann, however, identifies wholeheartedly with others, never asking whether or not they deserve to suffer. When Ann tries to raise money to replace a house destroyed by fire, Keturah is outraged that Ann would "be running to the relief of all the lazy and shiftless folks in the country" (20), insisting that Mr. Morris should have helped himself beforehand, or that "They could go to the poorhouse, where you'll go if some of your friends don't take you in hand and have a guardian appointed over you!" (21). Receiving no help from other villagers, Ann pays for the new house herself. Ann's other charities include sharing her inheritance with her good-for-nothing brother Jack (who soon dies), nurturing Jack's dog, taking in a shipwrecked parrot, paying for cataract surgery for "old Master Sullivan," cosigning a loan for her other brother Luke, whose financial failure leaves her very poor, and then paying her nephew's way through college. Then the nephew drowns, Ann's health fails, and the parrot starts a fire that burns down her house, leaving her entirely destitute as well as helpless, and fulfilling Keturah's prediction that Ann might have to go to the poorhouse. But at this critical moment, Keturah decides to take Ann into her own home.

"Miss Moggaridge's Provider" begins with the death of the minister-father and the break-up of his family, evolves through Ann's life-long persistence in defying her father's example of strictness, and ends with a new family, Ann and Keturah. Early in the story, Keturah flatly rejects Ann's suggestion that they might someday live together, but her perspective slowly changes because she loves Ann, and her gradual relenting is signaled by tears in her eyes: "and there Miss Keturah whisked herself out of sight, possibly to prevent any such catastrophe as her friend's seeing a tear in those sharp eyes of hers unused to such visitants" (24). At the end, Keturah is willing to share all she has: "I think we shall get along very well together for the rest of our lives, if you're not as obstinate and unreasonable—" (26–27). The religious perspective that underwrites panoptic charity is revealed to be selfish and cold. Spofford suggests that it be replaced by a generous, sympathetic charity that does not demand "worthiness" or even expect gratitude or other returns.

In Mrs. H. M. Field's "A Queer Mistake," published in the *Overland Monthly and Out West Magazine* in 1875, a "pair of old-maid sisters" (407) double the size of their family by adopting twin girls from the poorhouse. The narrator brings her sister with her to claim the babies, knowing that she will gaze on them with sympathy: "that very morning I coaxed Rachel over to the poor-house. . . . The sight of [the pink babies] in their utter helplessness and woful [*sic*] need was too much for Rachel's dear womanly heart to withstand" (410). Their charity brings its own reward in their increased domestic happiness: "I believe those babies gave me the purest and deepest pleasure of my life" (410). Field's story explicitly defends the value of females who are not living in relation to men, be they spinsters or orphaned babies, and shows a family complete without husbands, fathers, or brothers. Like other stories that contrast a matriarchal domesticity to a disciplinary poorhouse, "A Queer Mistake" suggests that one alternative to the poorhouse can be creative re-conceiving of family beyond blood ties, marriage, and child-bearing, a vision of family that can bond and thrive without men.

Mary Wilkins Freeman's "A Gentle Ghost" suggests a similar creative alternative to the poorhouse; in this story, a family replaces a dead child with a poorhouse orphan. Women represent both the sentimental and the disciplinary responses to the poorhouse child: the poorhouse is run by the masterly, unemotional Mrs. Gregg, and the Dunn home presided over by a warm mother. The Dunns live in "a large square building, glossily white, with green blinds," while the poorhouse, with walls nearly touching the Dunns', is "low, with a facing of white-washed stone-work reaching to its lower windows, which somehow gave it a disgraced and menial air; there were, moreover, no blinds" (367). The absence of blinds on the poorhouse emphasizes the exposure of its inmates to the outside world, while the Dunns' green blinds can shut out unwanted gazes. Furthermore, the poorhouse is not "glossily white" but merely "white-washed." In other words, a poorhouse is a mockery of a real home.

A reciprocal sentimental gaze establishes a loving bond between the poorhouse orphan Nancy Wren and the bereft mother Mrs. Dunn, in contrast to the complete lack of sympathy between the poorhouse mistress Mrs. Gregg and her charge. Nancy escapes from the poorhouse to the graveyard as often as she can, imagining that a long-deceased family is her own, and making friends with a ghost-child. Mrs. Dunn and her surviving daughter hear a girl crying every night and fear that it is their Jenny's ghost. When they discover that the nightly crying comes from the frightened Nancy, whose window is right next to Jenny's old room, Mrs. Dunn takes Nancy home from the poorhouse. Mrs. Dunn is moved by the sight of "little Nancy sitting up in bed, her face pale and convulsed, her blue eyes streaming with tears, her little pink mouth quivering." Mrs. Dunn's sentimental response opens the way to the new family: "A great wave of joyful tenderness rolled up in the heart of the bereaved woman," and she feels "almost as if she held her own Jenny" (372). Nancy takes Jenny's place, the family is again complete, and the ghosts disappear.

Whereas both "A Gentle Ghost" and "A Queer Mistake" feature girls being adopted into families, the "baby" in Annie E. P. Searing's "Mandy's

Baby" (published by the *New England Magazine* in 1896) is an elderly grandmother. Mandy is a middle-aged woman who gave up education and then marriage in order to care for family members who subsequently died. She "toiled in a factory to help support an invalid mother, and brothers and sisters left fatherless" and renounces "her matrimonial visions at the old call of duty" (16). Mandy's "baby" is a helpless but generous-hearted eighty-six-year-old woman sent to the poorhouse by family members tired of caring for her. Mandy finds herself renewed and redeemed by the love that develops between them: "If Mandy gave material attention of the most exacting nature, she also received a hundredfold in spiritual benefit" (18). The sentimental connection between Mandy and Grammer Great is stressed by their gazes. Mandy's "severe expression" is belied by her eyes, which reveal "the presence of feeling and fire beneath the icy surface" (16). As for Grammer Great, "everything about her seemed old but her eyes, and they were of that deep blue which we only expect to see in children's eyes." Through their eyes, perceptive and powerful in such different ways, the two women are drawn together. When Mandy reluctantly returns Grammer Great to a long-lost grandson, fearing another loss, the grandson miraculously turns out to be Mandy's lost beau. The story ends with their belated wedding, and the three of them form a family.

Compared to the disciplinary gaze that typifies the *Ladies' Repository* treatments of poorhouse problems, where sentiment reinforces the punitive role of the poorhouse and a panoptic religious perspective, the domestic poorhouse stories, especially taken together, emphasize the humanity of poorhouse residents and their need for true homes. Furthermore, they demonstrate how women who lead households and have adequate economic support can fill and warm their homes by opening them to destitute girls and women, not merely out of a duty to be charitable, but from a bond of genuine feeling. These authors do not directly confront the economic system that spawns so much deprivation, or the misguided public relief efforts that build and staff the poorhouses, but they obliquely critique the gender and age discrimination implicated in that economic system. In each of these stories, a sentimental gaze establishes a bond of mutual care, and the benefits of the new home are shared between the privileged woman and those rescued from the poorhouse.

While I have found no short stories that represent the worst abuses of the poorhouse system, or that encourage readers to identify with insane, disabled, or mentally incompetent characters, or that consider the additional problems that burdened poor immigrants and black Americans, a few stories convey the discomfort felt by an observer who attempts to sympathize with poorhouse residents who are marked as different from them. In "The Three Marys of Sharpsville" and "Sunday Afternoon in a Poor-House," the poor refuse to play the role assigned to them by the charitable middle classes, leaving those who desire to help them feeling awkward and confused.

One example of a troubled sentimental gaze is found in Corinna Aldrich Hopkinson's "The Three Marys of Sharpsville," published in 1873 in the *Atlantic Monthly.* Hopkinson sketches the stories of "three unmarried Pollys," one of whom ends up in the poorhouse. This Polly, Sharpsville's "Mary Magdalen," "had fallen from her high estate of maidenhood . . . and, as the custom was, had been discarded by all her large circle of unspotted relatives . . . she died among us, an honest, industrious woman, a Pharisee of the Pharisees, and a respected member at last, with three others, of the town's poorhouse" (664). Hopkinson's narrator explains that "to the poorhouse we all sent her friendly contributions of green tea, loaf-sugar, and such delicacies as are not provided by the selectmen; as also, from time to time, whatever garments she seemed likely to need. These she accepted with a lofty grace, quite her own, leaving us only humble that our offerings were not twice as many and better" (664). The women attempt to ameliorate Polly's condition and make up for the stinginess of the selectmen, but Polly conducts herself with dignity rather than the expected servile gratitude, denying the women a feeling of complacency.

The narrator also criticizes the church for a disciplinary gaze that recalls the *Ladies' Repository* panoptic church: Polly sits "in the front pew, where the town's poor were paraded, in what seemed to me an indelicate and inconsiderate manner" (664). Also, the deacons refuse to serve communion to Polly because "she had never given what was called 'satisfactory evidence' of her fitness to sit at the Lord's table. . . . Rather than confess, Polly asserted with her grand air, 'My skirts are clean'; from which oracular saying the deacons might have inferred much, if they had been less eager or curious, or more Christ-like" (664). Polly does not find true charity in the male deacons' church or in the selectmen's poorhouse. The gaze of the narrator reveals the inadequacy of both institutions, but creates discomfort with sympathetic charity at the same time. The discomfort is not resolved.

"Sunday Afternoon in a Poor-House," published in Mary Mapes Dodge's story collection *Theophilus and Others* in 1876, describes a Friendly Visit to a poorhouse. Through the story of two genteel visitors, Dodge conveys the discomfort that may emerge when a sentimental gaze replaces an objectifying one. The visit begins as a lark: "I was surrounded by luxury and could hear the sweet voices of a score of church-bells, [and] my enjoyment reached such a height that I concluded to go to the Poor-House" (243); however, the narrator's blithe desire to share her enjoyment through a visit, or perhaps to enhance her own comfort by visiting the miserable, quickly turns to awkwardness as the poorhouse residents reject her effort at Friendly Visiting.

The narrator, much like Fry in her *Ladies' Repository* report, presumes to understand the poorhouse residents. But they reject her sympathetic overtures and return assertive gazes. At first, the narrator believes that she can read the "revelations we saw in those rows of pauper faces!" (244). She imagines that one "crazy" woman is "tortured with inward bitterness," and tries to reach the pauper woman with a sentimental gaze; however, when she smiles, "trusting to the magnetism of kindness and sympathy," the pauper "glowered at me with a hideous grimace that sent the blood running back icily into my heart" (244). She then notes that another woman's "possible history opened before me like a revelation." But this woman also repulses the visitor, turning "stiffly away, as if with a haughty sense that I did not belong to 'her set' " (245). One "grand old pauper" does talk with the narrator about geraniums and religion, but even that cheerful elderly woman makes the visitor uncomfortable, "staring at me in that uncompromising way peculiar to paupers" (245).

Dodge's narrator begins to lose her confidence that the paupers welcome her Friendly Visit. Her gaze becomes more hesitant, and she "peer[s] about with a vague dread that I might see something which it would not be pleasant to discover" (246). She is horrified by the sight of two women on an outdoor bench, neither of whom seems fully human to her: one looks "more like a huge, gray, half-dead bat than a woman," and the other was "a brazen-looking thing [who was] either an idiot or a lunatic." The second woman, "the half-witted thing," takes a sponge from a pail of dirty water and begins washing "the other woman's bowed face. There was no remonstrance, only a wretched jerk of the head, which ceased with the second stroke of the sponge" (246). This unwelcome vision may emblemize the failure of poorhouse charity, as a despondent person passively submits to being futilely "washed" with dirty water.

The narrator and her friend have divergent reactions after their poorhouse visit. Whereas the narrator has tried to reach out to the residents, her companion, who has spent the afternoon talking with the overseer, comes away "filled with grand, philanthropic ideas" (246). The narrator, whose attempts at sympathy have chilled instead of warmed her, has no grand ideas: "As I looked back at the great red building, a choking sense of human misery came over me. [I said] 'Let us walk fast. There'll be a bright fire at home; and they'll all be sitting around it, waiting for us' " (246). Human misery cannot be ameliorated by sentimental connections, through "grand philanthropic schemes," or by any remedy she can imagine, and she is simply grateful to have a home safe from poverty, cold, and the gaze of condescending visitors.

In the final two decades of the nineteenth century, some women writers began to turn distrust of philanthropy and discomfort with sentimentalism into attacks on elements of their culture that created or exacerbated the problems of poverty. These texts include an 1881 study by Octave Thanet and several polemics by Ida M. Van Etten. In addition, three short stories examine systemic causes of poverty from a woman's perspective. First, "Among the Rose Roots" (*Harper's New Monthly Magazine* 1882) exposes the exploitation of women workers. Second, "Sealskin Annie" (*Overland Monthly and Out West Magazine* 1890) points out how a church panopticon of the sort espoused in the *Ladies' Repository* might itself be partly to blame for women's misery. Finally, "Ebb and Flow" (*Harper's New Monthly Magazine* 1894) recreates the panoptic poorhouse in order to contrast the masculine, disciplinary gaze with a feminine, sentimental gaze, identifying limitations in both and suggesting a new metaphor through which to perceive and respond to class difference and the realities of pauperism.

Thanet, in her extensively researched two-part study of "The Indoor Pauper," details the horrors of poorhouses yet remains invested in panoptic assumptions about the causes of poverty. She cites a New York report from 1874–75 that announces "The number of persons in our poorhouses who have been reduced to poverty by causes outside of their own acts is . . . surprisingly small" ("The Indoor Pauper: A Study" 756). The circular thinking required to uphold the notion that paupers cause their own problems is concisely illustrated in this comment: "the bathing arrangements were most primitive; but, judging from the paupers' aspect, they did not bathe often enough to be troubled by any deficiencies" (755). Thanet does not ask whether or not they might wash more frequently were the means to do so available.[3] Thanet re-inscribes the line between worthy and unworthy poor, arguing that the bad paupers only add to the miseries of the good ones, and inviting our sympathy for the worthy poor: "The class which suffers at all our almshouses is the class for whom almshouses are presumed to be maintained, the unfortunate and self-respecting poor."

However, much of Thanet's direct evidence belies her disciplinary premise. At a rural almshouse in Illinois, she intercedes in a quarrel between an elderly blind woman, a middle-aged man, and two younger women, none of whom appear to be content in the squalor of the poorhouse. The blind woman "had come to the almshouse, her husband and she, because he had been ill for years, and she was blind, and they had no living children" (754). Thanet does not try to explain how these problems can be blamed on the residents, nor does she demonstrate how the mildly insane men hobbling about the yard with chains on their feet or "a twisted creature who had lost both legs, and was shuffling himself along on his back with his hands" are responsible for their misfortunes. She also introduces us to an elderly man, "a tailor by trade," who was in the almshouse because of "ill health and partial blindness," yet who worked constantly sewing and mending for poorhouse residents ("The Indoor Pauper" 754). He is, she insists, an exception to the rule, as is "a colored woman [who] injured her leg in such a way that it had to be amputated below the knee," and who persistently "asked the officials for a wooden leg" so that she could "go out again and earn her own living" ("The Indoor Pauper" Part II 247).

Thanet is particularly focused on poorhouse women. For example, she is dismayed at the number of babies conceived and born in almshouses, sometimes through consensual sex and sometimes through rape (in particular of mentally ill women by male inmates). While she criticizes a German immigrant who admits that the father of her baby is not her husband ("She gave the abrupt giggle which in her class sometimes does duty for a blush"), she also reveals, using the woman's own language, that this mother loves her children: "I had little girl born here, but she die; I'm so 'fraid dis one die, too, but I take just so good care of him I can" (755). Thus her images of the poorhouse residents, and particularly poorhouse women, frequently encourage a sympathetic gaze that her own premises will not allow her to fully share.

Other women reformers explicitly reject disciplinary assumptions and blame abusive economic practices and bias against women. Ida M. Van Etten demonstrates how the "sweating system" exploits women's labor and she advocates women's labor unions, but she also harshly criticizes charity itself: working women "have truly become the *victims of charity and philanthropy.* So great has this evil become that I hold that charity should be classed as *one* of the direct causes of the wretched industrial condition of working-women" (330). Van Etten maintains that "the evils of charity are both moral and economic." Whereas charity "undoubtedly had its origin in the noblest and most unselfish motives of human conduct, it has, in later times . . . become the most powerful ally of the competitive system of industry and forms one of the strongest bulwarks of its support and continuance" (331). Charitable institutions are complicit in the abuses of the sweating system because they enable employers to offer outrageously low pay: "Charity has only succeeded in making it easier for the unscrupulous employers of women to exploit them safely and respectably. By the side of the huge factory, whose owner is growing enormously rich upon the spoliation of his women workers, it builds the Lodging House or Christian Home, and this enables the manufacturers to pay wages below the living point" (331–32).

Thanet's images of poorhouse residents and Van Etten's argument provide contexts in which to read the stories written near the end of the century. In "Among the Rose Roots," whose author is identified only as "A Working Girl," the narrator Dolores tells the story of Nettie (short for Marie Antoinette) to a lady of leisure, Felicia. Dolores, who manages a sweatshop for male employers, is very well educated (she alludes to

English, French, and classic literature). She introduces the title metaphor, which challenges Felicia to be aware that privileged women draw their life from thousands of working women:

> In our social system that Felicia and all of her ilk have their appointed place there is no doubt. For a dozen perfect roses lifted heavenward there must be a thousand rootlets delving in under-ground darkness. Do the roots envy the glowing blossoms? Nay, but they demand that they too shall do their duty. (105–6)

The factory scenes in "Among the Rose Roots" compare closely to those described in an article published five years later in the *North American Review* by Van Etten, who details the struggles of three million working women who are classed as "laborers, mill operatives, seamstresses, domestic servants, and teachers." These options offer women "a field of labor so circumscribed as to afford employment for not more than one-tenth of the number. Enormous overcrowding, fierce competition, and a consequent undue pressure on wages must necessarily follow such a state of things" ("Working Women" 312). Among the worst abused are the seamstresses:

> The trades dependent upon the needle form a history of human misery unequaled by the industrial condition of any working class the world has ever seen. . . . Miserable attics and cellars form the only homes of these women, and their tenure even of these is precarious, depending upon the uncertain fortunes of an employment in which, owing to the enormous overcrowding, the most frivolous reason serves as a pretext for a dismissal. (314)[4]

Dolores and Nettie of "Among the Rose Roots" work in just such a factory. Dolores hires Nettie during a day when "I had interviewed a small army of poor women and girls; for while we wanted two dozen, hundreds applied. . . . Work they asked for, and my business was to select the most likely to become useful, and give them a trial. . . . All were willing to try it, and all were driven by hard necessity." Dolores has learned to gaze empathetically: "I have not looked into so many faces without having learned to read something of the souls behind the masks, so I knew this one was in trouble," and Nettie, despite her ill health and desperation, returns the sympathy: "You look so tired, and there are still so many for you to talk to" (106).

The sentimental bonds between women extend throughout the factory, and they aid one another rather than looking for charity: "We come from all parts of the world to this work-room, and are as well assorted in nationality as in religion, but when help for a suffering companion is asked, you see only common sisterhood" (109). Nettie's kindness to the other women wins their friendship, and this "Marie Antoinette" loses her head figuratively rather than literally as her blinding headaches develop into a fatal illness. Eugenie, the "little Jewish handmaiden" who runs errands in the factory, reports to Dolores: "Nettie can not help herself at all, and indeed it is all they [the people with whom she boards] can do to keep her in bed. She gets up in her delirium and tries to go to work" (109). Because the working women owe almost all of their time to the factory, they are unable to save Nettie from being taken "'*To the almshouse!*' 'Oh, impossible! Cold horror seized us every one. Now, oh, Heaven, for just two of those precious hours which I had sold in labor's market!'" Eugenie, "with eyes both flashing and streaming," reports that "Miss Nettie was in her right mind just long enough to understand what they were going to do, and she fell down on her knees and begged them for the dear God's sake not to take her *there;* she would pay every cent if it took a hundred years! . . . But they took her away, and she is dying now, and we can't get her out of that place if we want to" (109).

The poorhouse is indeed a chamber of horrors. The doctor, whose gaze is cruelly panoptic, threatens Nettie with shock treatment: "This woman . . . is evidently assuming hysteria. If she does not make up her mind to get better shortly, I shall have her removed to another ward, and shall use the battery." These are the last words Nettie hears as she dies of "acute meningitis": "How did she die? How do people die in such a place? They had strapped her to the bed to keep her from forever wandering to her work" (110). Nettie's friends rescue her body from threatened dissection: "A day or two ago she was with us, worked, ate, clasped hands with us, and will fill a pauper's grave—if the pit where dissected bodies are flung can be called a grave—unless we her sisters demand her." Nettie's friends are warned that "though numbers of women die [in the poorhouse] they are of a different class—old or bad, mostly—and the doctors do not get a chance like this very often" (110). But with the help of generous laborers and one well-off sympathetic woman whose soul "melts in pity" when she hears "how we wished to save our companion from the coarse sack, the dissecting-table, and the 'dead-pit,'" they place Nettie's nicely dressed body in a secure grave, relieved that the people in the poorhouse had stolen only her treasured ring, but not her beautiful hair.

The author of "Among the Rose Roots" closes by pleading with Felicia to identify with the seamstresses: "Imagine . . . the misery of working all day with tears thick in your eyes, and such a load on your heart!" A few of the women sneak away from the factory for Nettie's funeral: "Protestant, Jewess, Catholic, sisters all, with clasped hands and wet eyelids we knelt and said, 'Our Father'" (111). Felicia and the story's readers are asked to share the sentimental gaze and identify with the thousands of women on whose labor their own luxury thrives. Furthermore, they are prompted to acknowledge that an unfortunate rose might find itself tangled and buried among the roots, nourishing the next generation of beauty and leisure.

Flora Haines Loughead's "Sealskin Annie" retells the old seduction story: a young woman falls prey to a rake, suffers physical and emotional hardship, and then dies, forgiven, in her father's arms. But while the seduction plot frequently warns young women about their own weak natures and preaches to them about the necessity of salvation, Loughead blames the very religious perspectives promoted in the *Ladies' Repository* for Annie's misery. Annie is introduced as a "feeble, witless creature" who always wears a worn-out sealskin coat, an emblem of lost wealth that carries the same meaning for its wearer as the scarlet letter did for Hester Prynne. She speaks only to name herself "Annie," makes no attempt to be useful, and wanders aimlessly around the poorhouse buildings and grounds. Her father "was one of the most rigid Calvinistic preachers . . . never satisfied unless preaching hell and damnation to all unbelievers." He tried to raise Annie "in the old orthodox way: no pleasures, no indulgence, no liberty." When "his child went astray" and the mother died of grief, the father is transformed: "[It] broke his pride, bred mercy, tolerance, pity in his heart," and he becomes one of "the most unselfish workers" in the cause of benevolence, and is looked to "for sympathy and advice; yet when he made the most impassioned appeals, when he spoke the wisest words of counsel, he wore an air of gentle deprecation and his bright eyes had a wistful look, as of one perpetually pleading for mercy at an unseen Bar" (48). Annie's father rejects judgmental theology and turns instead to a religion based on a sentimental gaze that identifies with the suffering.

Loughead extends her critique of the panoptic view of the poorhouse beyond Sealskin Annie's own pathetic story by encouraging the reader to sympathize with, but not to idealize, the other residents:

> The place was already teeming with Annies, and confusion untold resulted from the repetition of names. There was Annie Olsen, the one-legged and one-armed Norwegian girl, who had been a very decent servant, but who had attempted to kindle the fire with kerosene one morning, and who had retired from active service in consequence. Then there was Annie Donovan, the unfortunate young wife, whose husband had deserted her and her six children, and who had forthwith taken up quarters in the almshouse, with all her little brood. There was little Annie, her daughter . . . Annie the fat Dutch girl, and Annie the shrunken old paralytic, and miscellaneous Annies, old and young and large and small. (45)

Poorhouse residents may not be as grateful as they should be, but contrary to popular assumptions, most of them "made at least some pretense of being of use." Unlike most of the other poorhouse writers, Loughead represents the hopeless paupers humanely:

> Sorrowful old men, to whom past and present were hopelessly confused, worked patiently in the garden or about the stables, or cut hay in its season, albeit with weak backs that called for frequent rest, or trembling hands that could scarce grasp sickle or hoe. Old women with all their faculties dulled, and only a lingering spark of vitality animating their enfeebled frames, found comfort in performing simple menial tasks. Even old Betsy, who was nearly one hundred years old and who had been

> an inmate of the establishment for upwards of thirty years, was always wandering about the yard picking up fagots for an imaginary fire . . . yes, all who were able to be about busied themselves with real or fancied tasks, down to Jackanapes, the idiot, more ape than boy, who took a weird delight in hollowing graves in the little cemetery. (45)

Loughead's catalogs of poorhouse residents undermine the panoptic viewpoint that would label them with their specific problems and group them as "a pauper class," as does her statement that all of them "had reached their present estate accompanied by some tradition of past comfort or affluence" (46). In discussing how many of "the poor creatures . . . consoled themselves for their present misfortunes with faithfully nourished hopes of what the future might bring to them," she details some of the causes for pauperism:

> Some were patiently awaiting the appearance of wayward sons. Many among the women looked forward to the return of recreant husbands, or to the reform of lazy ones, or the repentance of those who had gone wrong. . . . A few of them held titles to land in remote and inaccessible places . . . treasured shares of wild-cat mining stock, or held mining claims. (46)

Loughead even goes so far as to recast religious language to demonstrate how inadequate are the prescriptions of religious panopticism for dealing with the miseries of a poorhouse. For example, she puts a common religious phrase in a secular context, as she describes the residents "who studied the stock reports and mining reviews in the daily papers, in a pathetic faith that some day they would read the blessed assurance that their lives of humiliation and dependence were at an end" (46). And she specifically challenges the comfortable notion on which the *Ladies' Repository* story "Bread upon the Waters" is based:

> Some had cast bread upon the waters in years gone by, and were always hoping against hope that it might some day come back to them, forgetting that it must have long ago mouldered, and been dissipated in impalpable decay; for the memory of human kindness will no more survive neglect than will perishable material substance. (46)

An interrogation of the panoptic gaze is most explicitly developed in Eva Anstruther's story "Ebb and Flow," published in *Harper's New Monthly Magazine* in 1894. The premise of "Ebb and Flow," which is set in England, is that a titled family has suffered a severe reversal of fortune and their property is now owned by a man whose "grandfather broke the stones to mend their roads" (219). The current owner shows a casual guest an almshouse where he carries on his father's hobby of collecting "relics of old families who had once lived in this and the neighboring counties and had fallen from their high estate" (220). These "relics" include the former owner and his wife, who were found "hidden away in some wretched slum" (220). The young woman who is visiting hesitates to observe the collection of people, asking the proprietor, "Isn't it cruel to force ourselves upon them because we have the power? They cannot like it." But the man, who does not share her qualms, reassures her that, "We will go straight to the musicians' gallery. . . . there you can see without being seen" (220). The residents are watched without their knowledge, and are completely within the power of the proprietor; in other words, Anstruther's fictional almshouse is indeed a panopticon.

Anstruther explores the reversals between rich and poor from multiple perspectives. First is the current landowner's pragmatic assessment that, "They went under, we came up; they were forced to sell, my father pleased to buy—that is the whole history in a word" (219). His pragmatic viewpoint corresponds to his security within the panoptic gaze of privilege. Second is the young woman's compassionate sympathy and longing to understand the almshouse residents, the "great pity in her voice," her declaration that "It's bewildering; it sounds like some old, old story, doesn't it? I want to think—to understand it" (220). Despite the woman's reluctance to watch the residents, she is unable to help gazing at them: "the girl shivered and drew back; but the scene had a fascination for her, and she looked down again" (221). The visitor experiences an uncomfortable sentimental gaze that the owner does not share. The reader, who has "watched" everything through these characters' eyes, is implicated in both of these perspectives: the arrogant and unselfcritical view of the landholder, and the sympathetic but awkward perspective of the young woman visitor.

The third perspective moves beyond both of these gazes. It comes from the narrator, and is captured in the final image of the story: "Past and present and future mingled in the dream-world. . . . And through the gap between the trees the young moon, with the old moon in her arms, looked down upon them silently" (221). The moon image is compelling: the young moon cares for the old moon as these youths attempt to care for the aged, but the appearance of two moons, one old and one young, is an illusion, so youth and age must be one thing as the moon is one body. Furthermore, the moon changes are cyclical, not linear, so when the narrator writes that "past and present and future are mingled," she suggests that the pattern of rising and falling, of youth and age, of wealth and poverty, is also cyclical, and that the young and strong may one day need care, that the rich may one day be poor. Finally, the moon is a feminine image that stands in opposition to the panopticon, an emblem of patriarchal domination. The man is oblivious to the message, the young woman senses it, but it is left for the reader to interpret the silent moon.

As women wrote poorhouse stories throughout the second half of the nineteenth century, they worked through and against cultural narratives about poverty that at first persuaded them that the poor deserved their fate, needed to be shut up in panoptic poorhouses, could be blamed for their failures and miseries, and should be disciplined to prevent them from asserting themselves. As women's use of sentiment to identify with one another evolved, an increasingly empathetic gaze grew uncomfortable with panoptic discipline and developed toward empathizing with the poor. This empathy moved writers toward identifying and attacking some of the social injustices that foster poverty. And finally, writers start to imagine new metaphors through which to comprehend the troubling interconnectedness of the wealthy and the laboring classes, of the privileged and the powerless. The metaphors of rose roots and of the moon move readers away from thinking in terms of sharply demarcated classes. If we accept the organic and feminine images of rose bush and moon cycles as metaphors for class relations, then we have to move beyond even a sympathetic gaze to imagine being one with people who are useless, miserable, and utterly rejected. The story of poorhouse stories reveals the complexity of cultural and rhetorical strategies through which we attempt to comprehend or excuse or resist or react to the abuses and oppression for which a society is responsible, problems so complex and so embedded that no one within the ideological maze of that culture can clearly see how to resolve them.

Notes

The Graduate College of the University of Northern Iowa supported this project by providing the author with a Professional Development Leave in Spring 2004.

1. Those interested in the history of poorhouses will find abundant images and documents on the Web site titled "The Poorhouse Story": <http://www.poorhousestory.com>.

2. The frequent abandonment of the elderly to poorhouses caught the popular imagination, as illustrated by Will Carleton's well-known poem "Over the Hill to the Poorhouse," which was set to music and inspired several "sequels."

3. Michael Katz analyzes how the authors of the New York report manipulated data and ignored evidence in order to arrive at their conclusions (89). Katz explains that, "Poorhouse demography did not match official images of paupers or the goals of policy very well. Inmates did not come from a degraded culture of poverty marked by illiteracy and intemperance. They were not, by and large, apathetic, unwilling to work, and permanently pauperized" (94). But Thanet reiterates this "official image," insisting that "it is a liberal estimate to put down one-tenth of the paupers as people deserving of sympathy; the other nine-tenths are in the almshouse because they have not wit enough or energy enough to get into prison." Such undeserving people "do not have a hard life in the almshouses. The squalor does not disturb men and women who have known nothing else" (757).

4. For an extensive discussion of the figure of the seamstress as a victim of poverty, see Lori Merish's essay in this volume.

Works Cited

Anstruther, Eva. "Ebb and Flow." *Harper's New Monthly Magazine* 89.530 (July 1894): 219–21.

Baker, Osmon C. *A Guide-Book in the Administration of the Discipline of the Methodist Episcopal Church.* Rev. ed. New York: Carlton and Porter, 1860.

Bentham, Jeremy. *Panopticon; Or, The Inspection-House: Containing the Idea of a New Principle of Construction.* 1787. Ed. John Bowring. *The Works of Jeremy Bentham,* Vol. 4. New York: Russell and Russell, 1962. 37–172.

"Bread upon the Waters: A Sketch from Life." *Ladies' Repository* 27.8 (August 1867): 462–64.

Carlin, Deborah. "'What Methods Have Brought Blessing': Discourses of Reform in Philanthropic Literature." *The (Other) American Traditions: Nineteenth-Century Women Writers.* Ed. Joyce W. Warren. New Brunswick: Rutgers UP, 1993. 203–25.

Dobson, Joanne. "The American Renaissance Reenvisioned." *The (Other) American Traditions: Nineteenth-Century Women Writers.* Ed. Joyce W. Warren. New Brunswick: Rutgers UP, 1993. 164–182.

Dodge, Mary Mapes. "Sunday Afternoon in a Poor-House." 1876. *Nineteenth-Century American Women Writers: An Anthology.* Ed. Karen L. Kilcup. Cambridge: Blackwell, 1997. 243–246.

Field, Mrs. H. M. "A Queer Mistake." *Overland Monthly and Out West Magazine* 14.5 (May 1875): 407–18.

Freeman, Mary E. Wilkins. "A Gentle Ghost." *Harpers New Monthly Magazine* 79.471 (August 1889): 366–73.

Fry, Mrs. Sue M. D. "Charities of Philadelphia: The Alms-House." *Ladies' Repository* 11.5 (May 1873): 352–55.

Foucault, Michel. *Discipline and Punish: The Birth of the Prison.* Trans. Alan Sheridan. New York: Pantheon, 1977.

Hazard, Thomas R. *Report on the Poor and Insane in Rhode Island.* Providence: Joseph Knowles, 1851.

Herbert, Miss M. J. "Poor-House Jan." *Ladies' Repository* 9.4 (April 1872): 248–52.

Herndl, Dianne Price. "Style and the Sentimental Gaze in *The Last of the Mohicans.*" *Narrative* 9.3 (October 2001): 259–82.

Hopkinson, Corinne Aldrich. "The Three Marys of Sharpsville." *Atlantic Monthly* 31.188 (June 1873): 663–69.

Howard, June. "What Is Sentimentality?" *American Literary History* 11.1 (Spring 1999): 63–82.

Katz, Michael B. *In the Shadow of the Poorhouse A Social History of Welfare in America,* Rev. ed. New York: Basic Books, 1996.

Loughead, Flora Haines. "Sealskin Annie." *Overland Monthly and Out West Magazine* 16.91 (July 1890): 44–49.

Searing, Annie E. P. "Mandy's Baby." *New England Magazine* 20.1 (March 1896): 15–21.

Spofford, Harriet Prescott. "Miss Moggaridge's Provider." *Atlantic Monthly* 27.159 (January 1871): 17–27.

Thanet, Octave. "The Indoor Pauper: A Study." *Atlantic Monthly* 47.284 (June 1881): 749–64.

———. "The Indoor Pauper: A Study, II." *Atlantic Monthly* 48.286 (August 1881): 241–52.

Van Etten, Ida M. "The Sweating System, Charity, and Organization." 1890. Ed. Nancy F. Cott. *Root of Bitterness: Documents of the Social History of American Women.* New York: Dutton, 1972. 327–32.

———. "Working Women." *North American Review* 144.364 (March 1887): 312–16.

A Working Girl. "Among the Rose Roots." *Harpers New Monthly Magazine* 66.391 (December 1882): 105–11.

2

Representing the "Deserving Poor"

The "Sentimental Seamstress" and the Feminization of Poverty in Antebellum America

Lori Merish

In Fanny Fern's *Ruth Hall,* the eponymous heroine, an impoverished widow, is cast off by her male relatives after her husband's death and must work as a seamstress to support her two young children and herself. In a scene midway through the novel, Ruth gazes out the window of her boardinghouse at a "large brick tenement" across the street—a "prospect," Fern notes, not designed to inspire "cheerful fancies" (90). A different kind of window scene from the type commonly found in domestic fiction, Fern's Ruth observes not the stuff of "life"—meditated experience to compensate for the deprivations of domestic privacy (Brodhead 65–66)—but the makings of a cautionary narrative. Although Ruth surveys several poor residents, "emigrants and others," inhabiting the tenement's dingy rooms, the figure that arrests her attention (and commands her sympathy) is a young seamstress, wanly and wearily performing her painstaking labor. Notably, Ruth readily constructs a narrative for the image before her: "There . . . sat a young girl, from dawn till dark, scarcely lifting that pallid face and weary eyes—stitching and thinking, thinking and stitching. God help her!" (90). Underscoring the tragic fatalism of the seamstress's conventional story, Fern makes a point of emphasizing the tenement's proximity to the neighborhood brothel—the unfortunate conclusion, the text implies, of many such poor women's tales (91).

In *Ruth Hall,* Fern both borrowed from and contributed to a growing body of "seamstress literature" (Reynolds 355) that gained widespread popularity in the 1840s and 1850s.[1] In this essay, I examine the construction of the figure Christine Stansell terms the "sentimental seamstress" (110) in three emerging, and overlapping, textual sites: the discourses of poverty, evangelical moral reform, and popular fiction. While most writers in Jacksonian America defended white male economic equality and had increasing difficulty imagining men as guiltless victims of capitalism and, thus, deserving objects of charity, they regularly depicted working women as overcome by uncontrollable economic forces. The era's predominant example of the "deserving poor," the seamstress was a figure whose economic dependency was seen to be dictated by the laws of capital as thoroughly as the "natural" strictures of femininity.[2] Referred to as "poor helpless females" in the proceedings of the National Trades' Union and denominated "poor and sickly" in the pages of the *Advocate* (the publishing organ of the New York Female Moral Reform Society) (Sumner 141), seamstresses were conventionally, and melodramatically, portrayed as beings hemmed in on all sides.

Sympathy played a key role in representations of impoverished seamstresses. Indeed, sentimentalism, usually understood as a "feminine" language of racial reform in antebellum America, was also central to discourses of class and, especially, poverty. The seamstress was the privileged object of sympathy in the writings of reformers concerned with moderating what was perceived to be a growing gap between rich and poor. The sentimental seamstress was decisively inflected by the literature of evangelical reform, which merged evangelical conceptions of the redemptive value of sympathy for the weak with traditional conceptions of social interdependency, and a paternalist "moral economy," that had historically provided a vocabulary of working-class resistance to laissez-faire capitalism and individualism (Thompson).[3] As a code for representing and managing class differences, sympathy was used in seamstress stories to negate the threat of class conflict and violence—ultimately, by translating class differences into gender.[4] In depictions of the sentimental seamstress, class victimization was representationally submerged within increasingly influential gender norms: seamstress stories fashioned an eroticized image of what was increasingly perceived to be an inherently *feminine* condition of economic dependency and embedded that image within a highly conventional narrative structure. The inscription of the sentimental seamstress's economic downfall, as a progressive condition narrated through time, became a gendered locus of particular forms of economic determinism, and a means of managing deep-seated cultural anxieties about workingwomen's (sexual and economic) autonomy.

Like her working-class contemporary the "factory girl," the seamstress was the subject of substantial debate about women's roles in the emerging industrial economy. However, unlike female mill workers, seamstresses had few opportunities to engage in acts of literary self-definition: there were no established media, such as the *Lowell Offering* or the *Voice of Industry,* in which needleworkers could articulate their experiences and publicly voice their concerns. Perhaps because of this discursive absence, there was surprising homogeneity in depictions of seamstresses, and the sentimental seamstress became a conventional "type" in fiction and poetry, as well as several discourses of social reform. "Real" seamstresses resisted such literary codification; contesting material and ideological forms of feminine dependency, militant seamstresses—like radical millwomen—mobilized languages of radical democracy to protest inequities based in gender as well as class.[5] While the non-labor press castigated them for defying the "natural" dictates of gender—for example, the *Boston Transcript* characterized a speech by Lavinia Wright, secretary of the United Tailoresses' Society of New York, as containing "clamorous and unfeminine" declarations of woman's rights, which "it is obvious a wise Providence never destined her to exercise"—labor leaders in the sewing trades, like millwomen such as Sarah Bagley, challenged such gender strictures. They encouraged female workers to act independently of men, defend their rights, and unmask paternalism as mere rationale for sexual injustice. For example, Sarah Monroe urged her sisters, "Let us trust no longer to the generosity of our employers; seeing that they are men in whose heads or hearts the thought of doing justice to a fellow being never seems to enter." She concludes, "It needs no small share of courage for us, who have been used to impositions and oppression from our youth up to the present day, to come before the public in defense of our rights; but, my friends, if it is unfashionable for the men to bear oppression in silence, why should it not also become unfashionable with the women. Or do they deem us more able to endure hardship than they themselves?" (as seen in Foner 5–6). Like radical workingmen, Monroe seized upon the democratic potential of economic modernization, endeavoring to fashion an activist identity for female needleworkers and demanding access to new social and economic opportunities. Indeed, Monroe points to the increasing public presence of workingmen as a potential model for workingwomen, and dismisses as mere "fashion" those gender conventions that would stifle female public speech. (At the same time, she hints that such strictures are imposed, in part, by workingmen themselves: it is those men who "come before the public in defense of [their] rights" who evidently consider workingwomen "more able to endure hardship than they themselves.") More frequently, however, the seamstress was typified within literary and political discourse as just the sort of emblem of endurance Monroe repudiates: represented as a figure incapable of change, she was textually marked as the primary victim of the "free market" and urban life.

Inscribed in a host of popular fictions, including William English's *Gertrude Howard* (1843), T. S. Arthur's *The Seamstress* (1843), Charles Burdett's *The Elliott Family* (1847), Mary Denison's *Edna Etheril, the Boston Seamstress* (1847), and George Lippard's "Jesus and the Poor" (1848), the sentimental seamstress's characteristic plot was one of unrelenting, and devastating, decline. For example, T. S. Arthur describes seamstress Mrs. Gaston as "struggling with failing and unequal strength against the tide that was slowly bearing her down the stream" (10); using natural imagery to signify the seamstress's fate, Arthur opposes nature's force to the weak, and hopelessly inadequate, female body. Seamstress narratives can be seen to dramatize and exorcise what Barbara Ehrenreich terms a "fear of falling"—anxieties about losing class status—that many felt in fluctuating economic times. As Carroll Smith-Rosenberg has observed, the 1840s were a decade when "downward economic mobility far exceeded upward movement," at least in major cities (86). Artisans and journeymen were especially affected; Stuart Blumin has shown that, as opportunities for advancement narrowed in the four decades preceding the Civil War, artisans were more likely to experience downward rather than upward mobility (as seen in Laurie 48). However, while expectations of masculine entrepreneurship and competition—best exemplified in popular "rags to riches" narratives—constituted one, increasingly normative, ideological response to economic insecurity, anxieties about economic failure and downward mobility were largely projected onto women.[6] The seamstress's "unfreedom" and diminished economic agency were produced through the confluence of several discourses; for example, the conventional downward path of the seamstress borrows some sense of inevitability from the plight of the fallen woman—a figure with which she was regularly linked in reform literature.[7] But the seamstress's economic helplessness was emphatically signaled by her privileged place within the discourse of poverty—evident in Mathew Carey's foundational texts of the 1820s and 1830s and firmly established in the writings that proliferated during the early 1840s, in what amounts to an American version of the English Poor Law debates.[8] Beginning with Adam Smith, laissez-faire theorists had represented poverty as an inevitable product of capitalism—a widely acknowledged inevitability that surely lent its weight to the seamstress's downward narrative. But a key historical effect of the English Poor Law debates, as Mary Poovey has shown, was the differentiation of pauperism from poverty; pauperism was increasingly specified as a moral and physical designation, while poverty was seen by many to be a structural part of the national economy deemed essential to capitalist production (11). Through the seamstress, pauperism was decisively feminized; the seamstress was a figure whose economic vulnerability, and specifically the need for (public or private) support, was deemed an inherent part of her moral and physical being, one closely aligned with—indeed, viewed as an extension of—her "natural" and irremediable gender dependency.

As depicted by writers from Mathew Carey forward, the seamstress appeared as the primary victim of market laws, exemplifying the social category Carey designated the "deserving poor." A being "ground down to the earth by [her] employers" (*Essays* 285), the "ill-fated" seamstress is, for Carey, a worthy object of charity: "There are those, who from principle, as they say, refuse assistance to the man who can obtain the means of supplying all his wants by his daily labour. But can they withhold relief from her who comes in her desolation and weakness—woman, who, by the law of her being, is excluded from paths in which coarser men may make a livelihood?" Grounding a gender division of labor in "the law of [woman's] being"—the natural strictures of gender, here appearing as weakness and refinement—Carey apparently makes her gender the basis of her claim to public assistance and the inevitability of her economic dependency ("Plea" 1).[9] Even Walter Channing, who theorizes poverty as a "social condition" and not the "result of the direct, willing agency of him who suffers it," invokes women workers, most notably seamstresses, under "constant pressure of comparatively light work," as most vulnerable to pauperism: "here is not only sure exhaustion of the body, but the very moral and mental power that may be bought into use, do little or nothing by such use of them to invigorate themselves. On the contrary, does not such use of them impair their powers; and when failure comes, *as come it must,* are not hopelessness and helplessness, their sure and close companions?" (20, 36–38; emphasis added). It is the female seamstress who makes the downward path of economic abjection both visible and seemingly inevitable, the constraints and "train of contingencies" palpable and affecting. Referring again to the "amount of time demanded of women who live by daily work, and to the very small compensation they receive for it," Channing writes, "They . . . can do no more than supply the daily returning want, and this only while remaining strength enables them to continue their long, and exhausting toil. When sickness comes, then comes that which to industry is more terrible than all pain. . . . Pauperism is here in the train of contingencies which cannot be controlled, and it often comes in its saddest forms" (38–39). As the victim of a "train of contingencies" she is helpless to prevent or alter, the seamstress becomes the locus of economic determinism, while distancing a sense of economic helplessness and lack of control from men. Channing's text suggests how paternalism was being refashioned in these writings to accord with antebellum gender norms; the basis of the seamstress's irresistible claim to support is, precisely, her femininity, and especially her feminine weakness and delicacy—a construction that at once eroticizes dependency, and anchors poverty's social claims in the inherent appeal of the appropriately "feminine" woman.[10] Feminizing dependency, writers such as Channing also helped to *privatize* that economic condition, insulating the persistence of poverty and economic inequity from the prospect of systematic or structural economic reform.[11]

The feminization of dependency[12] owed much to the emerging ideology of domesticity. Jeanne Boydston has demonstrated that a central feature of antebellum gender constructions was an emphasis on women's non-productivity. In domestic advice literature and women's fiction, as well as political and economic treatises, women were increasingly defined as leisured and non-productive, while productive work was envisioned as that which took place outside the home (and was compensated with wages) (142–63). (Notably, what Marxist feminists have termed the "invisibility" of women's work inside the home, and the absence of wage compensation for that labor, exerted a downward pull on all female wages: the conventional perception of sewing as unpaid and "unskilled" [i.e., *female*] domestic work had a depressing effect on the labor market faced by needleworkers.) These economically organized gender arrangements—as well as the contemporary tendency to ground them within the psyche—were memorably captured by Alexis de Tocqueville: American men, Tocqueville observed, are motivated by an "ardent and restless" desire for prosperity and the "constant excitement" and unpredictability of economic pursuits ("Men . . . continually change their tack for fear of missing the shortest cut to happiness"), while women superintend a home life that supplies the "tranquility," "order," and the "deep, regular and quiet affection which constitutes the charm and safeguard of life" (as seen in Barker-Benfield 45–46). According to the tenets of domestic ideology, male economic expansiveness and progress were routinely opposed to female rootedness, constancy, and stability. The conflation of femininity and dependency was evident in the very terms of the emerging Jacksonian consensus about outdoor relief (economic support of the poor at home). Such relief, it was widely believed, could "relax individual exertion by unnerving the arm of industry" and weaken the "desire of honest independence," engendering a state increasingly equated to the "natural" weakness, delicacy, and dependency of femininity (Rothman 166–67). Crucially, as David Rothman observes, "In the pre–Civil War period, women filled the outdoor relief rolls, men, the almshouse" (40).[13] The antebellum feminization of poverty helped consolidate emerging (but not uncontested) norms of gender, while explicitly curtailing female economic agency. The production of feminine dependency was not considered something public policy should, or perhaps could, seek to avoid; in fact, it was increasingly normalized.

The eroticized image of feminine dependency exemplified by the downtrodden seamstress was challenged by radical workingwomen and some workingmen, especially those who envisioned a redistribution of property and who questioned the role of the family in its consolidation and transmission. For example, in two controversial pamphlets published in 1840, *The Labouring Classes* and *Defense of the Article on the Laboring Classes,* Orestes Brownson argues for the abolition of hereditary property as an inherently anti-republican, monopolistic, and oppressive institution. In the tradition of Tom Paine, Brownson advances a plan for redistribution that involved reappropriating each citizen's property at the time of his death, so that each new citizen could receive, as national birthright, a certain portion when he (or more radically, she) would reach his (or her) majority. Brownson demonstrates how sympathy for a man's "dependents" was conventionally used to defend private property and a wage and inheritance system that itself disadvantaged women and children, essentially by producing the very dependency it was called upon to remedy. In the *Defense,* Brownson observes that one "objection" to his plan that "we had not anticipated" was that it "would bear exceedingly hard upon the widow and the orphan. As soon as a man dies, the state takes his property, and the widow and the orphan must be sent to the almshouse." This argument, as Brownson owns, "appeals to our sensibilities," mobilizing social anxiety on the part of "dependent" women and children. However, according to the plan, children would be "provided for in school, where they fare the same [as] they would were the father living"; while apropos of the widow, Brownson boldly argues that "in the reappropriation, the distinction of sex should not play the important part it does now. In all that concerns property, woman should share equally with man, and like him be an independent proprietor, a relation which marriage should not necessarily affect." Powerfully, Brownson asserts that "the idea of dependence should never necessarily attach to the one more than to the other. Marriage . . . should never be regarded as a marriage of estates, but of persons, and hearts. Each should have the means of living independent of that relation." To the inevitable concern that "our proposed reform will break up the family relation," Brownson, while he admits "great respect" for "the family feeling," argues for a reformation and expansion of social sentiment in accord with a truly democratic social order: "we have been taught by our religion, and by our philosophy, that the family is subordinate to Humanity, and that, though it is the centre of our affections, and the sphere in which lie our special duties, still it is in our love and action always to give place to mankind at large, and to universal justice"

(79, 80, 85).[14] Like many radical workingwomen, Brownson proposes a reformation in social sympathies, boldly imagining a new erotics that would not be governed by a Victorian gender binary of masculine independency and feminine dependency.

But while some protested this new social arrangement, it was rendered conventional in narratives of workingwomen's subjection to market laws. In the pages that follow, I read seamstress narratives, and the forms of "fallenness" and determinism they inscribe, as discursive efforts to curtail workingwomen's agency and diffuse the erotic and economic challenges female workers were posing to the Jacksonian social, economic, and political order.

Narrativizing Feminine Dependency

It is crucial to point out that the seamstress's downward path, as well as the peculiar temporality of her experience, distinguishes her from the male protagonists of much nineteenth-century urban fiction, as well as those memorably enterprising eighteenth-century fictional heroines, such as Daniel Defoe's Moll Flanders and Roxana. Indeed, Defoe's female protagonists exemplify economic ambition: ably navigating the market as independent female entrepreneurs, they make and break contracts (including marriage contracts) readily when they do not accord with their independent interests, sacrifice children easily, envision feminine "virtue" as an inconvenience and a stay upon female independence, rise and fall easily (and repeatedly) in their fortunes, capitalize on economic exigencies by resourcefully turning circumstances to their own account, and, overall, confront the world with optimistic expectations. Thus can Moll Flanders state gamely midway through her eventful and tumultuous story, "though I was a woman without a fortune, I expected something or other might happen in my way that might mend my circumstances, as had been the case before" (Defoe 112).

Such economic resourcefulness is abundantly evident in nineteenth-century urban literature. In *Signs Taken for Wonders*, Franco Moretti argues that intensified opportunities for mobility—spatial and economic—afforded by the modern city work to subordinate the city as discrete physical place to the city as "network of developing social relationships—and hence as a prop to narrative temporality" (112). Because the "meaning of the city . . . [only] manifests itself through a temporal trajectory" (112), the city becomes during this period the privileged object of narrative: indeed, nineteenth-century fiction generated a new rhetoric of temporality, culminating in the "suspense plot of the novel," which captured the dynamic nature of urban experience (109). For Moretti, the unpredictability of urban life—especially its economic and social contingencies—favors the adaptability of urban subjects, their ability to capitalize on what is provisionally available, to translate urban stimuli into opportunities or "'chances' to be seized" (117):

> City life . . . arms itself against catastrophe by adopting ever more pliant and provisional attitudes. It is no accident that the city dweller has always appeared as a typically "adaptable" animal. . . . In tragedy everything conspires concertedly *in only one direction.* In [urban fiction,] . . . the high number of variables inherent to the systems of the city and the novel brings about the conclusion through a continuous and highly unpredictable series of ups and downs. In this way, suspense and surprise encourage city dwellers to believe that only rarely is "*everything* lost." Even in the middle of catastrophe they are induced to perceive, and hence rejoice in, all surviving potentiality. . . . [T]he novel, and the city dweller's entire "education," do not hinge on the shock image of potential impact—but rather the know-how necessary to avoid it, on competence in "alternative paths" of every kind, and on the ability to latch on immediately to the possibilities that these very often disclose. (117–18, 123)

Moretti's description of the adaptability and improvisational facility unleashed and rewarded by the urban context, qualities perhaps best apparent in American literature, in the realist fiction of William Dean Howells, Henry James, and Theodore Dreiser, is a far cry from the character (and usual narrative trajectory) of the sentimental seamstress, whose story follows the contours of tragedy more closely than urban fiction. While Dreiser would later assign his working-class protagonist, Carrie Meeber, positioned on the threshold of urban life, essentially two choices—that she should "become better" or "become worse" (3–4)—in antebellum seamstress stories, the heroine's trajectory is decidedly and inevitably downward. Not "pliant" and self-transforming but fixed and unwavering, the sentimental seamstress is ascribed a tragic fatalism that borrows from a theological sense of feminine fallenness and determinism; and her characterization suggests that the exemplary urban subject described by Moretti is markedly masculine. Rather than capitalizing on urban, especially economic opportunities, the seamstress is immobilized by them; hers is a decidedly antimodern, or premodern, sensibility and subjectivity. In an important sense, the seamstress's economic ineptitude, her tendency toward self-effacement and passivity rather than self-promotion and entrepreneurial agency, signifies her virtue and especially her *modesty*—called by Joseph Addison and Richard Steele "the only Recommendation" in women, but "the greatest Obstacle to [men] both in Love and Business" (as seen in Yeazell 9). As Ruth Bernard Yeazell observes, "the gendering of modesty . . . follows from the separation of spheres—a division of labor that will increasingly free men for the aggressions of the marketplace by assigning certain 'beautiful' but inconvenient virtues to the safekeeping of women" (9). In seamstress narratives, the virtuous seamstress (as distinct from her degraded counterparts) shuns public attention and the competitiveness of market negotiation; her veiled figure characteristically shrinks in a dark corner of the tailor shop. In this way, the modest seamstress's economic decline is psychologically guaranteed, and envisioned as both sign and product of her virtue, while she is decisively distanced from the type of modern urban subject described by Moretti. Hers is a protonaturalist narrative; she is subject to a determinism at once economic and moral/psychological.[15] Edith Wharton's Lily Bart (driven to millinery work late in the novel) might be seen to embody the culmination of this antebellum narrative tradition: Lily's delicacy about economic matters, as fully as the unforgiving economic environment she inhabits, ensures her economic victimization.

This gendering of economic success and agency as masculine, as well as the association of poverty and economic decline with "virtuous" femininity, is identified with shrewd insight by Fanny Fern, who writes in one newspaper sketch: "There are few people who speak approbatively of a woman who has a smart business talent or capability. No matter how isolated or destitute her condition, the majority would consider it more 'feminine' would she unobtrusively gather up her thimble, and, retiring into some out-of-the-way place, gradually scoop out her coffin with it, than to develop that smart turn for business which would lift her at once out of her troubles, and which, in a man so situated, would be applauded as exceedingly praiseworthy" ("Injustice" 318). Importantly, for Fern, the figure who best embodies the condition of feminine destitution is the seamstress, "unobtrusively" retiring to domestic privacy ("some out-of-the-way place"), who "scoop[s] out her coffin" with her thimble. Implying that this figure is the product of popular prejudice rather than feminine nature, Fern attributes the "majority['s]" appetite for narratives of feminine economic decline rather than success to specific cultural assumptions about gender. Presented with an isolated, destitute woman, the "majority," Fern states, will approve of, and normatively expect, her fall rather than her rise—a temporal, narrative development designated in spatial terms in this passage. In Fern's sketch, the economic subjectivity of the seamstress is demarcated through loss and diminishment rather than expansion or growth—a diminishment written on her very body. Edgar Allan Poe's famous dictum, that the death of a beautiful woman is the most poetical topic in the world, appears subtended by particular economic, as well as aesthetic, expectations.[16]

As suggested above, the seamstress's downward path was patterned after that of the fallen woman—an association that served, simultaneously, to evoke and allay the suspicion of working-class female "immodesty" and active sexual (or economic) desire.[17] Indeed, the fallen woman can be seen to be the seamstress's double in these narratives, and if the condition of sexual "fallenness" is not explicitly personified it is implicitly presented as a possible outcome of female economic independence, a possibility that can be staved off through the rigors of self-denial and scrupulous curtailment of desire. Always shadowing seamstress narratives is the possibility of women's active, calculating self-commodification—the prospect of the kind of female entrepreneurial ambition Fern alludes to, exercised in both the labor and sexual markets. By sentimentalizing the seamstress and emphasizing her dependency, helplessness, and "feminine" submission, crafters of the seamstress image assuaged pressing cultural anxieties about working-class female agency—especially women workers' "immodesty," and the prospect of their sexual-economic independence. Sentimentality is an important tactic in these narratives' reformations of working-class female desire.

Class and the Politics of Sympathy

The "sentimental seamstress," like the "factory girl," had a transatlantic genesis: the seamstress as literary type was forged in British as well as American fictions of labor. Indeed, by far the most famous literary production about seamstresses is English author Thomas Hood's "The Song of the Shirt," which first appeared in *Punch* in 1843.[18] Hood introduces the seamstress, the singer of the "Song," as follows: "With fingers weary and worn, / With eyelids heavy and red, / A woman sat, in unwomanly rags, / Plying her needle and thread. / Stitch—stitch—stitch! / In poverty, hunger, and dirt, / Stitch—stitch—stitch! / She sang the 'Song of the Shirt!" (11.1–8). Using popular ballad meter, but placing the stresses to emphasize the monotony and rigor of the seamstress's task, Hood relies on contemporary ideals of womanhood to generate outrage at the "unwomanly" nature of the seamstress's plight. Hood depicts the trials of the seamstress's labors in the poem's middle stanzas:

> Work—work—work!
> Till the brain begins to swim;
> Work—work—work!
> Till the eyes are heavy and dim!
> Seam and gusset and band,
> Band and gusset and seam,
> Till o'er the buttons I fall asleep
> And sew them on in a dream!
>
> O! Men, with Sisters Dear!
> O! Men, with Mothers and Wives,
> It is not linen you're wearing out!
> But human creatures' lives!
> Stitch—stitch—stitch
> In poverty, hunger, and dirt;

Sewing at once, with a double thread,
A shroud as well as a shirt. . . .

Work—work—work!
My labor never flags;
And what are its wages? A bed of straw,
A crust of bread—and rags. (11.17–32; 41–11)

Here and throughout the "Song," the poet emphasizes the devastating irony that the seamstress who spends her life sewing garments can afford to dress in nothing better than "unwomanly rags." The diminishment of life that is the consequence of this ceaseless drudgery is powerfully conveyed: the seamstress lives in abject poverty, with insufficient food to support her body and spare furnishings and domestic comforts. Her very subjectivity is threatened by her work—the monotonous labors steal her consciousness, and even penetrate her dreams. By highlighting the figure of the suffering worker, the true nature of commodities is sensationally revealed: fabric is here the very stuff of life; the shirt is in actuality a shroud. Like the fates, the seamstress measures out the length of life with her thread—but the death she prophecies in the poem is her own. The remainder of the "Song" amplifies these motifs, casting the seamstress's labor as both imprisonment and enslavement, and extending the daily monotony of the labor to the cycle of the seasons: while the seasons change, the seamstress's unending work goes relentlessly forward. (She is deprived even of the relief of tears, "For every drop / Hinders needle and thread!") The poem concludes with the poet's plea, "Would that its tone could reach the rich! / She sang this 'Song of the Shirt!'" Reinforcing the poem's message of social paternalism, Hood appeals not to women as consumers but to men: "Oh, Men, with Sisters dear! / Oh, Men, with Mothers and Wives! / It is not linen you're wearing out, / But human creatures' lives!" (11.25–28).

Hood's poem not only spawned a wealth of literary imitators, it also helped create a "new iconographic vocabulary" of the seamstress in Victorian painting. As T. J. Edelstein notes, painting devoted to "social themes" was a trend that emerged in the late 1830s, and "by far the most popular of . . . social themes in Victorian painting was the seamstress." These works, beginning with Richard Redgrave's *The Sempstress* (exhibited at the Royal Academy in 1844) employ a recurring "symbolic vocabulary" that stresses the seamstress's identity "as a figure exploited by Victorian society" (183–84). Indebted to Hood, Redgrave, through his compositional choices, established the elements of this visual vocabulary: the seamstress is a solitary figure; the room is illuminated by a single candle or the dawn light; she is surrounded by a few meager possessions—including a spindly plant; a broken bowl; a bed, table, and chair; and an empty fireplace—all of which "acquire meaning by [their] constant repetition" in the era's theme painting. Importantly, traditional artistic associations added resonance to this imagery (188). Images of saints found in Italian Renaissance paintings—sweet, pious women turning their eyes to heaven—was one such artistic reference. The seamstress, with her pale, illuminated face and upturned gaze, is thus identified as a martyr to modern urban society. Further, "the seated female figure recalls not only piety but melancholy, Albrecht Dürer's version of this theme being the most important example" (192). The doleful expression of Redgrave's needlewoman alludes to this psychological state; other painters depict her with head in hands, the standard visual symbol. Additional, and conventional, compositional elements include a cup of tea (seamstresses were widely shown to need the stimulation of tea to complete their labor); the view of a church steeple or the placement of a clock (to signal the passage of time and the ceaseless rhythms of work); medicine bottles, to signal her illness and perhaps imminent death; and often a single flower (to mark the contrast between country and city, and as a symbol for the seamstress herself). This visual vocabulary certainly shaped, and was shaped by, literary representations of the seamstress, while melodramatic plays such as Mark Lemon's *The Sempstress* (1844) popularized this figure as well. Victorian paintings, plays, and narratives about the seamstress thus fashioned a figure that exemplified—and could generate popular sentiment about—industrial victimization, a figure with resonance on both sides of the Atlantic.

The suffering seamstress was adapted to the American context by a variety of writers, while the visual iconography of the seamstress influenced a host of cultural representations. (For example, in E. D. E. N. Southworth's *The Hidden Hand*, the seamstress Marah Rocke, frequently seen gazing out the window and lost in dejection, clearly embodies the seamstress's characteristic melancholy and meekness, while the aforementioned Mrs. Gaston in Arthur's *The Seamstress* is characterized through several of the details Edelstein enumerates.) Most important in shaping the figure in antebellum America were the influential writings of middle-class moral reformers, who translated the sufferings and poverty of needlewomen, depicted by such writers as Mathew Carey, into a distinctly moral register. Giving wide circulation to the seamstress's narrative of decline, moral reformers' writings interpreted that downfall in particular ways, heightening certain aspects of needlewomen's oppression (especially the understanding of the capitalist market as a realm of gender struggle) while downplaying or effacing others. In stories and sketches in the *Advocate,* discussed below, as well as more extensive narrative treatments such as Burdett's *The Elliott Family,* moral reformers read the scandal of female needlework through the lens of evangelical gender relations. Applying evangelical reformers' analysis of prostitution and sexual reform to the sphere of labor, these writers codify a gendered vocabulary of sexual desire as the frame for understanding—and reforming—capitalist and industrial practices. Middle-class reformers borrow from the melodramatic repertoire (and its paternalist social imagery) to tell the seamstress's tale; at the same time, they give sympathetic, pious middle-class women an important place in the seamstress's story, foregrounding their philanthropic role in reforming illicit male power. I argue below that moral reformers offered in their writings limited analyses of the nature of workingwomen's oppression; furthermore, they present a model of gender relations that ultimately undermines workingwomen's economic and sexual agency. Notably, moral reformers' rhetorics tended to diminish class differences among gender groups. For example, poor tailors appear as economically accountable as wealthy capitalists (indeed, often more so) for seamstresses' oppression and thus worked to displace class by gender—a displacement with crucial political effects. Most importantly, they seemed to assimilate economic practices of exploitation and victimization to sexual appetites and practices (e.g., male lust and aggression and female "passionlessness") that were increasingly naturalized during this period, while, in a circular fashion, locating the remedy for such exploitation in gender itself. In the final section of the essay, I examine the anonymously authored serial novella "Stray Leaves from a Seamstress's Journal" (1853–54), published in the feminist journal *The Una,* in which an emphasis on needlewomen's agency and self-determination—their (collective) identity as workers—contests their sentimentalization and challenges their inscription as the "feminine" and feminized poor.

Assimilating Labor to Sexual Reform: The Seamstress in the *Advocate*

In the 1830s, the figure of the seamstress was decisively taken up in the literature of moral reform, most influentially by the New York Female Moral Reform Society, an organization founded in 1834 that sought to rehabilitate prostitutes and expose the social effects of the sexual double standard. Through its publishing organ, the *Advocate* (one of the nation's most widely read evangelical papers), the Society circulated countless narratives of seduction and the devastating plight of "fallen" women. Melodramatically splitting villains and victims, these narratives emphasized the lascivious, sexually aggressive nature of American men, and construed women as "innocent and unsuspecting" victims of male sexual predations (*Advocate* [Vol. 2, 1836] 18). (Terms such as "budding," "lovely," "fresh," and "unsuspecting lamb" were frequently used to describe innocent women before their seduction, and men were assigned such epithets as "murderer of virtue.") One writer captured the *Advocate*'s characteristic argument: "It cannot be concealed that the treachery of man, betraying the interests of . . . woman, is one of the principal causes, which furnishes the victims of licentiousness. Few, very few . . . have sought their wretched calling" (as seen in Berg 181–82). The Society was especially important in drawing well-publicized connections between women's economic situation—the low wages drawn in traditional female occupations such as seamstresses, domestics, and washerwomen—and prostitution, and was among the earliest critics of the New York garment industry. Seamstress narratives clearly bear the imprint of the Society's accounts of fallen women; indeed, the *Advocate* expressly assimilated the seamstress's story into its conventional sexual melodrama of male exploitation and female victimization, thus consolidating gendered constructions of economic dependency.[19] As Carroll Smith-Rosenberg observes, "The Society's editors and officers placed the responsibility for the low wages paid seamstresses and other female workers on ruthless and exploitative men. Much the same tone of anti-male hostility is evident in their economic exposes as in their sexual exposes" (321n62). Indeed, moral reformers' rhetoric of sexual antagonism—a violent, predatory masculine sexuality available to reform by virtuous women (especially mothers), and an innocent, sexually vulnerable femininity—became an important analytic through which poor women's exploitation was understood and represented. Most importantly, this paradigm foregrounded gender and sexuality at the expense of class and labor. Moral reformers' blindness to these matters is evident in the fact that they generally envisioned the greatest sexual dangers in jobs that offered workingwomen the greatest opportunity for financial gain (Hobson 64), while they depicted domestic service as the most useful, safest employment for women; indeed, they routinely placed prostitutes "rescued" from brothels in Christian homes as servants.

The seamstress was a figure for the worst abuses of female labor in a range of moral reformers' writings. An example of virtue in distress, she was a recognizable heroine; in a sense, she was a working-class version of the "tragic mulatta" of antislavery stories, a figure endowed with attributes of middle-class subjectivity—sensibility, refinement, virtue, and beauty—that middle-class readers could recognize and readily identify with. Charlotte Elizabeth Tonna's influential book about suffering seamstresses, *The Wrongs of Women* (1842), received the following notice in the *Advocate:* "A Sketch designed to illustrate the wrongs and oppressions to which the . . . apprentices of the milliners and dress-makers of England are subjected" ([Vol. 8, 1842] 172). Using adjectives such as "poor," "sickly," "unprotected," "hapless," and "desponding" to characterize needlewomen, writers in the *Advocate* emphasized the wrongs and oppressions of garment workers—their sufferings and struggles as well as their subjection to powerful and oppressive economic forces.[20] An 1836 article, "Tailoresses and Seamstresses," told of "10,000 females in this city dependent upon their needles for support. . . . [A] valuable, worthy, and indispensable class of the community . . . laboring under a cruel and iron handed oppression . . . [they are] driven by the hand of a merciless oppression into the cellars and garrets of old, worn out, leaky . . . tenements, for which they have to pay an exorbitant rent, and there compelled to toil from 16–20 hours a day to gain a bare subsistence. . . . Here is labor without compensation—labor extorted from our own sisters . . . whom every principle of honor calls us to protect" ([Vol. 2,

1836] 171). Importantly, the connection between sewing and prostitution became a convention of this literature. Assimilating the seamstress's plight and economic distress to their existing analysis of female sexual victimization, the *Advocate* declared in 1845 that "it is a fact universally admitted that the ordinary rate of wages for female labor is unjust and oppressive. In this single fact lies the germs of woman's degradation in unnumbered instances" ([Vol. 11, 1845] 110). The previous year, one writer postulated that "In every large community and especially in cities there are multitudes of the young who . . . are thrown on their own resources and obliged to earn a subsistence . . . or become prey to the tempter. . . . Shame on . . . men who, by oppressing the hireling in her wages, drive the young and unfriended to dens of shame, while they fill their coffers with the avails of unrequited toil" ([Vol. 10, 1844] 165). The passive construction of the grammar (women are "thrown on their own resources" and "obliged to earn a subsistence"; they are "drive[n]" by men to "dens of shame") emphasizes the helplessness and passivity of poor women, compelled by forces beyond their control. Prostitution is the consequence of male activity and a desire that is alternately economic and sexual; men figure here as "tempters" and seducers, and as those who oppress the female "hireling" to increase their profits. Drawing on the Victorian theory of female sexual passivity, the *Advocate* thus stressed the active, aggressive sexuality of men in order to exculpate women from the stain of licentious desire. In addition, by equating capitalist acquisition and exploitation to their binary of sexual exploitation, moral reformers rewrite class in the language of gender.[21] The sexual vulnerability of the seamstress, and the connection between fallenness and women's wage employment, was emphasized in popular lore. It was a cultural commonplace that young country girls were regularly entrapped into prostitution by recruiters who cloaked their intentions with the promise of training and work in millinery and other sewing trades; and it was also widely held that agents and madams seeking new recruits often operated in conjunction with employment businesses, known as intelligence offices, where women were told they were being hired as seamstresses, milliners, or domestics. The *Advocate* reported that many houses of infamy were connected with millinery establishments, partly to conceal the true character of the houses from the young women hired and from the public ([Vol. 2, 1836] 19).

Thus moral reformers emphatically constructed the industrial labor market as a realm of gender struggle. At the same time, they assigned key roles to pious, middle-class women in reforming male sexuality and redeeming fallen women. (As the author of "Tailoresses and Seamstresses" makes clear, the "hand of merciless oppression" can only be stayed by the "protect[ing]" arm of middle-class women.) Positioned as privileged object of sympathy, the suffering seamstress enabled, and helped legitimate, the expansion of what the *Advocate* termed "the magnitude of woman's mission" and the growing sphere of middle-class women's social influence ([Vol. 21, 1855] 93). Gone are the democratic accents of militant needlewomen's rhetoric: the only female agency legible in these accounts is that of the evangelical reformer/rescuer. It is crucial that the status of sexual fallenness, and the seamstress's seemingly inevitable downward path, borrow from the same cultural logic. In each case, poor women are envisioned as helpless and abject, and bear the burden of narrative determinism.

Contesting the Sentimental Seamstress: "Stray Leaves from a Seamstress"

Both the feminization of dependency embodied by the sentimental seamstress and the authority of middle-class reformers to define that figure were attacked in a remarkable literary revision of the seamstress image, "Stray Leaves from a Seamstress." Written in first person, "Stray Leaves" fashions the seamstress not as suffering object but as resisting subject. Notably, the issue before the first installment of "Stray Leaves" contained Lizzie Lynn's suggestively titled "Dependence: Or What Made One Woman Meanly Penurious," a story that recounts the trials of a devoted, hardworking housewife, one Mrs. Dean, whose husband, a wealthy businessman, holds the family purse-strings too tightly. Unconscious of the painful position in which he places his wife, Mr. Dean prides himself on "the possession of wealth, and his large income, and his economical wife" ("very few persons spend as little as we do, and live as handsomely"); however, to maintain the family's handsome "exterior," Mrs. Dean must haggle relentlessly with sales clerks and "consume her life-force in elaborate needle-work," all the while masking the contradiction between "outward splendor and hidden poverty and want."

The story makes starkly explicit how female economic "dependence"—directly tied to the male breadwinning wage—was understood as a way to regulate female desire. While Mrs. Dean finds it "humiliating to ask, as though you were a beggar, and receive as though it were a charity, every cent you spend," her husband "thought . . . [that] the smallness of the sums given to his wife would be a wholesome check to any propensity to extravagance she might acquire. He was somewhat tinctured with the very common idea that women are reckless of expenditure whenever they have the means." Mrs. Dean counters her husband's paternalism with a democratic rhetoric of rights; she "chafe[s], and fret[s], and rebels" against being placed in the position of "a mere dependent upon his bounty," thus "receiv[ing] as a gratuity what is [hers] by right." Her plea depends on making visible her economic contribution, her valuable physical and emotional labor: "If we are going to settle accounts, I will go to the past and bring in a bill that you seem to have forgotten.—Who struggled with you in poverty? Who toiled early and late for the comforts that you were unable to procure? When our first-born cried for bread, and there was none to give him, whose hands earned it?. . . . Who labored in every way to promote your pecuniary interests?" Recognizing that "to her he owed everything; she made him what he was, and he knew it," Mr. Dean is reformed: affairs are "amicably adjusted," and he henceforth supplies more appropriate sums for monthly expenses, an arrangement with which his wife is "abundantly satisfied" (33–34).

The anonymously authored "Stray Leaves" similarly contests female economic dependency; indeed, the narrator at the outset vows "never to be dependent on those who would make me feel they grudged me my bread." "Stray Leaves" starts as a familiar narrative of downward mobility: narrator Lucy Vernon's father has recently and suddenly died, ending the family's comfortably middle-class existence and leaving her primary breadwinner for her invalid mother and two young sisters. As she states early on in the text, "How is it, that with all my toil, we grow every day poorer?" However, while at one point Lucy fears that her life will "waste away in gloomy loneliness," "Stray Leaves" re-writes the seamstress's characteristic "destiny," recounting not its narrator's victimization by circumstances but her ability to triumph over them. The story ends with the narrator an independent and contented "old maid" possessing "a small competence, the fruit of [her] own industry," with which she has "purchased a little cottage" in the country.[22] To, in the narrator's apt words, "gain independence and conquer 'circumstance, that unspiritual God,'" the narrator resists feelings of "tender dependence" toward her former beloved, a Dr. L., and stoically dedicates herself to her "duty." Possessing a "fierce pride and unbending spirit," she declares her resolution at the outset, "I am strong, full of life and vigor. . . . I must not make my own theories a failure, for I have said that woman was equal to any emergency, that she had worlds of latent strength to be developed at the right time." While activist workingwomen were often pejoratively depicted in popular culture as "de-sexed" and "unfeminine," the narrator proudly embraces what society would deem her "masculine" traits, stating that "God . . . planted in my very soul all the desperate earnestness of man, with the unchanging, patient constancy . . . of a woman."[23]

That "desperate earnestness" is strikingly manifest in the text: using the format of a journal, "Stray Leaves" presents, with surprising intensity and force, a bold and independent working-class feminist voice—one relatively unmarked by conventional melodramatic or sentimental cadences. (Indeed, in its confessional intensity and its record of psychic conflict it is surprisingly modern, closer to *Notes from the Underground* than nineteenth-century "woman's fiction" or popular melodrama.) Envisioning her journal as an intimate "friend" and "sole confident [*sic*] of my thoughts, my aspirations and desires," the narrator records the daily struggles and pains of poverty and endless work, as well as her intellectual and often sharply conflicted emotional responses to those experiences. At times expressing resignation that, as "child of the people," she is "made for [labor]," she more often records her outrage at class inequity and the callous disregard of her middle-class, and mostly female, employers; resentment at the wounding slights she regularly experiences from employers, landlords, and shopkeepers; and gratitude for the generosity of other workingwomen ("poor seamstresses have . . . hearts that are easily touched with the griefs of others"). While she expresses romantic desire and does pine for the loss of Dr. L., an older man whose proposals she had earlier rejected and for whom she now bears a "long buried" passion, the "aspirations and desires" she voices are mainly those for radical political and economic change; indeed, her writing is infused with revolutionary fervor and "haunt[ed]" by "the grand idea . . . of cooperative industry." In an expression of what Michael Rogin terms the "American 1848," the narrator powerfully imagines seamstresses not as passive economic victims but as agents of violent revolt: "Are women to be born for this, to toil, shrivel, die and rot? Is there never to be an avenue opened for their powers? . . . My very soul is roused with indignation. The women of France once rose in rebellion. Their cry was 'bread for our babes'; will the women of our country ever utter this cry as they gather in crowds from attics, cellars, by lanes, and dark dens of filth and squalor? Alas! Yes, if no change comes for the better, they too will thirst for the purple cup of revolution." And instead of melancholy figures pining in solitary, nun-like domestic retreat, she imagines seamstresses living and working together in "cooperation." Writing of her domestic partnership with another seamstress, Maria L., she muses, "if two can thus combine their interests for economy, why not more? Why could not a dozen join their slender means, and make shirts and caps, or any other articles demanded in the market, and have the profits? . . . The ants and the bees alone could understand me. I wonder if I was not once a bee." At one point figuring a young bride as a lamb "decked . . . for a sacrifice," the narrator constructs for herself an alternative plot to the standard melodramatic one of decline and (paternal) rescue. Indeed, the absence of a romantic plot both serves to register the multiple privations and losses seamstresses experience, and enables the narrator to dedicate herself liberally, and publicly, to "the good of humanity."[24]

Throughout the text, the narrator voices outrage at middle-class women's inability to imagine in a complex way the experiences of working-women or psychologically surmount the boundaries of class. In interactions with female clients, she characteristically utters "some biting [and] . . . wholesome truth" to "startle" them into "momentary feeling" (227). The narrator's critique of what she terms middle-class women's "narrow bigotry" (179) extends from her female employers to feminists such as Margaret Fuller (whose idealism creates "a veil . . . between her and the rude, practical, every-day working world. She may . . . call herself a laborer, but this brings her only into distant relationship with us" [150]), and, especially, to moral reformers such as those discussed in the previous section. During a visit to "Mrs. Broadson" to collect on a long-outstanding bill, she rejects the woman's effort to pay her in cast-off clothing and demands interest on the amount due; embodying the retributory violence she presages above, the narrator describes how "my feelings of scorn, contempt, and burning indignation, for the woman held me silent for a moment; I felt as though I could annihilate her with one breath" (69).[25] Attending the "rigidly moral" "Mrs. L." who spies her watch and questions "whether a virtuous girl could get articles of that kind," the narrator decries religious women's sexual suspicion of workingwomen, and indeed shrewdly suggests that middle-class women's "charitable" preoccupation with their "fallen" working-class sisters entails a projection of their own repressed sexual longings. Vowing that "she should have no power over me," the narrator declares, "I might . . . tell you how I came in possession of this watch . . . but I scorn to enter upon a self defence [*sic*] when there is only a coarse and cruel suspicion against me. You madam, are a sensualist, you have a nature low enough to prostitute yourself for gold, or you would never suspect one of your own sex of unworthy acts" (101). As with Mrs. Broadson, she here envisions herself as an instrument of class vengeance: "Woman, I have been tempted; the tempter still trails along my path; I know the weakness that comes from hunger and weariness; Beware, lest at the last, the blood of my soul be found in your skirts that you deem so pure and spotless" (101).

But it is especially when two moral reformers visit the narrator and Maria L. at home, bearing tracts and questioning the seamstresses' moral and spiritual practices, that what passes for the (cross-class) feminine "sympathy" of middle-class women is most severely undercut. The women interrogate the seamstresses, expressing the usual preoccupations of moral reformers—do they attend church? Are they taking the necessary precautions to avoid temptation and preserve their virtue?—and the narrator's responses are recorded in illuminating detail. When the women express shock at the narrator's admission that she does not attend church, she enlightens them on the causes of her (and other workingwomen's) absence: she can not afford a seat—and the free seats provided for the poor, in the galleries, "have few of the comforts with which the seats for the rich are furnished" (179); she has no appropriate clothing; she has no time ("I worship perpetually, if labor is worship"). The reformers seem alarmed at her nondeferential, indeed defiant stance, and endeavor to bolster their authority with spiritual threat: "It seemed evident . . . that I was in the 'gaul of bitterness and bonds of iniquity'; that I hated the blessed Savior, and I would make my bed in hell at the last" (179). Attempting to persuade the narrator to mend her ways and value spiritual over material concerns, one reformer quotes scripture, "Seek ye first the kingdom of heaven, and all these things shall be added unto you," (to which the undaunted narrator replies that the application of this text to her situation is "perverted"); while the other reproves her, "you are most of the time engaged in such—vanity . . . as this [dress], and more in earnest about it, than about your precious, undying soul" (179). In response, the narrator reaffirms her commitment to the material realm: "I am always in earnest to fulfill my promises, and for this kind of work I get good and prompt pay; and now allow me to say, ladies, that if you would do good, and save souls, your best mode of doing so is to give women work, pay them well. . . . Stretch out your hands, *extend your sympathies to their bodies,* and then you may point them to the Infinite Father's love, more successfully. . . . Go to the boardinghouse, at the end of this court. Look at that miserable, haggard crowd, there struggling . . . and then demand of society relief, not a pittance doled out as charity, but demand for the homes, where through attractive industry, they may be made useful, healthy and happy" (179; emphasis added). Demanding not charity and spiritual uplift for individuals but justice effected through collective political action, the narrator contests the authority of moral reformers to understand, as well as to represent, the seamstress's identity, experiences, and needs. Indeed, refocusing reformers' attention to the material realm and the real exigencies of seamstresses' lives, the narrator challenges their simplistic, socially distanced portrait of needlewomen; in doing so, she aims to refashion, and re-form, middle-class women's sympathies.

Writing in the *New York Tribune,* Horace Greeley affirmed that "the worst features" of needlework "are its hopelessness and its constant tendency from bad to worse. . . . Small as are the earnings of . . . seamstresses, they constantly tend to diminish" (as seen in Sumner 136). A decade later, in the *American Woman's Home,* Catharine Beecher and Harriet Beecher Stowe observed, American readers continued to be "harrowed with tales of the sufferings of distressed needle-women" (322). "Stray Leaves" unravels the popular image of the sentimental seamstress and her conventional downward plot. In particular, its narrator—like the text as a whole—reverses relations of discursive control established by middle-class reformers and other crafters of the seamstress image, wresting control—if only temporarily—of the seamstress's story. By the end of her encounter with the moral reformers, the narrator notes, "In my vehement earnestness . . . I was standing before them, the preacher . . . of the three" (179).

Notes

1. On the popularity of seamstress literature in England, see Gallagher (126–46). For Gallagher, seamstress tales exemplify the "feminization of the image of the working class in [English] industrial fiction" that helped refunction the ideology of social paternalism under contest by Chartists and other radical workingmen (129, 130).

2. Joan Scott examines the "production of women workers' marginality" in the nineteenth century, which she identifies as a key way in which "the meaning of work has been constructed" (163). As Scott observes, political economy was imbued with moral categories: "Analyses of wages linked gender and economics: the 'natural dependency' of women on men within families explained the differential between male and female wages; the 'natural laws' of supply and demand explained why women would always have to depend on men. One set of 'natural' laws articulated and constructed the other" (148). According to Michèle Barrett, "the concept of 'dependence' is, perhaps, the link between the material organization of the household and the ideology of femininity: an assumption of women's dependence on men structures both of these areas" (214).

3. On the legacy of this tradition in America, see Gutman.

4. Noting that "the sentimentalist imagery of female poverty became a convention of nineteenth-century urban thought," Stansell observes that sentimentalism "reinforced the categories of worthy/unworthy and fleshed them out with a specifically female content" (72–73). The construction of the seamstress as sentimental figure, and the deployment of sympathy as a means to domesticate workingwomen and diffuse or assuage the antagonisms and potential violence of class conflict, is ideologically crucial. Just as political writers, especially Whigs, employed a rhetoric of the "harmony between the classes" to justify protectionist policies and state supported capitalist expansion, literary fashioners of the sentimental seamstress diffuse class conflict and present the spontaneous ministrations of sympathy as a means to correct the abuses of the market system and bring its elements into harmony. Sympathy can thus be seen as a vehicle of class domestication. As Lynda Nead notes, "if you feel sympathy rather than fear towards a group which challenges the dominant social order, its power may be diffused" (138).

5. Starting in New York in 1825, seamstresses came together and held meetings to organize to secure higher wages and to form unions, cooperatives, and associations. These organizations included the United Tailoresses' Society in New York in 1831, the Female Improvement Society for the City and County of Philadelphia in 1835, and the Shirt Sewers' Cooperative Union in New York in 1851. On several occasions the seamstresses'

activities culminated in strikes. Between 1825 and 1855 newspapers reported several strikes by seamstresses in Boston, New York, Baltimore, Philadelphia, and other cities. On the history of needlewomen's activism, see Foner (1–17).

6. On new norms of masculinity generated by market conditions, see Leverenz (60, 72). Joseph Kett observes that, by 1840, the isolated, ambitious male self was expected to rise beyond his father in a world where everyone felt "marginal and insecure" (as seen in Leverenz 60). Seamstresses were often widows or unmarried women bereft of paternal protection, so that the fall into poverty simultaneously entailed a fall from domesticity. As Carey noted, many women "have been gradually reduced from a state of comfort and affluence to penury, and thrown upon the world, with no other dependence than their needles to support themselves and their offspring" (*Letters* 9).

7. As narratives of feminine economic helplessness and dependency, antebellum seamstress stories also borrow a sense of inevitability from the figure of the fallen woman—an association conventionalized in philanthropic writings as well as fiction. Analyzing the "idea of fallenness as a predelineated narrative" (12), Anderson reads narratives of fallen women as exemplifying the ways in which culturally specific anxieties about determinism—especially the idea that circumstances determine character, or that acts bring inexorable consequences—were projected onto women. According to Anderson, the Victorian preoccupation with fallenness "can be understood only if one is careful not to reduce it to female sexuality"; exploring a "rhetorically supple and historically overdetermined conception of fallenness as attenuated autonomy," Anderson sees the fallen woman as "a charged site for Victorian concerns with the question of agency itself" (15, 6). In particular, "fallenness should be understood principally in relation to a normative masculine identity seen to possess the capacity for autonomous action, enlightened rationality, and self-control" (13). The narrative structure through which women's sexual fallenness is delineated guides depictions of the seamstress's economic decline as well.

8. On the emergence of "systematic discussion[s]" of poverty and its sources by the 1820s, see Stansell (19ff). As Montgomery notes, "a rapidly rising tide of urban poverty in the 1810s [a consequence of the War of 1812] and 1820s provoked widespread controversy over the costs and purposes of poor relief" and undermined patrician confidence in the effectiveness of traditional forms of urban benevolence (20).

9. Notably, Carey was criticized by the labor press for demanding charity instead of justice (Sumner 133).

10. Of the constitutive erotics of feminine "dependency," Lynda Nead writes, "the [Victorian] notion of dependency should not be seen in terms of a repressive exercise of power; rather, dependency was believed to be a natural and gratifying component of respectable femininity" (29). As deployed in seamstress narratives, this naturalized model of feminine dependency operated to manage the threatening "otherness" of working-women and contravene their assertions of economic autonomy, while enforcing the normative erotics of the "family wage" endorsed by many workingmen. On the sexual politics of working-class culture, see especially Stansell and Lott.

11. On the antebellum privatization of economic relief and its insulation from demo-

cratic control, see Montgomery. Observing that "gender profoundly shaped the everyday experience of class in the distribution of public charity," Montgomery recounts how "free markets, a safety net of abstemious relief to the worthy poor, and the suppression of 'idleness' and 'dissipation' . . . framed the historic alternative to working people's claims to benevolence from the rich and from town magistrates" (21).

12. The rhetorical feminization of dependency dated back to the Revolutionary period, when full citizenship was routinely associated with masculine economic "independency," but it was consolidated during the 1830s when, as Nancy Fraser and Linda Gordon have shown, the traditional status of dependence was markedly disassociated from white workingmen—a consequence of new rhetorics of white male "free labor"—and transferred onto women, who—along with children, slaves, and Native Americans—began to serve as what they term "personifications of dependency." What had been the traditional status of dependency in preindustrial societies was thus translated into a moral and psychological register, and "dependency as political subjection" was transformed into "dependency as psychology" and assigned markers of class, race, and gender (129). The feminization of dependency is quite evident in antebellum social discourses (see Boydston). For example, William Sanger, author of the first major American study of prostitution, pointedly called workingwomen "dependent women," and assumed that, by not living under a father's or husband's roof, women "would have to look to the state for care" (28).

13. Carey, in "A Plea for the Poor," notes that the vast majority (498 of 549) of Philadelphia's "out of door paupers" are women, and heading that list are seamstresses (1, 8).

14. Brownson's essays, republished as pamphlets, first appeared in the *Boston Quarterly Review.*

15. As Yeazell suggests, women were assigned the task of embodying residual social values and communal sentiments deemed inconvenient in a market economy. This was certainly true in antebellum America; indeed, the cult of domesticity defined the ideal of "woman" as the antithesis of the active, and ambitious, market subject. For instance, that women were seen to possess a "home feeling" in the midst of capitalist transformation has more than mere gender significance; it signals an attachment to person and place antithetical to processes of modernization. On the "creative destruction" of the bourgeoisie and its replacement of the "bonds of personal dependency" with an abstract "community of money," see Harvey (167–68). Seamstress narratives project forms of sentimental attachment and personal dependency onto women, removing them from the dynamism of modernity.

16. For Brooks, economic "ambition" is a "dominant dynamic of plot" in nineteenth-century fiction; Fern's analysis makes it clear how distinctly masculine was this scripting of what Brooks terms "narrative desire" (39ff).

17. The link between seamstress and fallen woman was conventionalized in philanthropic writings and the burgeoning medical literature on prostitution, as well as in seamstress fictions themselves.

18. In addition to Hood's influential poem, important British examples of seamstress literature include Elizabeth Stone's *The Young Milliner,* Elizabeth Gaskell's *Ruth,*

G. W. M. Reynolds's *The Seamstress; Or, The White Slave of England,* and especially Charlotte Elizabeth Tonna's reformist writings (e.g., "Milliners and Dressmakers"). When an American edition of Tonna's complete works appeared in the mid-1840s, Harriet Beecher Stowe wrote the introduction attesting to Tonna's great fame—a fact that suggests important connections between sentimental fictions of class and better-known abolitionist fictions.

19. Focusing on Boston's New England Female Moral Reform Society, Hobson observes that antebellum moral reformers treated the economic exploitation of women workers as an extension of their metaphor of male dominance and female submission.

20. *Advocate* (Vol. 9, 1843): 24; (Vol. 2, 1836): 17–19; (Vol. 11, 1845): 109.

21. The connections between seamstress and prostitute were forged in canonical literary texts as well. In addition to the obvious example of Hester Prynne, Hawthorne's Priscilla, in *The Blithedale Romance,* embodies this conjuncture: a seamstress, she is also the narrative's "white slave" and object of Westervelt's nefarious designs; while the purses she sews—a resonant sexual image—exemplify the seamstress's characteristic conflation of eroticism and labor.

22. The narrative of seamstress as "fallen woman" does appear in "Stray Leaves": the narrator relates the story of "Laura L.," whose "long[ing] for rest, for freedom" from labor is exploited by her married seducer, and who, after being abandoned, dies in childbirth (*The Una* 1.8 [August 20, 1853]: 117; 1.9 [September 1853]: 132). This narrative structure, however, is dialogized and critiqued by and through the narrator's story.

23. *The Una* 1.4 (May 2, 1853): 68, 69; 2.1 (January 1854): 195; 1.7 (August 1, 1853): 100; 2.3 (March 1854): 228; 1.9 (September 1853): 133; 1.4 (May 2, 1853): 69, 68; 2:1 (January 1854): 195.

24. *The Una* 1.4 (May 2, 1853): 68; 1.10 (October 1853): 150; 1.9 (September 1853): 133; 1.7 (August 1, 1853): 100; 1.4 (May 1853): 69; 1.8 (August 20, 1853): 117; 1.12 (December 1853): 178, 179; 1.9 (September 1953): 134; 1.10 (October 1853): 150; 1.12 (December 1853): 179; 2.3 (March 1854): 227; 2.12 (February 1854): 211.

25. *The Una* 2.3 (March 1854): 227; 1.12 (December 1853): 179; 1.10 (October 1853): 150; 1.4 (May 2, 1853): 69; 1.7 (August 1, 1853): 101; 1.12 (December 1853): 179, emphasis added; 1.12 (December 1853): 179.

Works Cited

Anderson, Amanda. *Tainted Souls and Painted Faces: The Rhetoric of Fallenness in Victorian Culture.* Ithaca: Cornell UP, 1993.

Anon. [Hood, Thomas.] "The Song of the Shirt." *Punch* (December 1843): 42.

Arthur, T[imothy]. S[hea]. *The Seamstress: A Tale of the Times.* Philadelphia: R. G. Berford, 1843.

Barker-Benfield, G. J. *The Horrors of the Half-Known Life.* New York: Harper and Row, 1976.

Barrett, Michèle. *Women's Oppression Today.* London: Verso, 1980.

Beecher, Catharine, and Harriet Beecher Stowe. *The American Woman's Home.* New York: J. B. Ford, 1869.

Berg, Barbara J. *The Remembered Gate: Origins of American Feminism.* New York: Oxford UP, 1978.

Boydston, Jeanne. *Home and Work: Housework, Wages, and the Ideology of Labor in the Early Republic.* New York: Oxford UP, 1990.

Brodhead, Richard. "Veiled Ladies: Toward a History of Antebellum Entertainment." *Cultures of Letters: Scenes of Reading and Writing in Nineteenth-Century America.* Chicago: U of Chicago P, 1993. 48–68.

Brooks, Peter. *Reading for the Plot: Design and Intention in Narrative.* New York: Vintage, 1985.

Brownson, Orestes. *Defense of the Article on the Laboring Classes.* Boston: William H. Greene, 1840.

———. *The Laboring Classes.* New York: Elton's, 1840.

Carey, Mathew. *Letters on the Condition of the Poor.* Philadelphia: Haswell and Barrington, 1835.

———. *Miscellaneous Essays.* Philadelphia: Carey and Hart, 1830.

———. "A Plea for the Poor." *The Jacksonians on the Poor: Collected Pamphlets.* New York: Arno Press, 1971.

Channing, Walter. "An Address on the Prevention of Pauperism." *The Jacksonians on the Poor: Collected Pamphlets.* New York: Arno Press, 1971.

Defoe, Daniel. *Moll Flanders.* Ed. Juliet Mitchell. New York: Penguin, 1987.

Dreiser, Theodore. *Sister Carrie.* Introd. Alfred Kazin. New York: Penguin, 1981.

Edelstein, T. J. "They Sang 'The Song of the Shirt': The Visual Iconology of the Seamstress," *Victorian Studies* 23.2 (Winter 1980): 183–210.

Ehrenreich, Barbara. *Fear of Falling: The Inner Life of the Middle Class.* New York: Pantheon, 1989.

Fern, Fanny [Sara Parton]. "A Bit of Injustice." *Ruth Hall and Other Writings.* Ed. Joyce W. Warren. New Brunswick: Rutgers UP, 1990. 318.

———. *Ruth Hall and Other Writings.* Ed. Joyce W. Warren. New Brunswick: Rutgers UP, 1990.

Foner, Philip S. *Women and the American Labor Movement: From the First Trade Unions to the Present.* New York: The Free Press, 1982.

Fraser, Nancy, and Linda Gordon. "A Genealogy of 'Dependency': Tracing a Keyword of the U.S. Welfare State." *Justice Interruptus: Critical Reflections on the "Postsocialist" Condition.* New York: Routledge, 1997. 121–49.

Gallagher, Catherine. *The Industrial Reformation of English Fiction.* Chicago: U of Chicago P, 1985.

Gutman, Herbert. *Work, Culture and Society.* New York: Vintage, 1977.

Harvey, David. *The Urban Experience.* Baltimore: Johns Hopkins UP, 1989.

Hobson, Barbara. *Uneasy Virtue: The Politics of Prostitution and the American Reform Tradition.* New York: Basic Books, 1987.

Laurie, Bruce. *Working People of Philadelphia, 1800–1850.* Philadelphia: Temple UP, 1980.

Leverenz, David. *Manhood and the American Renaissance.* Ithaca: Cornell UP, 1989.

Lott, Eric. *Love and Theft: Blackface Minstrelsy and the American Working Class.* New York: Oxford UP, 1993.

Lynn, Lizzie. "Dependence: Or What Made One Woman Meanly Penurious." *The Una: A Paper Devoted to the Elevation of Women* 1.3 (April 1, 1853): 33–34.

Montgomery, David. "Wage Labor, Bondage, and Citizenship in Nineteenth-Century America." *International Labor and Working-Class History* 48.6 (Fall 1995): 6–27.

Moretti, Franco. *Signs Taken for Wonders.* Trans. Susan Fischer et al. New York: Verso, 1997.

Nead, Lynda. *Myths of Sexuality: Representations of Women in Victorian Britain.* London: Blackwell, 1988.

Poovey, Mary. *Making a Social Body: British Cultural Formation, 1830–1864.* Chicago: U of Chicago P, 1995.

Reynolds, David S. *Beneath the American Renaissance: The Subversive Imagination in the Age of Emerson and Melville.* Cambridge: Harvard UP, 1989.

Rothman, David J. *The Discovery of the Asylum: Social Order and Disorder in the New Republic.* Boston: Little, Brown, 1971.

Sanger, William W. *The History of Prostitution: Its Extent, Causes and Effects throughout the World.* New York: Harper and Bros., 1858.

Scott, Joan Wallach. *Gender and the Politics of History.* New York: Columbia UP, 1988.

Smith-Rosenberg, Carroll. *Disorderly Conduct: Visions of Gender in Victorian America.* New York: Oxford UP, 1985.

Stansell, Christine. *City of Women: Sex and Class in New York, 1789–1860.* Urbana: U of Illinois P, 1987.

Stray Leaves from a Seamstress. The Una: A Paper Devoted to the Elevation of Women. 1.4 (May 2, 1853); 2.3 (March 1854).

Sumner, Helen L. *History of Women in Industry in the United States.* New York: Arno, 1974.

"Tailoresses and Seamstresses." *Advocate of Moral Reform* 2 (1836): 171.

Yeazell, Ruth Bernard. *Fictions of Modesty: Women and Courtship in the English Novel.* Chicago: U of Chicago P, 1991.

Thompson, E. P. "The Moral Economy of the English Crowd." *Past and Present* 50 (1973): 76–136.

3

"Dedicated to Works of Beneficence"

Charity as Model for a Domesticated Economy in Antebellum Women's Panic Fiction

Mary Templin

When the wildly speculative economy of the mid-1830s collapsed in panic in the spring of 1837, causing widespread bankruptcy, loss of property, and unemployment, a number of American women writers responded with novels and stories about the effects of financial failure on the home. Fiction by authors such as Catharine Maria Sedgwick, Hannah Farnham Sawyer Lee, and Eliza Lee Cabot Follen presented strikingly similar narratives of middle-class families whose assets were lost through speculation, thus forcing them to economize in their domestic arrangements in order to protect or regain financial and social position. Although these authors' explanations for the economic catastrophe often resemble those found in newspapers of the time—most frequently blamed are greedy speculators and a bloated paper currency—female-authored "panic fiction" differs significantly from journalistic accounts of panic in assigning to women a major role in their families' and the nation's economic recovery. Seeking to mitigate middle-class women's vulnerability to economic loss at such a precarious time, these authors imagined an enhanced economic role for women that would protect their middle-class identity even in the face of loss, while simultaneously promoting a female-guided route to restored financial prosperity.

Given the extraordinary level of financial distress resulting from the Panic of 1837, it is perhaps not surprising that a key element of this proposed new role for women was charity.[1] While small property owners and mid-level merchants and manufacturers suffered significant losses from the crisis, those hardest hit were the working poor of industrial cities like New York and Boston, dependent for survival on their pay from manufacturing jobs and other manual labor. Precise figures are hard to come by, but historians have estimated that somewhere between one-third and one-half of urban laborers in the Northeast were put out of work by the massive business failures, many remaining unemployed throughout the early 1840s. Those fortunate to retain their jobs suffered sharp cuts in pay, as wage rates in New York, for example, fell by about one-third between 1836 and 1842. In an era without federal or state welfare systems—it was not until two decades later, following the Panic of 1857, that a public employment program was even proposed (but not adopted) in New York—joblessness often meant starvation and overcrowded conditions for the poor. Thus panic produced an increased need for both private and institutional charity, especially in the cities.[2]

We see these needs being met in numerous scenes of charity in the panic novels of the late 1830s. Hannah Lee's pair of novels about the Fulton family, *Three Experiments of Living* and its sequel *Elinor Fulton*, published just months apart in 1837, both feature middle-class female characters who circulate "subscriptions" among their friends and acquaintances to raise money for destitute families. They also visit the poor, bringing food and medicine to those unable to work or feed their children. In other panic novels, including Lee's *Rosanna, or Scenes in Boston* (1839) and Eliza Follen's *Sketches of Married Life* (1838), female characters plan and carry out longer-range projects of poverty relief, especially schools for poor children designed to educate them for middle-class life while enabling their mothers to be gainfully employed outside the home.

Such attention to charity in novels about financial loss might seem to suggest an acknowledgment that the middle-class dispensers of charity—only steps away from poverty themselves—and the recipients of their aid shared a similar condition as a consequence of panic. But that is rarely the case, at least in terms of any explicit recognition of such connection. Even though, historically, both middle and working classes clearly suffered from the economic losses resulting from panic, panic authors strain to differentiate the significance of their respective plights, portraying middle-class women as victims of economic fluctuations, and the poor as occupants of a fixed status, unrelated to panic. One brief exception to this occurs at the end of Lee's *Three Experiments of Living,* when Jane Fulton, the middle-class wife of a recently bankrupted speculator, takes comfort in the observation that, because her husband's creditors are rich men who won't feel their loss, "we have injured nobody but ourselves" in their financial failure. A friend then replies ironically, "I am glad to hear you say you owe only those who will not feel it. Of course, there are no butcher's or bakers' bills unpaid;—no carpenters, masons, or tradesmen of any kind;—no mantua-makers or milliners;—no women who go out to daily labor, and who have families of children depending upon them for bread" (137). By having the friend thus confront Jane with the potential results of her inability to pay her tradesmen's bills, Lee draws attention to the effects of business failures on the working class, implicitly suggesting that readers in Jane's position remember the "trickle-down" effects of economic loss. Nevertheless, Lee's narrative focus remains on the sufferings of her middle-class family, putting them at the center of the crisis.

Thus charity does figure as a solution to the effects of panic, but primarily for the giver rather than for the receiver. One of the principal threats that panic authors seem to be defending against is the potential for panic, in altering middle-class women's economic circumstances, to also alter their sense of identity. In order to bolster a sense of self that relied heavily on class identity, panic authors tend to emphasize the individual agency of their protagonists above their relationality to members of the poorer classes. Aimed at assuaging the anxieties of a primarily middle-class readership, panic fiction employs philanthropy as a signifier of, and a means of exercising, economic power for the middle-class female protagonists whose economic and social status is threatened.

In the narratives that this essay examines, charitable acts protect middle-class women's social identity and bestow increased economic agency in three distinct ways. First, by constructing separate roles for the "giver" and the "receiver" of aid, philanthropy helps to preserve the social distinctions between financially threatened middle-class women and the poor they are afraid of becoming. Scenes of charity in panic fiction tend to mark the poor as identifiably different from the middle class and emphasize the moral or intellectual superiority of the female philanthropist who has lost her money but retains internal markings of class. Second, the financial aspects of charity—raising and distributing money or material goods to the poor—emphasize women's capacity for business, thus justifying increased economic agency in other areas. Many authors of panic fiction depict charity as an economic act as well as a moral one, demonstrating women's ability to handle financial resources responsibly.

Finally, envisioned on a national as well as local scale, charity, or benevolence, serves as a symbol for a "domesticated economy" that panic authors advocated in place of the speculative system they depict as irrational and immoral. Using their novels and stories as an entry into national economic discourse, the authors of panic fiction advanced their agenda for women by appealing to prevalent public distrust of speculation and calling for an economic system based on moral principles. With "works of beneficence" as the ultimate goal of commerce rather than greedy accumulation, panic authors argued, public welfare would be served as the American economy thrived. By thus proposing benevolence—already beginning to be regarded as a feminine domain—as an integral part of the national economic agenda, they simultaneously imagined a more humane economic course for the nation and a system more conducive to women's economic participation.

Reinforcing Middle-Class Identity

Much of the recent groundbreaking work on women's benevolence in the nineteenth century has noted its function in the process of social class formation. Lori Ginzberg argues, for instance, that "early benevolent work and rhetoric were vehicles for the emergence of a new middle-class identity" (7). In part, this was because the benevolence practiced by predominantly white, middle-class reformers was essentially an extension of the domestic ideals of order, nurturance, and moral virtue already linked to the middle-class home. Even in the late nineteenth century, Deborah Carlin notes, philanthropists' principal goal was to instruct the poor in "the domestic and religious values of the middle class" (211). The difficulties posed for those without money to emulate the values of a middle-class household, however, simply reinforced domesticity and virtue as elements of specifically middle-class feminine identity.

Charity also aided in middle-class formation by creating class relationships based on distinctions. Although benevolence in its different forms theoretically was employed to elevate the poor and thus diminish the separation between classes, the inherently unequal relationship between benefactors and recipients, added to a general failure to address the economic origins of poverty, tended to keep class differences intact.

For the authors of panic fiction, this aspect of benevolence provided them with a way to shore up the middle-class status of their female characters by depicting them in paternalistic relationships with the poor, even as their own financial resources were being depleted. One of the great anxieties that underlies panic fiction is that financial failure may threaten the social identity of middle-class women as it destroys the economic underpinnings of their lifestyle. Thus panic authors work hard to define a middle-class identity that is not based solely on money, a project that includes identifying non-material differences between poor and middle class. As traditional distinctions such as income, assets, and living spaces are obliterated by panic and economic failure—and many middle-class women are even forced to engage in some form of paid labor, thus erasing that crucial distinction from the working class—panic authors instead invoke biological and cultural differences that could not be erased by economic fluctuation.

In the case of panic novels' depictions of domestic employment—another form of hierarchy that serves to uphold the social status of middle-class panic victims—ethnicity and race often serve as highly visible and ineradicable markers of class difference. While the employers generally have English surnames, domestic servants are predominantly Irish, with their ethnic heritage emphasized in the narrative as well as denoted in their speech. Less frequently, servants of African descent appear, such as the "coloured" cook in Catharine Sedgwick's *Live and Let Live* (1837). Such racial distinctions play a lesser role in depictions of charity relationships, however. Some of the poor who receive aid from the hands of panic fiction heroines are specifically Irish, but many are of indeterminate ethnicity. More often, recipients of charity are distinguished from their benefactors through moral character—displaying failings such as drunkenness, sexual lasciviousness, lack of industry or prudence, or untidiness in contrast to the consistent virtue of the middle-class philanthropists. In Sedgwick's *The Poor Rich Man, and The Rich Poor Man* (1836), for example, the charitable protagonists come to the aid of a former classmate, identical to them in ethnic and social origins, but marked by weak character. Paulina has fallen into drunken destitution as a result of vanity, exemplified in childhood by a desire for "handsome" clothes, and in adulthood by her "filthy lace cap," "tattered French cape," and "soiled silk gown" (130). Those on the receiving end of charity are also frequently marked by an attitude of helplessness and dependency that serves to accentuate their benefactors' competency and ability to render aid.[3] These moral and psychological qualities are usually implied to be fixed, not merely situational, thus marking distinctions between classes that provide the basis for stable class relationships.

In Hannah Lee's novel *Rosanna,* for instance, published two years after the Panic of 1837, the philanthropist is a middle-class woman, Mrs. Jones, who recruits children from poor neighborhoods for an "infant school" and rescues the title character from prison by giving her a second chance as a chambermaid in her house. Throughout the novel, Lee emphasizes the social and moral distance between Mrs. Jones and the poor that she helps, who in this case are Irish. While Mrs. Jones is portrayed as morally upright, compassionate, and wise, the Irish Rosanna demonstrates her lack of either fiscal prudence or sexual control by insisting on marrying before she and her husband have the financial means to support themselves. When Rosanna, predictably, ends up on the streets, she turns to drink for solace, reinforcing the stereotype of the drunken Irish. Rosanna's utter failure to thrive on her own, and her dependence on Mrs. Jones's kindness, exemplifies an unequal relationship between classes that rhetorically elevates the middle-class philanthropist. Even the names Lee uses for her characters, with Mrs. Jones always referred to by her title and surname and the women of the Irish ghetto by their first names alone, signal a fixed social gulf between them, characterized by paternalism.

Sedgwick uses a similarly paternalistic model of charity to shore up her characters' vulnerable social identity in *The Poor Rich Man, and the Rich Poor Man.* Although published in the year preceding the actual panic, *Poor Rich Man* typifies an era of great financial insecurity, and shares with post-panic novels their authors' apparent desire to ward off the dangers of financial failure. The "rich poor man" of the novel, Harry

Aikin, and his wife, Susan, practice a philanthropy of time and moral influence rather than money. In contrast to the selfish "poor rich man" of the novel, who refuses to help a destitute old man on the grounds that he "made it a rule never to give to strangers" (91), but also in opposition to a second gentleman who contributes five dollars but cannot spare the time to tend to the man's needs, Harry takes the man home with him, providing him with the comfort of a loving family as well as food and shelter. When they arrive at the Aikins' house, Susan "opened the inner door, drew Charlotte's rocking-chair to the fire, threw a dry stick into the stove, and received the stranger with that expression of cheerful, sincere hospitality, which what is called high breeding only imitates" (93). In similar instances throughout the novel, Harry and Susan give of themselves rather than money—their home, their time, their talents, and their moral wisdom.

While on one level such an approach to charity is more leveling than either handouts or that described by Lee in *Rosanna*—the Aikins and their beneficiaries share a standard of living and become a kind of family—it also reduces the physical and moral autonomy of those that the Aikins help. Whereas gifts of money can presumably be spent in any way the recipient chooses, the Aikins' kind of philanthropy is designed precisely to mold the very thoughts and characters of their recipients. Similar to the "maternal" model of charity that Jill Bergman observes in Elizabeth Stuart Phelps's fiction (in this volume), the Aikins' approach grants them a sort of parental authority over those they take in.[4] Thus, while the physical and material distance between philanthropist and recipient is lessened in Sedgwick's model, the moral gap is actually reinforced, emphasizing the importance for the middle-class philanthropist to control the behavior of the poor and to impose middle-class moral standards.

Philanthropy of both types provides a model for relationships between the middle class and the poor that maintains the superior status of the middle class, either in terms of resources, intelligence, or moral direction. The poor remain dependent, while middle-class women (and in Sedgwick's novel, men as well) exercise economic agency and display moral virtue. Sedgwick even suggests that "inequality of condition" is divinely mandated in order to encourage the practice of benevolence: "Has not Providence made this inequality the necessary result of the human condition, and is not the true agrarian principle to be found in the voluntary exercise of those virtues that produce an interchange of benevolent offices? If there were a perfect community of goods, where would be the opportunity for the exercise of the virtues, of justice and mercy, humility, fidelity, and gratitude?" (39). While in this formulation, the poor also benefit morally from philanthropy, the obvious implication that the middle-class givers exercise justice and mercy as the poor recipients express gratitude maintains even a hierarchy of virtues.

Expanding Economic Agency

Although Lee describes Mrs. Jones's philanthropy in *Rosanna* in nonmonetary terms, and Sedgwick specifically favors a benevolence of time and influence over one of money in *Poor Rich Man*, most panic authors do emphasize the economic aspects of charity, showing their middle-class protagonists raising and spending money to benefit the poor. In their efforts to rhetorically construct ways for middle-class women to be less economically vulnerable, panic authors counteract characterizations of women as financially ignorant and helpless by endowing all the different facets of women's traditional domestic role—housekeeper, caregiver, conjugal sympathizer—with an economic dimension. Rather than simply keeping house, for instance, the matron of panic fiction is a domestic manager, carefully budgeting household expenditures, supervising the purchase and use of domestic consumer goods, and directing the labors of domestic employees, much as a businessman oversees the financial affairs of his factory or counting-house. Such financial expertise similarly extends to women's role as confidant to their husbands. In addition to providing emotional support and spiritual guidance, the wives and daughters of panic fiction serve as competent and knowledgeable economic advisers as well, helping to decide on wise investments and steering male relatives away from foolish speculative schemes.

The financial dimension of charity seems rather obvious—those who have more money and material possessions give to those who have less. But nineteenth-century characterizations of money as crass, as well as genteel ideals of a feminine sphere of activity ruled by the heart and not by economic considerations, meant that the pecuniary character of women's benevolent work was consistently disguised by a rhetoric of feeling. Charity was often characterized as an extension of women's natural urge to nurture, an outflowing of sympathy for the sick and the poor, manifested not in money but in pails of soup and a gentle, soothing presence at the sickbed.

Nevertheless, as Ginzberg has documented, most nineteenth-century charity work—women's as well as men's—revolved around money. The image of the lone matron on a mission of mercy is overshadowed by the reality of large benevolent organizations in which women raised funds, directed investments, distributed grants, disbursed pay to employees, and occasionally even received wages for supposedly voluntary work (42). Many antebellum charities operated like businesses, Ginzberg notes, seeking and receiving incorporation. Corporate status allowed married women to control funds in the name of the corporation, despite their legal inability to direct their own individual financial affairs (50). Regardless, then, of whether women's fundamental motivation for charity was sympathy or a desire for self-development, benevolence required substantial financial expertise and demonstrated women's competence in monetary matters.

Although none of the novels discussed in this study portray the comprehensive "business of benevolence" that Ginzberg has uncovered—and they do depict women dispensing soup and sympathy—their female characters' attention to budgeting and distributing money for charity does reflect this conception of benevolence as a form of economic agency. Just as the domestic manager makes decisions about household expenditures, she also allocates money or other resources to promote the well-being of those in need outside her home. In *Three Experiments of Living*, for example, Hannah Lee juxtaposes charitable giving and spending on household goods as competing budget items, marking failure to give as a sign of a poor domestic manager. The novel's female protagonist, Jane Fulton—whose husband is, in the beginning of the novel, a rising but still only moderately prosperous physician—is contrasted with the wealthy Mrs. Hart, who lives in a "splendid apartment" filled with the most elegant furnishings (28). When Jane appeals to Mrs. Hart to "subscribe" five dollars to a fund to supply clothes and schooling for some poor children—a request that Jane herself matches from her slender budget—the merchant's wife pleads poverty:

> "How benevolent you are, my dear Mrs. Fulton! Would to Heaven I had the means of being equally so! But my time is wholly engrossed, and the claims upon my purse are constant. Perhaps none are so heavily taxed as the rich, or have less right to be called affluent. I declare to you," said she, drawing forth her elegant crimson silk purse, and holding it suspended on her jeweled finger, "I cannot command a farthing; you see how empty it is. But I approve your plan. Perhaps you will be so kind as to advance the same sum for me that you pay for yourself. We will settle it when we next meet." (31)

Ironically, the "claims upon [her] purse," as we know from a previous scene, include a luxurious camel's-hair shawl that Mrs. Hart has just purchased for three hundred dollars on credit. The moral contrast between the two claims on Mrs. Hart's pocketbook is evident, but Lee is equally interested in exposing the lady's financial mismanagement. Wasting money on frivolous luxuries that one cannot afford prevents expenditure on more worthy objects. Mrs. Hart must go into Jane's debt for her charitable contribution, just as she has for the shawl. Her failure to appropriately manage her household funds plays up by contrast Jane's competence in balancing charitable and household expenses. As Jane's husband later comments, "[If] . . . you would have a pelisse as costly as Mrs. Hart's, then you would be as poor as she was to-day, and could not afford to give any thing away, instead of becoming her creditor" (32). Even with a small income, Jane is able to direct the family's resources to where it is needed most.

Jane's role in raising the funds also typifies panic heroines' execution of the financial aspects of charity. In Lee's sequel *Elinor Fulton,* Jane's daughter Elinor similarly takes charge of a project to aid an impoverished family. A previous attempt by another woman—consisting primarily of an emotional appeal for funds—has already failed, paving the way for Elinor's more business-like approach. By investigating the family's economic situation and drawing up a detailed accounting of their earnings and expenses Elinor demonstrates her financial expertise. "She had accurately made out her statement, had arranged the industrious earnings of the family opposite their necessary expenses for rent, clothes, food, light, and fuel, and fully proved, that, though their daily labor was sufficient to enable them to live from day to day in a state of health, when sickness came, nothing remained for such exigences [*sic*]" (30). Elinor is subsequently not only successful in raising the needed money but is also praised by an observer for her "exact statement of the case, [which] was worth a hundred elaborate descriptions of their wants, and pathetic appeals to the charity of the affluent" (31).

Perhaps the most financially autonomous panic heroine is Amy Weston, in Eliza Follen's *Sketches of Married Life.* Like the Fulton women, Amy raises funds for the poor by canvassing her friends and acquaintances for contributions, but also finances her project of a school for poor children with her own money, a small fortune inherited from her mother. Having her own source of income allows Amy to defy her father's opposition to her charity work and make independent spending decisions. Follen creates in the character of Amy both a mouthpiece for the moral and economic benefits of aiding the poor and a model for women's control over the philanthropic process—from the maternal origin of the funds to the implementation of an entirely female-conceived enterprise.

All of these women represent rational and responsible economic agents, implicitly arguing for the legitimacy of middle-class women's participation in a wider spectrum of financial affairs. The ability to manage a household budget and to oversee charitable projects that put poor families on a more stable financial footing suggests an equal capacity to rescue the failing marketplace and set the nation's finances in order. Without actually placing any female characters in public roles of economic responsibility, panic authors could suggest through domestic analogies that the economic chaos produced by rampant overspeculation and unsecured credit might be reduced to order in the same manner that properly executed domestic work brought order and harmony to the home. A combination of women's rationality and compassion could, in other words, counteract the masculine frenzy of greed that had produced the panic, and provide a model for a more cautious and humane national prosperity.

Revising National Economic Policy

Again, benevolence was key to this vision. Ultimately, I argue, panic authors' emphasis on the theme of charity had a far more ambitious purpose than simply demonstrating women's financial competence or reinforcing class distinctions, as important as these objects were in a time of profound financial crisis. A larger aim signaled in their narratives was to actually revise the economic and social paradigms that structured national debate over economic direction: first, challenging traditions of who could take part in that debate and, second, proposing that the ultimate goal of national economic policy be radically changed.

Early-nineteenth-century public discourse on economic issues was almost exclusively masculine. Women were barred by law and/or custom from the discussions that took place in governmental, legal, and educational institutions, and largely silenced in, if not excluded from, public meetings.[5] Economics, like politics, was widely assumed to be a masculine prerogative, unrelated to women's domestic concerns. But just as the genre of domestic fiction provided an outlet for women to join public discourse in print, the concept of benevolence provided them with a point of entry into specifically economic discussions. As women's historians have long argued and as several other essays in this collection document, by the early nineteenth century, benevolence, along with other manifestations of virtue, had come to be seen as a feminine domain.[6] Thus, focusing on benevolence as a legitimate and crucial aspect of any economy, whether of home or nation, gave female authors a platform from which to address the nation's financial distress following the panic.

An emphasis on benevolence also recast the very terms of current economic debate. Rather than asking by what means maximum economic growth could be achieved and maintained, as much of the debate over paper money and credit did, panic novels inquired into how economic practices might be made to conform to moral precepts. Their economic lessons were not in how to make a profit—although they were concerned with economic recovery from failure—but in how to manage money responsibly in ways that served public welfare.

Calls for morality within the marketplace were, of course, not new in the 1830s, nor were they unique to women's fiction. As the nation's economy expanded throughout the late eighteenth and early nineteenth centuries, and opportunities for individual gain in commerce, manufacturing, or land ownership increased, protests against greed and demands for restraint in the exercise of economic self-interest abounded in the pages of newspapers as well as economics texts. At times of crisis in particular, editors across the country railed repeatedly against the "villainy" of bankers and the extravagant excesses of speculators. The *New York Herald*'s declaration on June 14, 1837, that banks' refusal to pay out specie to customers in order to protect their own solvency was a "violation of truth, integrity, law, honor, and public faith . . . never before perpetrated in any country under heaven" is typical of the moral rhetoric found in the financial news pages. The very frequency of such journalistic denunciations suggests that by the 1830s the American economy was widely perceived as operating without concern for principles of fairness or restraint. In the view of many, the marketplace had abandoned any semblance of moral virtue.

But panic novelists' moral critique of current economic practices differed in at least one significant respect from that of masculine critics of economic excess. The male discourse of morality in economics focused almost exclusively on issues of "honesty" and "legitimacy." It called for investors to truthfully represent their financial positions and for financial institutions to operate within the extent of their capitalization. These were concerns for the female authors of panic fiction as well. The root financial cause of failure for the Fulton family in Hannah Lee's *Three Experiments of Living*, for example, is Frank Fulton's speculation with funds he has not yet earned. His honesty is called into question when he claims to own a house he has purchased on borrowed money. But panic authors added to these concerns an obligation to create and use wealth for the benefit of others rather than for oneself. A more fundamental problem with Frank's speculation is that it represents a surrender to self-interest—an abandonment of his socially beneficial calling as a physician in order to achieve greater gain for himself. The Fultons' return to grace is marked not by restored wealth but by Frank's resumption of his medical practice and Jane's renewed interest in helping others. A "moral" economy, in other words, would not only avoid the wrongs of fraud and greed but also would practice the positive virtue of benevolence.

Female panic authors claimed the right to participate in ongoing economic debates and also the right and obligation to influence the operation of the marketplace. While women's presumed moral authority provided one basis for such claims, a more immediate foundation was the impact of economic panic and failure on the domestic sphere. Repeated narratives of women and children who were forced out of their homes due to bankruptcies or who had to alter their daily lives as a result of lowered income demonstrate the permeability of the supposed boundaries between home and marketplace. Actions performed in banks and stock exchanges triggered very real consequences in kitchens and parlors. One of the principal aims of panic fiction, in fact, seems to be to demonstrate that the marketplace and the home are not two separate, mutually exclusive spheres, but are inextricably intertwined.

The implications of this claim are significant. If economic practices and decisions have such devastating domestic consequences, then women have both the right and the appropriate expertise to remodel the economic system in ways that will protect domestic interests. Rather than placing the home at the mercy of the market's erratic ups and downs, they suggest, the marketplace ought to be an extension of the household, operated according to domestic values of trust and morality. With the household as model for the nation's economy, concern for the welfare of all members, or benevolence, becomes an integral component of economic practice. Just as the domestic woman keeps her domain running smoothly by providing for the needs of others, the national economy prospers by seeking the well-being of all rather than maximum profit for a few. Thus panic authors depict investors speculating only to the extent of their existing capital (rather than risking their homes), merchants paying off their creditors on time (even at the expense of their own cash flow), and domestic employers paying generous wages to their servants.[7]

Benevolence and an Economy of Sufficiency

Catharine Sedgwick's *The Poor Rich Man, and The Rich Poor Man* demonstrates how a primary focus on benevolence creates an economy of sufficiency within the microcosm of the home, providing for the needs of an extended family circle and protecting against the dangers of an uncertain economy. As indicated earlier in this essay, the principal characters of *Poor Rich Man,* Harry and Susan Aikin, devote their lives to aiding those in need. In addition to sheltering the destitute old man, they also take in a child whose drunken mother cannot care for him, and give a home to Susan's improvident father and invalid sister. Susan, a seamstress, also trains a young orphan girl in the profession so that she will be able to make her own living.[8] While all of these forms of charity are clearly domestic in character—providing a home and nurturing for those without—the domestic and the economic are seamlessly interwoven in this novel, linked by an overarching attitude of benevolence. Harry, for instance, chooses the profession of "carman," or one who drives a cart, in order to have more time to spend at home than he would have had he remained a merchant. In doing so, he gives up the chance for greater income in exchange for expanded opportunities to influence his children and dependents. Harry's attitude of caring for others is reflected in his business ethics as well. When an earlier enterprise fails due to lack of experience, Harry insists on repaying his creditors in full, despite his partner's protest that partial settlements are accepted business practice.

While Harry's life within the marketplace is strongly influenced by domestic concerns, Susan's domestic work has an economic dimension. Her sewing, a quintessential domestic skill, is performed both for family and for money, while her supervisory role within the household blends mothering with professional instruction. As she watches her children with a "vigilant eye," she is simultaneously "tailoring and instructing in her art a young girl, who had just set the last stitch in a vest of the most costly material, and was holding it up for inspection" (82). Susan's "scrutiny" and ultimate approval of the girl's work combines maternal encouragement with the rigor of an employer readying her apprentice for a role in the marketplace. Both at home and in their work lives, the Aikins are what we might today call "other-directed"—pursuing the welfare of others.

As a consequence, the Aikin family economy is not one of affluence. Unlike many panic novels, in which financially distressed families ultimately regain wealth through economizing measures and rational investment, the Aikins remain relatively poor to the end. But they always have enough to share with others as well as to supply their own needs and, most importantly, they are content with what they have. Harry's reminder that "till we are conscious of employing, and *employing well,* the means we have, we ought not to crave more" (112) underscores the novel's twofold lesson that one should strive not for maximum gain but for sufficiency, and that even limited resources can enable benevolence.

Lest Sedgwick be accused of attributing benevolence only to the poor, however, she does include a wealthy family who manifest a similar attitude and practice of charity. The Beckwiths, who, like the Aikins, demonstrate their domestic values by spending time with their children, use their wealth to design and build model housing for the poor. Their construction of low-cost but spacious and healthy apartments serves as an example of investment that brings a monetary return (in the form of rents) while providing a public benefit. Once again, Sedgwick unites the economic and the domestic—making money by building homes—through a project that is centered on the welfare of others. The Beckwiths prosper, in part, through improving the lives of the poor and, in turn, reinvest their profits in a continuous cycle of benevolence.

Both the Aikins and the Beckwiths serve as models for how benevolence, when an integral part of the family economy, promotes overall welfare through sufficiency for all, as well as a moral satisfaction that is worth more than money. Such an economy based on benevolence helps to ward off the anxieties attendant on financial panic by removing both the potential for huge losses and the danger of destitution. Striving only to have "enough" rather than to accrue maximum profit reduces the financial fluctuations that result from risky attempts at gain. If there are no excessive gains, there will, presumably, be no catastrophic losses. At the same time, a commitment to mutual care among members of a community serves as an insurance policy against poverty. If everyone is benevolent, no one will suffer the direst effects of financial failure.

It is important to note that both families' charity is neither a solely masculine nor solely feminine enterprise, but a male-female partnership that includes the children as well. The Aikin children mimic their parents' generosity by speaking kindly to a poor orphan girl and offering to fill her pail at the pump, while Mr. Beckwith enlists his children's assistance in drawing house designs, "not so much to test their skill in draughting as their knowledge of the wants of the poor, and their zeal for their accommodation" (146). Sedgwick thus envisions an economic system that is not divided into separate gendered spheres of home and marketplace, with charity as a feminine activity outside the bounds of the public economic realm, but rather includes benevolence as an essential component of economic life that brings home and marketplace together in a partnership that protects both from the ravages of panic.

Benevolence and an Economy of Abundance

While Sedgwick's novel remains centered in the home, Eliza Follen's *Sketches of Married Life* shows how a male-female partnership in benevolence might operate on a wider scale. The novel essentially takes Sedgwick's domestic model and expands it to the national stage of commerce and industry. Follen, the daughter and granddaughter of successful eighteenth-century Massachusetts merchants, differed from many other panic authors in her optimism about economic expansion. While the economic anxiety produced by the Panic of 1837 spurred most panic authors to conservative stances on speculation and commercial risk, Follen embraced the opportunities for gaining wealth that mercantile enterprises presented, as long as that wealth was achieved with integrity and employed for the general welfare of all. At the same time, she revised notions of commerce as a solely masculine realm, antithetic to the domestic concerns of women, by envisioning women as fully engaged partners with men in economic decision-making. Although male and female roles remain distinct in Follen's novel, both are dedicated to a vision of economic enterprise that positions benevolence, not profit, as the ultimate goal.

The main characters in *Sketches of Married Life* are Amy Weston and Edward Selmar, a young couple who marry within the course of the novel. Prior to their marriage, however, Edward suffers a financial failure that is brought on by the bankruptcy of others. Settling with his creditors for 75 cents on the dollar, he is released from the remainder of his debt, and leaves for a trading venture in China, where he ultimately recoups his fortune. During his absence, Mr. Weston also loses his money, propelling Amy into the role of "economist"—manager of the reduced household budget and financial adviser to her father. Throughout the Westons' move to a smaller house and process of "retrenchment," Follen emphasizes Amy's new position of responsibility: "In all their arrangements, she took care that her father's comfort should be especially consulted. All the sacrifices she managed should, as far as possible, fall upon herself; all the indulgences that she thought they could allow themselves were for his comfort. Her father had gradually acquired the habit, from seeing Amy so efficient, of consulting her about every thing. All his affairs were now known to her" (117–18). This economic agency, although acquired only in response to her father's loss of power and wealth, does not diminish upon Amy's later marriage to Edward, but expands into an active participation in her husband's business affairs. Although she does not literally join Edward in his mercantile office, she continues in her role as adviser, most notably in the couple's joint decision to repay Edward's creditors in full. Defending this decision to her disapproving father, Amy takes her share of the responsibility for what she calls "our conduct" in refusing to keep the money (202). Thus, in financial matters as well as household concerns, the Selmars share the responsibility of making decisions, manifesting a model of an equal marriage.

Like the Aikins in Sedgwick's novel, Amy and Edward center their family economy on benevolence. The importance of charity is established early on in *Sketches of Married Life,* as Amy and her father debate the value of her work among the poor. Mr. Weston objects to charity from the perspective of a wealthy man who wishes to maintain the economic inequalities that permit his privileged life: aiding the poor makes them "discontented," he asserts, and merely perpetuates poverty that would "die out, of itself, but for the mistaken efforts of benevolent enthusiasts" (77). Citing the Bible, he declares that "Jesus was careful never to meddle with any of the existing relations of society," even slavery, a view his daughter (and the author) deems a "perversion" of Christianity (78). For Amy, though—and hers is clearly the privileged voice in this debate—charity is beneficial to both the giver and receiver. The children in her school receive care and instruction, their mothers are enabled to work in order to support themselves and their families, while Amy herself gains discipline and a strengthened religious faith. Despite Mr. Weston's fears, altering the "existing relations of society" by aiding the poor promises a better society for all its members.

Unlike the Aikins, however, whose benevolence is linked to an economy of sufficiency, Edward and Amy's benevolence arises from, and motivates the continuance of, an economy of abundance. Although they practice charity even when hampered by reduced circumstances, their ultimate goal is to acquire wealth in order to "do good" with it. Defending Edward's profession of merchant against his own self-doubts, Amy emphasizes the opportunities it provides for righteousness—both in the resistance of temptation to extravagance, and in the practice of charity. "When I think of your profession," she muses, "it gives me pleasure to notice that merchants in general, as they acquire property more easily, are more disposed to spend it liberally." Agreeing, Edward observes that,

> the greater proportion of our public benefactors have been merchants. Their money has given eyes to the blind, and ears to the deaf, health to the sick, and peace and comfort to the forsaken; it feeds and instructs the ignorant poor; it sends the glad tidings of salvation to the unbeliever and the penitent; it takes little children in its arms, and blesses them. [And] all this glorious power supposes wealth. (191–92)

By the end of the novel, choosing their life in the urban world of commerce over the offered temptation of a rural existence, the Selmars resolve to turn financial success, and the benevolence it makes possible, into their mission. The narrator tells us that,

> Edward returned to his business with a new zeal for the accumulation of wealth, that he might be enabled to enjoy the luxury of changing tears of sorrow to tears of joy. . . . All of his earnings beyond a certain sum, which he set aside for the support and real good of his family, he solemnly dedicated to works of beneficence; not to a useless and enervating almsgiving, but to intelligent, thoughtful, consistent methods to alleviate the sufferings of the poor, by enabling them to raise themselves to a dignified independence. (290)

He also, we are told, worked for "the great cause of human freedom"—an allusion to Follen's own and her husband's dedication to the abolition of slavery. Thus Follen defines benevolence, or "works of beneficence," fairly broadly—as implicitly including political action that aims at improving the lives of others, as well as more direct modes of relief.

Given the novel's overall insistence on gender equality, it is perhaps curious that this passage is so exclusively devoted to Edward's philosophy of charity. Although the paragraph in its entirety concludes its account of Edward's efforts with the sentence "In all these duties and pleasures, Amy was his intimate adviser and efficient helpmate, his equal partner, his best friend," Edward's own commitment to benevolence is clearly the focus, with Amy relegated to a supporting role. In part, I see this as evidence of Follen's desire to legitimate her vision of a benevolent economy by voicing it through a male character. A similar instance occurs when it is Edward who first proposes repaying his creditors in full, an action prompted by moral considerations of fairness and obligation, but contrary to current financial custom. Although he consults with Amy before making a final decision, the idea is originally his, a fact that Amy reiterates when her father accuses her of influencing Edward with feminine—and therefore romantic—notions of perfectibility. Mr. Weston's complaint that "The wise and the experienced people of the world must sit still and listen, while boys teach them morals and women instruct them in political economy" (205) seems clearly to represent a criticism of female-authored panic fiction that Follen sought to sidestep by attributing some of her economic proposals to a male character. By focusing on Edward's commitment to benevolence in the book's final passage, Follen avoids the simple opposition between feminine morality and masculine business sense that Mr. Weston posits, and thus deflects potential criticism of women's effect on the economy if allowed to put moral concerns into practice. Masculine benevolence serves as a strategy of authorization for Follen's proposal of a benevolent economy.

Elsewhere in the novel, however, Follen clearly grants to women an important role in making the economy more benevolent by putting a human face on the consequences of financial decisions. In her argument with her father over charity, Amy responds to his disapproval with repeated "appeal[s] to [his] heart" (78). She attempts to make the poor real to him, to describe the mothers and the children whom she desires to help in order to make him see them as human beings for whom he has a responsibility. A bit later in the novel, Amy's cousin Fanny humorously contrasts her husband's interest in "rail-roads, and silk-worms, coal-mines, and sugar-beets, Swedish turnips and steam-boats" with the women's efforts on behalf of the "dirty, crying children," suggesting that women are more concerned with "the individual good of human beings," while men aim for a more abstract "public improvement" (87). Aiding the poor on an individual basis functions thus as a humanizing complement or corrective to commercial and industrial development as well as an appropriate means for spending the money that such development produces.[9] Follen herself participates in exposing the human side of economic decisions by showing how Edward and Amy's repayment of their creditors changed the lives of two affected families. Edward is personally able to witness the joy and gratitude of one boy who could now afford to go to college, while Amy receives an account of a girl reprieved at the last minute from going to Georgia as a governess to help her family's finances (207). Understanding how mercantile failures affect individuals such as these becomes something that Follen the author, as well as her female characters, can contribute to economic discourse.

Although Follen primarily addresses the opportunities for benevolence in the commercial world, she suggests that other sectors of the economy could be equally dedicated to charity. Toward the end of the novel, Amy and Edward visit friends who have established an idyllic industrial community in the country, thus combining aspects of manufacturing and agriculture. In their efforts to tempt the Selmars into leaving the city permanently, Fanny and William crown their glowing accounts with the story of how the community banded together to make up the losses incurred by a local carpenter in a construction disaster. This tale of communal benevolence marks the character of the factory town, providing a model for economic relations based on cooperation rather than competition.

In her idealized portraits of both commerce and industry, Follen affirms national expansion, and even rapid economic growth, but revises the ultimate goal of such growth from individual profit to benevolence. Such a change in economic direction will not necessarily prevent future panics, since for Follen, financial failure occurs primarily as a result of chance, but it will, Follen suggests, make the world a better place. Although Follen does not bring home and marketplace together quite as concretely as Sedgwick, she does link them through her portrayal of mutual decision-making in marriage and her vision of a marketplace that cares about individual people. By emphasizing benevolence as the ultimate aim of becoming wealthy and portraying the Selmars as partners in everything, including economic endeavors, Follen stakes a claim to women's rightful inclusion in a national economy that is operated in the interests of all citizens.

The authors of panic fiction vary considerably in their expressed attitudes toward the poor and in their proposals for appropriate methods of charity. Some depict poverty as resulting largely from either the poor's own moral failings—laziness, drunkenness, or gambling—or from misfortune such as a father's death or illness. Others acknowledge the role of social inequality and a lack of education. Likewise, some characterize charity as the relief of immediate physical needs, while others advocate aid designed to break a cycle of poverty. Both Susan Aikin and Amy Weston exemplify the latter approach, attempting to prevent future poverty by educating poor children and enabling women to support themselves financially.

What all these novels share is their vision of charity or benevolence as key to an economic system that protects both home and nation from the devastating effects of panic. Incorporating benevolence as an integral element of the family or national economy promises restraint of the unbridled pursuit of self-interest that causes financial instability, and ensures consideration of everyone's needs. At the same time, benevolence provides an economic role that middle-class women can play in their homes, communities, and nation, lessening the sense of vulnerability that results from enforced passivity.

In a sense, both benevolence and panic fiction itself are responses to economic circumstances that embed economic agency within moral and domestic narratives. We have seen how this works in panic novels: A middle-class home threatened by financial failure serves as a setting in which women can wield economic responsibility within their traditional roles in order to restore their family fortunes morally as well as financially. In a similar way, the economic character of women's benevolence plays out within cultural "narratives" of feminine kindness, duty, and caretaking. In both cases, moral and domestic imperatives provide a rationale for middle-class women to engage in economic activity. While the economic circumstance that benevolence "responds" to—a disparity between wealth and poverty—does not necessarily imply failure, fear of this disparity is precisely what motivates panic fiction. Panic narratives capture the middle-class anxiety about crossing the divide between wealth and poverty, moving from one side of the gap to the other through failure. Engaging in benevolence becomes a way for the female protagonists of panic fiction to show which side of the divide they are on; and while the desire to eradicate that divide is clearly ambivalent, benevolence also promises a society in which the consequences of failure are made less harsh.

This parallel between benevolence and panic fiction points to an intertwining of economics and morality in nineteenth-century domestic identity, despite rhetorical efforts to characterize them as separate or even mutually exclusive. Economic activity by middle-class women was dependent on moral narratives for legitimacy. At the same time, specific forms of morality, including benevolence within the home and community, relied on an underpinning of financial resources and expertise. Most importantly, economic decisions concerning both investment and expenditure had moral consequences, and thus required a process that would consider moral as well as financial factors. For panic authors, who sought to give women authority to speak about and enact economic policy by exposing the interconnections between economics and morality, benevolence provided both a narrative device and a blueprint for a domesticated economy. Whether that economy was envisioned as one of sufficiency or one of abundance, benevolence symbolized an opening of the marketplace—to wider prosperity and, especially, to middle-class women's increased participation.

Notes

1. I am using the terms "charity" and "philanthropy" more or less interchangeably in this essay to signify some form of direct aid to the poor, including money, goods, education, and so on. The term "benevolence" I am using in a somewhat broader sense—to signify a philosophy and practice of "doing good" that encompasses direct aid but also extends to a more abstract conception of public welfare.

2. Unemployment figures for the period come from Edward Pessen (84) and R. C. McGrane (130). Sean Wilentz has documented the dropping wage rates of the late 1830s and early 1840s in his history of the urban American working class (301). The story of New York's battle over whether to aid the city's unemployed with a public works program is related in Kenneth Stampp's *America in 1857* (228).

3. For more on the one-way nature of benevolence relationships, see Karen Tracey's and Monika Elbert's essays in this volume. Tracey's application of the concept of "panoptic discipline" to the moral scrutiny focused on the poor is particularly helpful here.

4. See Bergman's essay in this volume. Debra Bernardi's discussion of privacy and its forfeiture, although directed at later nineteenth-century fiction, also resonates with Sedgwick's model of charity.

5. By the 1830s some women were beginning to address mixed audiences on the lecture circuit, but often met with criticism for their "unnatural" behavior. The *New York Herald* satirically reports an unusual speech on commerce by Fanny Wright in its October 9, 1837, issue, mocking her views on bankruptcy legislation and the culpability of Jackson's "pet banks" even though her views coincided remarkably with the *Herald's* own philosophy.

6. Perhaps the most elegantly stated version of this point is Ruth Bloch's classic argument that eighteenth-century conceptions of virtue as masculine and public shifted by the early nineteenth century, with standards of virtue increasingly assigned to women's guardianship in a private sphere removed from the self-interest of the marketplace.

7. The "domesticated economy" envisioned by panic authors is less revolutionary than the economy of "abundant mother-love" that Gillian Brown reads in Harriet Beecher Stowe (23–24). Whereas Brown interprets Stowe as proposing to "abolish the marketplace altogether" and replace it with a maternal model, I read panic authors as primarily wanting to make market economics safer. Benevolence does not displace profitable exchange; rather, it coexists with it, taming greed and spreading the benefits of wealth.

8. Sedgwick's depiction of Susan Aikin and her protégée is clearly *not* within the tradition of the impoverished, dependent seamstress in danger of becoming a "fallen woman" that Lori Merish describes in her essay in this volume. Susan is married, self-sufficient, and a moral guide to the young in her care. Sedgwick may have been writing against the grain of popular conceptions, extending panic fiction's rhetorical empowerment of women to even such an entrenched symbol of feminine dependence.

9. Historians and literary critics have debated whether women's nineteenth-century charity and reform work was a genuine criticism of and alternative to male economic development that ignored (and created) human need, or whether it actually allowed such development to proceed untrammeled. Ruth Bloch and Gillian Brown both argue that the relationship between reform and capitalism was as much complementary as oppositional. Follen's own attitude about this seems ambivalent. While Fanny and Amy reprove male relatives for ignoring human need, Fanny is clearly proud of her husband's contributions to national industrial development. Combining benevolence with development as she does appears to be Follen's answer to this dichotomy.

Works Cited

Bloch, Ruth. "The Gendered Meanings of Virtue in Revolutionary America." *Signs: Journal of Women in Culture and Society* 13 (1987): 37–58.

Brown, Gillian. *Domestic Individualism: Imagining Self in Nineteenth-Century America.* Berkeley: U of California P, 1990.

Carlin, Deborah. "'What Methods Have Brought Blessing': Discourses of Reform in Philanthropic Literature." *The (Other) American Traditions: Nineteenth-Century Women Writers.* Ed. Joyce W. Warren. New Brunswick: Rutgers UP, 1993. 203–25.

Follen, Eliza Lee Cabot. *Sketches of Married Life.* 1838. Rev. ed. Boston: William Crosby and H. P. Nichols, 1847.

Ginzberg, Lori D. *Women and the Work of Benevolence: Morality, Politics, and Class in the Nineteenth-Century United States.* New Haven: Yale UP, 1990.

Lee, Hannah Farnham Sawyer. *Elinor Fulton.* Boston: Whipple and Damrell, 1837.

———. *Rosanna, or Scenes in Boston.* Cambridge: John Owen, 1839.

———. *Three Experiments of Living.* Boston: Wm. S. Damrell, 1837.

McGrane, Reginald Charles. *The Panic of 1837: Some Financial Problems of the Jacksonian Era.* Chicago: U of Chicago P, 1924.

New York Herald. June 14, 1837.

Pessen, Edward. *Jacksonian America: Society, Personality, and Politics.* Rev. ed. Urbana: U of Illinois P, 1985.

Sedgwick, Catharine Maria. *The Poor Rich Man, and The Rich Poor Man.* 1836. New York: Harper and Bros., 1868.

Stampp, Kenneth M. *America in 1857: A Nation on the Brink.* New York: Oxford UP, 1990.

Wilentz, Sean. *Chants Democratic: New York City and the Rise of the American Working Class, 1788–1850.* New York: Oxford UP, 1984.

4

Reforming Women's Reform Literature

Rebecca Harding Davis's Rewriting of the Industrial Novel

Whitney A. Womack

> Met Miss Harding, author of "Margret Howth," which has made a stir and is very good. A handsome, quiet woman, who says she never had any troubles, though she writes of woes. I told her I had lots of troubles; so I write jolly tales; and we wondered why we each did so.
>
> —Louisa May Alcott, 1862

Rebecca Harding Davis was never fully satisfied with her first novel *Margret Howth: A Story of To-Day* (1862), a view shared by many contemporary readers and literary critics.[1] When Davis first submitted the manuscript—then titled *The Deaf and the Dumb*—to the *Atlantic Monthly* in May 1861, editor James T. Fields rejected it. Just the month before, Davis had burst onto the national literary scene with the *Atlantic Monthly*'s publication of her short story "Life in the Iron-Mills," the story of the physical and spiritual starvation of factory workers in an anonymous industrial town. As a long-time resident of Wheeling, Virginia (later West Virginia), Davis was a firsthand witness to America's exploding Industrial Revolution, a phenomenon that had not yet entered the nation's literary imagination.[2] Her habit of taking "vagabond tramps" allowed the middle-class Davis to observe Wheeling's iron works, coal mines, cotton mills, and nail factories as well as the lives, habits, and dialects of their employees, which she incorporated into her short story. "Life in the Iron-Mills" was well received and heralded by critics for its realism, its industrial subject matter, and its raw, unpolished prose style. Its success brought the obscure thirty-one-year-old writer to the attention of America's literati, including Nathaniel Hawthorne, Bronson and Louisa May Alcott, Ralph Waldo Emerson, and Oliver Wendell Holmes.[3] Indeed, Fields was so impressed with Davis's story that he encouraged her literary efforts and offered her the substantial sum of one hundred dollars for another submission (Rose, *Rebecca Harding Davis* 22).

Considering Fields's unbridled enthusiasm for her fiction the month before, his negative response to *The Deaf and the Dumb* must have come as a great shock to Davis, who clearly had been at work on her first novel for some time. Davis later destroyed the original manuscript, but we know the plot of this draft, as well as Fields's objections to it, from what exists of their correspondence. Fields asserted that the text was written in a "pathetic minor" and that the "assembled gloom" of its conclusion—ending with the suicide of factory owner Stephen Holmes on Christmas Eve and the dedication of heroine Margret Howth to a quiet life of social reform work—was altogether too pessimistic for the *Atlantic*'s readers (qtd. in Yellin 287–88). While Davis provided an eloquent defense of her manuscript in her reply to Fields's rejection letter, she was clearly shaken by his criticism, asking "do you care to have me as a contributor?" In order to appease the powerful and influential editor, Davis promised, perhaps a bit sarcastically, that she would replace the novel's gloom with "a warm healthy light," transforming the "gloom" into a "perfect day in June" (288). Fields accepted the revised manuscript, delivered a mere eight weeks later, and retitled it *Margret Howth: A Story of To-Day*—a decidedly more optimistic title, one perhaps intended to be more appealing to a female readership. Although few readers would claim that this grim story of life in an industrial town is truly a "perfect day in June," Davis did weave in a marriage plot and more conventional happy ending. *Margret Howth* ran serially in the *Atlantic* from October 1861 to March 1862 and received several positive reviews, including one in *Peterson's* that favorably compares the novel to the works of Charlotte Brontë (Pfaelzer 57). It was popular enough to merit republication in book form later that year, selling a respectable, if not record-setting, 2,500 copies in three editions (Harris 82).

While Fields was disappointed with *The Deaf and the Dumb,* Davis was disappointed with *Margret Howth,* which she felt failed to convey the "true history of To-Day" that she intended to write. In an 1861 letter, she claimed the revised novel was "like giving people broken bits of apple-rind to chew"—in other words, not at all satisfying or fulfilling (qtd. in Yellin 289). She urged Fields to allow her the opportunity to revise the novel again before its publication in book form, a request he denied. Most Davis critics agree with the author's assessment of the novel. Tillie Olsen, who resurrected Davis's fiction in the 1970s after decades of critical neglect, pronounces the novel "sometimes embarrassingly bad" (95).[4] Sharon M. Harris laments Davis's compromises and declares that *Margret Howth* is "ultimately a failure in artistic terms precisely because of the insertions of 'full sunshine' into an otherwise stridently realistic work" (63). Many critics accuse Fields, the quintessential "Gentleman-Publisher,"[5] of undermining the "integrity of [Davis's] hard-hitting fiction" (Tichi 10) and containing her "narrative radicalism" (Pfaelzer 54) as well as attempting to feminize Davis's discussion of industrial capitalism by urging her to expel the "gloom" and add elements more typical of sentimental "woman's fiction."[6]

Fields, as well as contemporary critics, may have misunderstood Davis's intentions in both the early draft and final version of *Margret Howth.* I read Davis's novel as a direct response to and critique of the conventions and assumptions of the industrial reform novels that were commercially and critically popular in England during the mid-nineteenth century.[7] Like both "Life in the Iron-Mills" and *Margret Howth,* British industrial reform novels, a widely popular form of benevolence literature, sought to give a human face to the suffering of industrial workers and expose the injustices of industrial capitalism and laissez-faire policies. Today we tend to associate such male writers as Benjamin Disraeli, Charles Kingsley, and Charles Dickens with the industrial novel, yet it was in fact women writers like Frances Trollope, Charlotte Elizabeth Tonna, Elizabeth Gaskell, Charlotte Brontë (among Rebecca Harding Davis's favorite writers), and George Eliot who pioneered and sustained this subgenre throughout the mid-nineteenth century. As Joseph Kestner explains in *Protest and Reform: The British Social Narrative by Women,* "[n]ot only were many women part of this tradition; they also entered it far earlier than their male counterparts" (3). In industrial reform novels by both male and female novelists, so-called women's values—benevolence, empathy, compassion—are prescribed as the antidotes to the ills of industrial capitalism and utilitarianism. In almost every industrial reform novel, idealized women characters are empowered to act as moral guides, class mediators, and saviors of the industrial world. Industrial reform novels inevitably imagine middle-class women bringing about peaceful resolutions to England's industrial crisis and diffusing the very real threat of class revolution during the turbulent Chartist period of the 1840s and 1850s, in spite of the limited social and political positions of women in this era. Feminist literary critics—notably, Constance Harsh, Catherine Gallagher, Rosemarie Bodenheimer, and Barbara Leah Harman—have reshaped our vision of industrial reform novels, which had long been dismissed as heavy-handed and overly didactic, by exploring the radical possibilities embedded in the representations of middle-class women reformers and the novels' implicit critiques of separate spheres ideology.

Davis was undoubtedly familiar with the tradition of British industrial reform fiction.[8] These texts were widely available in authorized and "pirated" editions throughout the United States in the 1850s, making it very likely that the well-read Davis came into contact with them before or during the composition of *Margret Howth.*[9] Davis's Anglo-Irish father had instilled a love of British literature in his daughter, and her writing reveals a considerable knowledge of British authors. In *Margret Howth* alone there are allusions to William Shakespeare, Samuel Johnson, Fanny Burney, Maria Edgeworth, Percy Bysshe Shelley, Thomas Carlyle, Charles Dickens, and Charles Darwin. When Davis sat down to write about the United States' new industrial landscape, it is likely that she looked to British industrial reform novels as examples. Indeed, Davis recognized potential comparisons between herself and Brontë, author of the industrial reform novel *Shirley.* She expressed a concern about the association in a letter to Fields regarding *Margret Howth:* "You did not think I imitated Charlotte Bronte [*sic*], did you? I would rather you sent it back than thought that, but tell me candidly if you did. I may have done it unconsciously" (qtd. in Pfaelzer 59). Davis also had a strong desire to be published in England, where, according to Harris, she "felt she could have the political freedom to write as realistically as she desired" and was disappointed when Fields failed to locate a British publisher for *Margret Howth* (96–97).[10]

While American literary critics have hailed Davis as the pioneer of such American literary movements as realism and naturalism,[11] they have largely overlooked the fact that she was working within a well-established British literary tradition. Considering the longstanding, institutional resistance to transatlanticism in literary studies, this omission is perhaps not surprising. In the last decade, however, many scholars have argued for a dismantling of the traditional national canons and for a new focus on the complex and multiple cultural conditions in which texts have been produced, distributed, read, and critiqued.[12] In his recent study *Romantic Dialogues: Anglo-American Continuities,* Richard Gravil asserts that critics who continue to ignore the impact of transatlanticism on both American and British literature in the nineteenth century are guilty of "offering a bowdlerized literary history" (xx). It should come as no surprise that British and American writers engaged in dialogues about industrialization, especially given the significant transatlantic literary discussions regarding the abolition of slavery, the other major social reform movement of the early and mid-nineteenth century. Indeed, such recent studies of abolitionist literature as Audrey Fisch's *American Slaves in Victorian England: Abolitionist Politics in Popular Literature and Culture* and Helen Thomas's *Romanticism and Slave Narratives: Transatlantic Testimonies* document the fluid circulation of texts and cross-fertilization of abolitionist texts and rhetoric across the Atlantic.[13] Placing *Margret Howth* in the context of the British industrial novel compels us to rethink earlier critiques of the novel and helps to dismiss the mistaken, but all too common, notion that Davis was a literary enigma "without precedent or predecessor," writing about industrial issues in a vacuum (Olsen 10). In fact, we can see her as part of a larger "imagined community," to borrow Benedict Anderson's term.

I argue that Davis sought specifically to challenge and subvert Elizabeth Gaskell's novel *North and South,* published serially in 1854–55 in Dickens's journal *Household Words,* popular in both nations. There are striking, even uncanny similarities between the characters, settings, and plots of *North and South* and *Margret Howth,* which strongly suggest that Davis consciously set out to rewrite Gaskell's novel. From the Davis-Fields correspondence, it appears that in *The Deaf and the Dumb* Davis attempted to break with the typical plotline of industrial novels and complicate their often simplistic notions of reform and easy solutions to complex social and economic problems.

In particular, Davis initially refused to include a romance plot, which is used in *North and South* (and other industrial reform novels) to symbolize the union of opposites and suggest a reconciliation of masters and men. Even in the revised *Margret Howth,* with its reluctant romance plot,

Davis still manifests a critique, evidenced by the narrator's frequent disruptions and metafictional commentaries. These narrative asides serve to subvert the very romance plot that Fields requested Davis include. As Lisa Long notes in her article "Imprisoned in/at Home: Criminal Culture in Rebecca Harding Davis' *Margret Howth,*" Davis may have in fact "duped Fields" by "adding rather than subtracting narrative complexity" when she revised the text (83). Although Davis was clearly critical of many tropes and traditions of the industrial reform novel, I do not believe she set out to write an anti-industrial reform novel. With *Margret Howth* Davis sought not to destroy but to reform the industrial novel by exposing its fundamental flaws and fallacies and participating in ongoing, transnational conversations about women's roles in benevolent and reform work and the shape of industrial reform narratives.

Readers can recognize links between *North and South* and *Margret Howth* almost immediately, beginning with the remarkably parallel lives of the novels' protagonists. The heroines share the initials "M. H." and similar names: Margaret Hale and Margret Howth. Davis's clipped, two-syllable spelling of the name "Margaret" is significant, marking Margret Howth as different from a sentimental heroine who, the narrator claims, would have a "name *three-syllabled,* and a white dress that never needs washing, ready to sail through dangers dire into a triumphant haven of matrimony" (Davis 102, emphasis mine). In addition, the two women are almost exactly the same age—Margaret Hale is nineteen, while Margret Howth turns twenty on the opening day of the novel. Davis does provide a pointed contrast in the characters' social situations. At the beginning of *North and South,* Margaret Hale lives in her aunt's fashionable London home, in fact leading the sentimental heroine's charmed life, and seems destined to find her way into the "triumphant haven of matrimony." Davis, however, immediately saddles Margret, "a quiet, dark girl, coarsely dressed in brown," with real-life problems and practical concerns (9).

Both the Hale and the Howth families find themselves geographically and economically displaced, forcing Margaret and Margret to enter and negotiate the public sphere and forsake their own dreams for the future. Their ineffectual fathers are unable to deal with the new industrial world and yearn for the past: Reverend Hale is teacher of dead languages and literatures, while Mr. Howth, a former teacher himself, hungers for the age of feudalism and chivalry, a sentiment that echoes the ideals of British politician and reform writer Benjamin Disraeli and other members of the Young England movement (33).[14] Margaret Hale ventures out into the dirty streets of Milton-Northern (a thinly disguised version of Manchester, Gaskell's home) to make housekeeping arrangements for her family. She travels "up and down to butchers and grocers" in an effort to hire a suitable servant girl, a difficult task in a mill town where girls can earn better wages working in factories (109). At one point Margaret jokes that she has become more like "Peggy the laundry-maid" than "Margaret Hale the lady," but she never truly loses her middle-class, entitled position (115).

Middle-class Margret Howth, however, falls much further down the social ladder when she is forced to take a job as a bookkeeper at Knowles & Co., a monstrous, seven-story textile mill, a world away from the Howths' rural Indiana farm. This is also a much bolder step into the public sphere; while Margaret Hale makes only a few trips alone into public spaces, Margret is forced to travel alone each day to the factory, where she is subject to the gaze of male workers. Margret's experience working at the mill is described in sensory terms: her office is a cramped closet on the seventh floor; her one small window provides only a view of the wool-dyeing vats; she is inundated with the smell of sickening dyes; and the floor shakes with "the incessant thud of the great looms" (15). Margret soon learns the mind-numbing effects of the factory, for after just one day of monotonous copying work, she already handles herself in a "mechanical fashion" (10). Later Margret is described as having "dead, dull eyes" (59), and after several months in the mill she is like an "automaton" (225). Davis makes a point of showing how the factory system strips workers, even white-collar workers like Margret, of their identities, transforming them into anonymous "hands." In the happy endings of both novels, the protagonists are able to escape their reduced economic circumstances and finally marry, fulfilling a woman's proper destiny, due to unexpected cash windfalls. Margaret Hale is made an heiress after the death of her godfather, the ivory tower Oxford don Mr. Bell. Davis mocks Gaskell's deus ex machina conclusion with the timely but rather improbable discovery of oil on the Howths' central Indiana farm, which presumably will grant them a comfortable income and stable future.

Davis's resistance to Gaskell's narrative is also made clear in her representations of the domestic sphere. Despite their reduced circumstances, the Hales have a cozy home, which is more comfortable and inviting, in fact, than factory owner John Thornton's grand but sterile house. The majority of Gaskell's novel takes place in domestic spaces, with only a few forays into the public world of work and industry. Certainly Margaret's appearance before a mob of striking workers at Marlborough Mills is a significant moment in the history of female public appearance, but she quickly retreats to the domestic sphere. In contrast, very little of *Margret Howth* takes place in domestic spaces. Instead, Davis takes Margret and her readers into the bowels of a factory and on a tour of the "under-life of America," a world populated by society's "dregs":

> The room was swarming with human life. Women, idle trampers, whiskey-bloated, filthy, lay half-asleep, or smoking, on the floor, and set up a chorus of whining begging when they [Knowles and Margret] entered. Half-naked children crawled about in rags. . . .
>
> A girl of fifteen, almost a child, lay underneath [a sheet], dead,—her lithe, delicate figure decked out in a dirty plaid skirt, and stained velvet bodice,—her neck and arms were bare. . . . Margret leaned over her, shuddering, pinning her handkerchief around the child's dead neck. (150–53)

Even when we do enter the Howth household, Davis highlights the fact that the domestic, private sphere is not an idealized safe haven, immune from the effects of the public world and marketplace. As Jean Pfaelzer explains, Davis purposefully "blurs the public-private distinction from which the very notion of gender arises" (17). The slow dismantling of the Howth household, as the family pawns their most valuable possessions in order to keep from starvation, manifests this critique of the idealization of the domestic. Mrs. Howth and Margret cannot bring themselves to tell the blind Mr. Howth what they have done, and the old man continues to insist that Margret dust paintings and bric-a-brac the family no longer owns: "You can clean the pictures today, Margret. Be careful, my Child" (39). This "white leprosy of poverty" even leads the once domestic and genteel Mrs. Howth to forage for food in the fields around their house (38).

Davis also subverts Gaskell's idealized vision of the reformer-heroine, exemplified by Margaret Hale, who is an eager, benevolent social activist. In creating Margaret Hale, Gaskell herself was rewriting the long-standing stereotype of Lady Bountiful, a term describing those upper- and middle-class women who would condescendingly visit and dispense charity—along with a heaping dose of moral instruction as well as lessons in proper domesticity—to the "worthy" poor.[15] These benevolent women would work zealously on behalf of philanthropic societies but would never actually venture into factories, slums, or red-light districts to interact with the "objects" of their good works. Both Gaskell and Davis would have appreciated Dickens's caricature of such Lady Bountifuls in *Bleak House:* "They took a multitude of titles. They were the Women of England, the Daughters of Britain, the Sisters of all the Cardinal Virtues separately, the Females of America, the Ladies of a hundred denominations. . . . It made our heads ache to think, on the whole, what feverish lives they must lead" (93–94).

In contrast, Gaskell presents a very different image of the type of the benevolent work women ought to do. She grants Margaret Hale publicity, voice, and agency—transforming Lady Bountiful into a woman reformer. This reform work enables Margaret to maintain her class position, despite the Hale family's loss of status and income after her father resigns his position as a clergyman due to a crisis of faith. As Mary Templin notes in her study of "panic fiction," in this volume, such "charitable acts protect middle-class women's social identity" and "emphasize the moral and intellectual superiority of the female philanthropist" (82–83). Margaret feels entitled to do this work, considering it her right, even her moral duty to step into the fray and act as translator and mediator between the "masters" and "men" of Milton-Northern, represented by factory "hand" Nicholas Higgins and mill owner John Thornton. When she discovers that the root of class antagonism is a lack of communication, she easily and successfully forges a personal connection between the men. Because of Margaret, Thornton is brought face-to-face, man-to-man with Higgins, which enables him to see past the "mere cash nexus" (525). He decides to soften his policies and provide a communal dining room, where he can share an occasional "hot-pot" with his workers (446). This is an interesting example of instituting women's domestic values in the public sphere, yet ultimately it acts as a bandage on the gaping wound of class oppression. Gaskell imagines Margaret's benevolent work ameliorating her own life far more than it affects the conditions of Milton's industrial workers. Margaret becomes an active participant in the public world, continuing her reform work when she moves back to London after the deaths of her parents, and later gaining economic agency by becoming a factory owner when she purchases Thornton's financially troubled Marlborough Mills with her unexpected inheritance.[16]

Davis upsets readers' expectation that Margret Howth, like the female protagonists of other industrial novels, will stand up and lead the charge against the injustices of the factory system by easily slipping into the role of woman reformer. Unlike Margaret Hale, who has the time and the ability to argue with "masters and men" and mediate strikes, Margret Howth is exhausted from her long hours at the mill and shy about expressing her opinions (29). She feels "stifled" in her new position, and her "higher life" is "starved, thwarted" (71). Indeed, Davis compares Margret with the pathetic caged chicken kept in the mill office (11). In order to endure her current situation, Margret in effect buries herself: "She thrust out of sight all possible life that might have called her true self into being, and clung to this present shallow duty and shallow reward" (44). Although she clearly believes that "[s]omething is wrong everywhere," she does not believe she has the inherent power or strength to right this wrong (68).

Davis provides Margret with the opportunity to take on the role of social reformer when Dr. Knowles, a former factory owner turned socialist and philanthropist, asks her to serve as a benevolent worker in his planned "communist fraternity" for the poor (83). Throughout her life Davis was skeptical of organized and institutionalized forms of benevolence, particularly, as Pfaelzer explains, of "any formula whereby the dreams of a single man would shape a community" (20).[17] Davis objected to the nineteenth-century movement toward what Monika Elbert in this volume terms "scientific charity" or "philanthropology" (160). Davis was writing during America's great age of organized reform work; by the midcentury, there were literally thousands of local and national associations, societies, commissions, and institutions devoted to benevolence and philanthropy. As noted elsewhere in this volume, due to women's "peculiar influence," many of these organizations were led by, managed by, and composed of public-spirited, middle-class women. In *Women and the Work of Benevolence,* Lori Ginzberg chronicles the history and influence of such women's organizations as the American Female Anti-Slavery Society, the New York Moral Reform Society, and the Women's Central Association of Relief. A strong advocate of the abolition of slavery, Davis certainly could not have been blind to the political good that could come from organized agitation, but she also saw in these associations the potential for misuse and hypocrisy. Davis instead advocated concrete, immediate acts of charity, encouraging individual over collective activism. Davis exposes the difference between these two approaches to reform in an anecdote in her memoirs *Bits of Gossip:*

> One of our good friends, years ago, was Dr. J. G. Holland. . . . He had incessant disputes with me about almsgiving, I upholding the ancient lax methods of the good Samaritan, who, out of his own pocket, helped the man fallen by the wayside, not inquiring too closely as to his character. The Doctor maintained vehemently that all alms should be given through the agents of the Organized Charity Boards, and then only after close examination, to those whom they found worthy. (148–49)

Davis similarly blasts those people who would substitute institutionalized charity for individual benevolence and social responsibility in her editorial "Indiscriminate Charity": " . . . when a man shifts his personal responsibility for the poor wholly to legal action or organized associations, does he not rob his needy brother and himself of that reality of human brotherhood . . . ?" (qtd. in Harris 54).

By definition a "communitarian fraternity" should be a place of brotherhood/sisterhood and equality, but Davis makes it clear that Knowles envisions his role as the head of the commune, as the great paternalist leader of his own flock. His plans for the commune seem to come more out of his own desire for self-aggrandizement than any concern about the poor and marginalized whom he describes as mere "atoms," a swarming mass rather than as individuals (89). Knowles is reminiscent of the utopian visionary Hollingsworth in Hawthorne's *The Blithedale Romance,* whose "godlike benevolence has been debased into all-devouring egotism" (71) and has rendered him "not altogether human" (70). When Knowles takes Margret to the slums, he is shocked when she easily and unthinkingly picks up and kisses a little "pickaninny," admonishing her to "[p]ut *it* down, and come on" (151, emphasis mine). Margret refuses his offer of work, which in fact reads more like a command: "I want you to do your work. It is hard; it will wear out your strength and brain and heart. Give yourself to these people. God calls you to it. There is none to help them. Give up love and the petty hopes of women" (154). She refuses Knowles not because she doesn't care about the poor—indeed she seems to feel far more compassion for them than Knowles does—but because she is not convinced that benevolent work is her calling, because she already has a paid position, and because she is not willing to sacrifice herself completely, which is what Knowles demands of her. The clergyman Van Dyke astutely points out that Knowles sees Margret as a machine to do his work, claiming that "It is the way with modern reformers. Men are so ploughs and harrows to work on the 'classes'" (216).

Ironically, Davis offers up Lois Yare, the most abject figure in the narrative, as her model of a true social reformer, not Dr. Knowles or Margret Howth. As an African American, disabled, working-class woman, Lois is at the bottom of America's social hierarchy, one of the "dumb" Davis refers to in her original title *The Deaf and the Dumb.* Like Bessy Higgins in *North and South,* Lois's health has been ruined by her work as a child laborer. Lois, symbolically nicknamed "Lo," recalls her factory work: "I kind o' grew into that place in them years, seemed to me like I was part o' the engines, somehow" (69). She is left with "some deformity of her legs [that] made her walk with a curious rolling jerk" (55) as well as "an injured brain" (93). Using Elizabeth Grosz's theory of the human body as text, an inscriptive surface on which messages can be written, we can read both Bessy's and Lois's scarred and battered bodies as indictments of industrial capitalism, their bodily suffering representing class oppression (117). In her article "Benevolent Maternalism and Physically Disabled Figures," Rosemarie Garland Thomson argues that such disabled characters are an essential rhetorical element in benevolent literature, noting that these narratives inevitably are based on,

> mutually defining relationships between foregrounded, idealized versions of white maternal benefactresses and muted, marginalized female figures

> who require spiritual and material redemption. Distinguishing each of these subordinate figures is a visible physical disability. This mark of Otherness operates as a badge of innocence, suffering, displacement, and powerlessness that renders the disabled women sympathetic and alarming figures of vulnerability who cry out for rescue. (557)

Thomson also claims that these narratives are designed to showcase the able-bodied benefactresses, who "boldly enact voice, agency, and self-determination [while] the vulnerable figures languish on the narrative margins, ensnared by the limitations of their own bodies" (569).

Margaret Hale and Bessy clearly embody these roles, with Margaret providing spiritual and material comfort to the bedridden Bessy as she dies of "fluff," a disease caused by inhaling cotton fibers in textile mills. But in Davis's novel it is Margret Howth who suffers from soul starvation and Lois who is granted the power to save and redeem, emerging as the novel's unlikely "benefactress." Margret curses her life of sacrifice and work, which has left her with a "hopeless thirst" for "every woman's right—to love and be loved," and doesn't see how she could possibly help or encourage others (61). Lois, however, inspires people, for "some subtile [*sic*] power lay in the coarse, distorted body, in the pleading child's face, to rouse, wherever they went, the same curious, kindly smile. . . . No human soul refused to answer its summons" (76–77). After spending a day with Lois as she makes her rounds, Margret comes away spiritually nourished and transformed: "her morbid fancies were gone; she was keenly alive; the coarse real life of this huckster fired her, touched her blood with a more vital stimulus than any tale of crusader" (78). Her reference to the "crusader" alludes both to her father's medieval fancies and to the philanthropist Dr. Knowles, who fashions himself as a modern-day crusader. But neither Mr. Howth nor Dr. Knowles are able to combat what Davis sees as the true "enemy, Self"—their self-interested desires for money or position or self-fulfillment (7). It is only Lois Yare, with her focus on human interaction and her simple, optimistic message—"things allus do come right"—who can reform the crisis of soul starvation that Davis believes afflicted people of all social classes in an industrial world, not just the poor (68).

Davis further complicates representations of reform and benevolence by introducing the issue of race. While *North and South* focuses almost exclusively on issues of social class, with a brief allusion to ethnic tensions between British and Irish laborers, *Margret Howth* addresses the overlapping, and at times competing, issues of class and race in America. Davis's novel opens with explicit references to the conflict on every American's mind in 1861: the Civil War. In fact, it initially appears the novel will be about the war and the question of slavery from Davis's opening remarks:

> I write on the border of the battlefield. I find in it no theme for shallow arguments or flimsy rhymes. . . . Hands wet with a brother's blood for the Right, a slavery of intolerance, the hackneyed cant of men, or the bloodthirstiness of women, utter no prophecy to us of the great To-Morrow of content and right that holds the world. (3–4)

Davis literally was writing the novel from the "border of the battlefield"—Virginia was a slaveholding state, though Davis's region was a Union stronghold and seceded in 1862 to form West Virginia. However, Davis makes it clear that she will be addressing a different war, a war she has also witnessed firsthand: "the life-long battle for butter and bread" (20). Yet with the creation of Lois Yare and her father Joe Yare, Davis constantly reminds us of the nation's simmering issue of racial conflict, showing how intertwined racial and economic oppression are in the United States.[18] Davis makes Lois the most exemplary character in the novel, the one person not working solely for his or her own self-interest. We can read Lois as Davis's indictment of a racist society that would likely be blinded to the power of a figure like Lois due to prejudice. Pfaelzer, however, objects to Davis's depiction of Lois, claiming that Davis invokes a "racist stereotype of a childlike, physically handicapped, mentally retarded mulatto woman" (70). By making Lois an object of sympathy, she argues, Davis ultimately undercuts Lois's power.

Yet Davis grants Lois the ability to unite people, allowing her to transcend borders and barriers and mediate between different races and classes, between the rural and urban worlds: "everybody along the road knew Lois, and she knew everybody, and there was a mutual liking and perpetual joking, not very refined, perhaps, but hearty and kind" (73). Lois stops at houses even if there is no produce to pick or drop off, bringing mail, news, small gifts, or "'jes' to inquire fur th' fam'ly," and is inevitably urged to stay and share a meal with the family—with food serving as an antidote to both emotional and physical hunger (74). Lois, who has little to spare, helps feed the poor by selling them food at prices below those in the capitalist, male-dominated marketplace (76). Davis represents her belief in the reciprocal nature of charity, for in return for her good deeds Lois is showered with love and affection from all people in the community. Unlike Knowles's institutionalized approach to reform, Lois's reform efforts are personal, immediate, hands-on, and spiritual. Her relational bonds with the community, as well as her Emersonian connection to Nature (which is somehow "alive to her"), enable her to reform a heartless, mechanical society (93). Jean Fagan Yellin argues that Lois's "faith, hope, and charity (as well as the Christian suffering and transcendence)" are what will "save the nation" (282).

Christ-like Lois sacrifices her own body, rushing into the burning mill to rescue factory owner Stephen Holmes. The fire had been deliberately set by Lois's father Joe Yare, a former slave and ex-convict who has only recently returned to town and taken a job as a stoker in the mill's furnace room (162). Although Yare is desperately "tryin' to be a different man" (165), Holmes decides to reveal a forgery Yare committed years before. Despite Yare's pleas for mercy—"It'll kill my girl,—it'll kill her. Gev me a chance, Marster"—Holmes plans to turn him over to the authorities, who will inevitably return him to prison (166). Rather than leave Lois again, Yare sets the mill on fire, knowing that Holmes sleeps there and will be killed in the blaze. Pfaelzer claims that in this scene Davis is demonstrating her fear that "the rage of racism and poverty" could bring down "the industrial house" and that the factory system could literally implode (73). Davis surely meant to evoke images of violent slave revolts, in which slaves would rise up and burn down the master's house. Yare's plan goes awry, though, when selfless Lois awakens to see the fire; realizing that Holmes is within and remembering that he had always been "so kind to her," she rushes in (172). Despite her physical limitations and her desperate fear of the mill (which she envisions as "a live monster"), Lois manages to bring Holmes to safety (171). She pays the ultimate price for this selfless act of heroism; the fumes she inhales in the fire lead to her death on New Year's Eve. The narrator dwells on Lois's body, imagining her afterlife: "I like to think of her poor body lying there: I like to believe that the great mother . . . took her uncouth child home again, that had been so fully wronged,—folded it in her warm bosom with tender, palpitating love" (263).

Harris condemns Davis's decision to kill off Lois, claiming that the novel's "placebic happy ending" is "ironically accomplished at the expense of the single potentially redeeming figure in the novel" (67). Pfaelzer, however, acknowledges that Davis had few options, for "the traditional mid-century fictional ending of marriage and home is historically and imaginatively unavailable for a black woman character" (71). Lois has helped to reform the current social system by bringing people of all races and classes together, yet narrow-minded, racist American society is not ready to embrace her or allow her to lead a full and fulfilled life. It is the middle-class Margret, then, who is left at the novel's end to carry on Lois's mission. While Gaskell sets up the middle-class Margaret Hale as industrial society's savior from the beginning, Davis only reluctantly appoints Margret Howth to this role, and even then leaves us with real doubts about her ability to transform society.

The scene of Lois's bodily sacrifice provides an interesting parallel to the strike scene in *North and South* in which Margaret Hale uses her body to shield Thornton from a mob of striking workers. Margaret shames Thornton into facing these men, who have surrounded Marlborough Mills to protest being "turned out" and replaced with Irish scab labor:

> "Mr Thornton," said Margaret, shaking all over with her passion, "go down this instant, if you are not a coward. Go down and face them *like a man*. Save these poor strangers [the Irish], whom you have decoyed here. Speak to your workmen as if they were human beings. Speak to them kindly. Don't let the soldiers come in and cut down poor creatures who are driven mad. I see one there who already is. If you have any courage or noble quality in you, go out and speak to them, man to man!" (232, emphasis mine)

In a novel so intensely concerned with gender roles, it is interesting that Margaret urges Thornton to "act like a man," not to hide in the house like a coward—or a woman. As we soon see, Margaret decides she can embody this "man's role" herself. She watches as Thornton reluctantly stands, statue-like, in front of the rioters, then tears off her bonnet, throws open a window, and leans out—positioning herself half in and half out of the domestic sphere. But when she sees that the "infuriated men and reckless boys" (233) are armed with rocks and clogs and ready to explode into violence, she decides she must step onto the public stage, enacting what Elaine Hadley has termed "theatricalized dissent" (2). Margaret acts because something must be done, reminding us of British writer and reformer Harriet Martineau's observation, "when women are able to do they will do, with or without leave from men" (qtd. in Poovey 165). Using her body to shield Thornton from the angry workers, Margaret takes on the typically masculine role of protector:[19]

> The hootings rose and filled the air,—but Margaret did not hear them. Her eye was on the group of lads who had armed themselves with their clogs some time before. She saw their gesture—she knew its meaning,—she read their aim. Another moment, and Mr. Thornton might be smitten down,—he whom she had urged and goaded to come to this perilous place. She only thought of how she could save him. She threw her arms around him; she made her body into a shield from the fierce people beyond. Still, with his arms folded, he shook her off.
>
> "Go away," said he, in his deep voice. "This is no place for you."
>
> "It is!" said she. (234)

Bodenheimer reads this scene as the enactment of the "fantasy of female social rescue," in which women, by virtue of their womanhood, are able to save society: "[Margaret's] imperious maternal instincts, a proof of Margaret's special courage, demand that we redefine women as strong protectors . . . " (65). But Gaskell does show the inherent dangers of the public sphere; a stone clearly intended for Thornton strikes Margaret: "A sharp pebble flew by her, grazing forehead and cheek, and drawing a blinding sheet of light before her eyes" (235). While Margaret walks away relatively unscathed save for a scratch on the forehead, Lois dies as a result of her injuries at the mill—yet another example of the way that Davis seeks to replace idealized or romanticized moments in *North and South* with examples of harsh reality and suffering for workers and reformers.

In *North and South,* Gaskell employs what Lyde Cullen Sizer, in her book on Civil War–era women writers, terms a "rhetoric of unity," bringing together opposing factions and ideologies: North and South, public and private, industrial and domestic, masters and workers, capitalism and compassion. The novel's marriage plot, culminating in the engagement of Margaret and Thornton in the final chapter, symbolizes this union of opposites. Ruth Bernard Yeazell argues that industrial novelists like Gaskell invoke the sentimental novel's convention of the marriage plot to contain "social and political anxieties" (127). In *North and South,* the marriage plot redirects our attention, often at key moments in the narrative, away from the public sphere of industrialization and class strife to the private sphere of love, romance, and sexual politics. For instance, after the riot, Gaskell focuses on Margaret's relationship with Thornton, not on the conditions and demands of the workers, who are largely forgotten. Margaret's actions in front of the mob are read by virtually everyone as a sign of her love for Thornton, leading him to propose to her. Margaret, however, insists that love or personal feelings had nothing to do with her decision to join him on the public stage: "It was only a natural instinct; any woman would have done just the same. . . . [A]ny woman, worthy of the name of woman, would come forward to shield, with her reverenced helplessness, a man in danger from the violence of numbers" (252–53). Margaret refuses this first proposal, and the second half of the novel is more about their "pride and prejudice" relationship than about the very real threats of violence and class revolution that are simmering beneath the surface in Milton.

From what we know of *The Deaf and the Dumb,* it appears that Davis abandoned Gaskell's rhetoric of unity and marriage plot. Although in *Margret Howth* Davis does bring Margret and Holmes together, to appease Fields and perhaps to fulfill readers' expectations, she constantly undermines their romance through commentaries by the novel's confrontational narrator, the alter ego of the engaging narrator found in such reform texts as *Mary Barton* and *Uncle Tom's Cabin.*[20] This narrator confronts and challenges readers, who may want to escape reality through fiction: "You want something . . . to lift you out of this crowded, tobacco-stained commonplace, to kindle and chafe and glow in you. I want you to dig into this commonplace, this vulgar American life, and see what is in it. Sometimes I think it has a new and awful significance that we do not see" (6). Davis critics cite these frequent narrative intrusions in their discussions of the novel's aesthetic failures, largely overlooking the important and subversive role they play in this text. While Gaskell seamlessly weaves together reform and romance in *North and South,* Davis intentionally allows her seams and gaps to show, as the confrontational narrator comments repeatedly on the difficulty—and perhaps the futility—of combining these two story lines. Chapter five, for example, opens with the narrator wondering whether a traditional romance narrative even belongs in this novel:

> Now that I have come to the love plot of my story, I am suddenly conscious of dingy common colors on the palette with which I have been painting. I wish I had some brilliant dyes. I wish, with all my heart, I could take you back to that "Once upon a time" in which the souls of our grandmothers delighted. . . . How can I help it, if the people in my story seem coarse to you,—if the hero, unlike all other heroes, stopped to count the cost before he fell in love. . . . Of course, if I could, I would have blotted out every meanness before I showed him to you; I would have told you Margret was an impetuous, whole-souled woman, . . . but what can I do? I must show you men and women as they are in that especial State of the Union where I live. (101–5)

Davis recognizes, and even sympathizes, with her readers' desires for romance, but she argues that they nonetheless need to be instructed in the reality of the industrial world, despite its dingy colors. She notes that if she were to write a fairy tale about dashing heroes and radiant heroines, her readers would surely recognize the dishonesty of her story and insist on the commonplace, asking her to "tell us about the butcher next door, my dear" (102). *Margret Howth* concludes with more metafictional commentary that destabilizes the seemingly happy union of Margret and Holmes: "My story is but a mere groping hint? It lacks determined truth, a certain yea or nay? I know: it is a story of To-Day" (264). This coda leaves the novel intentionally indeterminate. We are left without assurance that the social, economic, and political crises the novel describes will be resolved with Margret and Holmes's marriage, just the opposite of the effect of Margaret and Thornton's marriage plans in *North and South.* This ending is more optimistic and conciliatory than it was in *The Deaf and The Dumb,* but it is not the promised "perfect day in June."

Margret Howth is a perfect example of a text that truly benefits from a transatlantic reading. Davis has too often been dismissed as an anomaly, an oddity in American fiction, left to lurk in the shadows of the canon. *Margret Howth* has long suffered from a lack of critical context and, according to the sales department of the Feminist Press, their 1993 reprint of the novel has sold poorly, making it likely that the novel will again be out of print and inaccessible. But when read in the context of Gaskell and other British writers, Davis can be understood as participating in an evolving tradition of industrial reform literature and a critical dialogue about the effectiveness of benevolent work in nineteenth-century England and the United States. Davis's novel critiques both the traditional Lady Bountiful figure and the idealized middle-class woman reformer figure common in British industrial reform fiction. Ultimately, Davis forces her readers to confront and question simplified images of women's benevolent work.

Notes

1. The epigraph is taken from an 1862 entry from Alcott's diary and is published in *Louisa May Alcott: Her Life, Letters, and Journals* (131).

2. There are certainly examples of American fiction that address the social injustices brought about by the Industrial Revolution before Davis's "Life in the Iron-Mills," most notably Herman Melville's diptych "The Paradise of Bachelors and the Tartarus of Maids" and stories by factory workers themselves that appeared in such journals as the *Lowell Offering* and the *Voice of Industry.* But industrial fiction in the United States did not yet have the wide readership and significant cultural impact that it did in England. I agree with Cecilia Tichi's recent claim that Davis "established the genre of industrial fiction in the United States," a genre Tichi traces from Davis through the works of such naturalist writers as Frank Norris and Upton Sinclair (21).

3. After repeated urgings by Fields and his wife Annie to visit Boston and repeated delays caused by the Civil War and her father's ill health, Davis was finally able to travel North in June 1862. She was introduced to her literary idol Hawthorne (and even given a rare invitation to stay at his home), and to Emerson, Holmes, Bronson Alcott, and Louisa May Alcott (whom Davis very much admired; Alcott's impression of this meeting is quoted in the essay's epigraph). Davis's memories of this two-week stay in Boston and Concord are recorded in the chapter "Boston in the Sixties" from her memoirs *Bits of Gossip* (28–64).

4. Tillie Olsen first discovered Davis's "Life in the Iron-Mills" when, at age fifteen, she read "three water-stained, coverless volumes of bound *Atlantic Monthlys* bought for ten cents each in an Omaha junkshop" (Olsen 157). Olsen looked to the anonymous

author of "Life in the Iron-Mills" (whose name she did not learn until some years later) for inspiration, for a sign that "[l]iterature can be made out of the lives of despised people" (158). Olsen's interest in Davis led to the republication of "Life in the Iron-Mills" by the Feminist Press in 1972, which prompted the movement to recover and republish other forgotten nineteenth-century women writers. The Feminist Press edition and the more recent Bedford Cultural Series edition of "Life" (edited by Cecilia Tichi) have made this story a fixture in American literature anthologies and syllabi, and given Davis at least a marginal position in the literary canon. The recovery of the rest of Davis's extensive corpus—which includes twelve novels, 275 short stories and pieces of serialized fiction, 125 juvenile stories, and over 200 journalistic essays—has been slow (Rose, "A Bibliography" 67). The Feminist Press reprinted *Margret Howth* in 1990, the New College and University Press reprinted *Waiting for the Verdict* in 1995, and the University of Pittsburgh Press published a Davis anthology (*A Rebecca Harding Davis Reader*) with fifteen short stories and sixteen essays in 1995. In 2001, Vanderbilt Press released *Rebecca Harding Davis: Writing Cultural Biography*, edited by Janice Milner Lasseter and Sharon M. Harris, which contains Davis's autobiography *Bits of Gossip* plus a previously unpublished family history by Davis.

5. In *Doing Literary Business: American Women Writers in the Nineteenth Century*, Coultrap-McQuinn describes the uneasy relationship between nineteenth-century women writers and their "Gentleman-Publishers," male publishers like Fields who positioned themselves as literary guides, moral guardians, and father-figures to their female charges, the writing "ladies." Their paternalism sought to replicate and reinforce the notion of separate spheres by keeping women away from the business side of publishing, and, in many cases, underpaying them (38). Davis suffered financially from this relationship; while it was common for writers to receive at least 10% of the profits for their publications, Davis was paid just one-half of 1% of the profits of *Margret Howth* (Harris 82). The *Atlantic*'s poor compensation led Davis to publish her work in more popular journals, especially *Peterson's*, *Harper's*, *Youth's Companion*, and later, the *Saturday Evening Post*. In *Rebecca Harding Davis and American Realism*, Sharon M. Harris provides a more detailed history of Davis's relationship with Fields, which lasted for well over a decade.

6. In *Woman's Fiction: A Guide to Novels by and about Women in America, 1820–70*, Nina Baym introduced her theory of midcentury "woman's fiction": novels that "are written by women, are addressed to women and tell one particular story about women, . . . the 'trials and triumph' . . . of a heroine who, beset with hardships, finds within herself the qualities of intelligence, will, resourcefulness, and courage sufficient to overcome them" (22). Such sentimental midcentury bestsellers as Susan Warner's *The Wide, Wide World* (1850) and Maria Susanna Cummins's *The Lamplighter* (1854) fit this model of female triumph over adversity. Davis's rejection of sentimentality can be read as a backlash against this type of popular woman's fiction.

7. The industrial novel—alternately referred to as the reform novel, the social problem novel, the Condition-of-England novel, the humanitarian novel, the political novel, and the novel with a purpose—thrived in England from the 1830s to the 1860s, gaining particular popularity during the "Hungry Forties" and the rise of the Chartist move-

ment. Industrial novelists, most of whom were middle class, imagined peaceful solutions to the nation's class crisis and prompted middle-class readers to social action. Certainly earlier novels had addressed social issues and injustices, but, according to Constance Harsh, "for the first time fiction felt it could compete with non-fictional genres such as essays and sociological documentation; it claimed to have as much authority as they did in representation as well as the analysis of social reality" (6). The best recent studies of the industrial novel are Catherine Gallagher's *The Industrial Reformation of English Fiction,* Barbara Leah Harman's *The Feminine Political Novel,* and Harsh's *Subversive Heroines: Feminist Resolutions of Social Crisis in the Condition-of-England Novel.*

8. A few critics have mentioned Davis's possible links to British literature in general and the industrial novel tradition in particular, though none have pursued these connections further. For example, in his article "Success and Failure in Rebecca Harding Davis" (1963), James Austin asserts that "Miss Harding's strong, crusading spirit suggests the influence of Elizabeth Gaskell" (45). In his biography *The Richard Harding Davis Years: A Biography of Mother and Son* (1961), Gerald Langford observes that "Rebecca was influenced by the humanitarian fiction of English writers like Charles Kingsley and Charles Reade, and especially Gaskell's *Mary Barton*" (17). More recently, Jean Pfaelzer has noted common motifs in Brontë's Jane Eyre and Margret Howth, suggesting that nineteenth-century American women writers "did not write in intellectual isolation" from their British counterparts (59).

9. Most British industrial novels were reprinted—in authorized as well as "pirated" editions, since authors were not yet protected by international copyright laws—by American publishers and were advertised and reviewed in American periodicals. Harriet Beecher Stowe wrote an introduction for a three-volume American edition of *The Works of Charlotte Elizabeth* in 1845, which included two early industrial novels (*The Wrongs of Woman* and *Helen Fleetwood*) and went through multiple editions in the United States in the 1840s and 1850s. *Harper's* published an authorized edition of Elizabeth Gaskell's industrial novel *Mary Barton;* Gaskell's works were popular enough in the United States that the *Nation* published a moving obituary after her death in 1865, claiming that her "novels [are] in book-stalls all over the union" (qtd. in Easson 518). As is clear from the immense popularity of his reading tours in the United States, Dickens was a favorite of American readers as well.

10. Davis did publish a story in England later in 1862, the only British publication of her work during her lifetime. Fields sent Dickens a copy of Davis's "Blind Tom," a biting and timely indictment of slavery. The story is based on the real life of a slave boy who was mentally incapacitated but possessed amazing musical talent, an idiot savant. Tom was displayed by his master and forced to play concerts throughout the South, one of which Davis attended. Dickens responded, "I have read that affecting paper . . . with strong interest and emotion. You may readily suppose that I have been most glad and ready to avail myself of your permission to print it" (qtd. in Harris 97). The story was simultaneously published in the *Atlantic* in the United States and in *All the Year Round* in England. Clearly Davis was familiar with Dickens's journals, in which he published

many British industrial stories and serialized novels, including Gaskell's *North and South* in 1854–55.

11. Ever since Olsen's recovery of "Life in the Iron-Mills," critics have debated where to position Davis within the existing American literary canon. Most Davis critics have championed her as a significant figure in the transition from romanticism to realism in American fiction. Previously, critics held up William Dean Howells, Frank Norris, and other male writers of the 1880s and 1890s as the forerunners of the realist aesthetic, largely ignoring the contributions of women writers. In *Rebecca Harding Davis and American Realism,* Sharon M. Harris notes that "Davis had a well-developed theory of the 'commonplace' nearly two decades before Howells shaped his own version of the concept," and was undoubtedly an influence on Howells, who worked as an assistant editor for the *Atlantic Monthly* during Davis's association with the journal (9–10). Focusing on Davis as perhaps the first American realist helps to give her, and women writers in general, a higher profile in the canon. While Harris, Pfaelzer, and others do recognize Davis's generic hybridity (particularly the ways she blends elements of romanticism, sentimentalism, and regionalism with realism), they do not look beyond the borders of the United States for literary traditions to which Davis may have been contributing.

12. There have been major strides in the field of transatlanticism in recent years. The journal *Symbiosis: A Journal of Anglo-American Literary Relations,* created in the mid-1990s, is dedicated to the growing field of transatlanticism, and its editors proclaim that their mission is to address "the artificial divide between literatures in English on either side of the Atlantic, a divide recognized by few creative writers but enshrined in the modern academic community." More recently, Heidi Macpherson and Will Kaufman's collection *Transatlantic Studies* seeks to define this interdisciplinary field of inquiry. Further, the January 2003 issue of *PMLA* devoted to the special topic "America: The Idea, the Literature" includes several articles on transatlanticism and transnationalism (Julia Ortega's "Transatlantic Translations," Paul Giles's "Transnationalism and Classic American Literature," and John Carlos Rowe's "Nineteenth-Century United States Literary Culture and Transnationality"), a sign of the field's mainstream acceptance.

13. One of the clearest examples of a transatlantic abolitionist text is Harriet Beecher Stowe's *Uncle Tom's Cabin,* which was an unprecedented bestseller in England, selling an astounding 1.5 million copies and leading to the cultural phenomenon the *Spectator* dubbed "Tom-mania" (Fisch 13). Interestingly, both Gaskell and Davis have ties to Stowe, perhaps the best-known reform writer of the nineteenth century. Stowe and Gaskell met during the London stop of Stowe's first European tour. In an 1853 letter, Gaskell notes, "Oh! and I saw Mrs Stowe after all; I saw her twice; but only once to have a good long talk to her; then I was 4 or 5 hours with her, and liked her very much indeed" (*Letters of Mrs. Gaskell* 237). The two women writers corresponded until at least 1860, and at one point Stowe even proposed that they collaborate on a travel narrative about their trips to Italy (Stowe, "Letter"). Stowe, who, like Davis, worked closely with James T. Fields, sent Davis a supportive letter in 1869 after Henry James published a scathing re-

view of Davis's *Waiting for the Verdict* in the *Nation*. Works by Stowe, Elizabeth Stuart Phelps, and other women writers had been similarly attacked in the *Nation*, and Stowe exposed this fact in Boston press, calling James "brutal" and "unmannerly" (Pfaelzer 156). In her letter to Davis, Stowe noted that the *Nation* had "no sympathy with any deep & high moral movement" (qtd. in Hedrick 345).

14. Before he became Prime Minister in 1868, Benjamin Disraeli published a trilogy of industrial reform novels: *Coningsby* (1844), *Sybil, or The Two Nations* (1845), and *Tancred* (1847). In the 1840s, Disraeli was part of the Young England movement, a loosely organized group of young conservatives in Parliament who split from Sir Robert Peel and the traditional Tory party. The Young Englanders held a romantic view of the Middle Ages and envisioned the creation of a neo-feudal hierarchy, in which paternal noblemen would take care of industrial "peasants," as the antidote to the dehumanizing system of industrial capitalism. Middle-class industrialists are figured as the true enemy, and the Young Englanders sought to strip them of their growing political, social, and economic power. See chapter three of Edgar Feuchtwanger's *Disraeli* for a more complete history of the movement.

15. As Jill Bergman and Debra Bernardi note in the introduction to this volume, American benevolent societies and workers often distinguished between the "worthy" and "unworthy" poor, a practice shared by their British counterparts (3). Worthiness was based on many factors, including the individual's "perceived morality," with sympathy and charity denied to those viewed as immoral or responsible for their own poverty (3).

16. When Margaret Hale learns of Thornton's business failures, she arranges with an attorney to lend him the money to reopen the mill. Significantly, Margaret demonstrates her business savvy by ensuring that "the principal advantage would be on her side" in this arrangement (529). With the loan, Margaret rescues Thornton, recreating her role as rescuer and savior at the workers riot, and allows him to continue his "experiments" with the workers at Marlborough Mills. Pamela Corpron Parker correctly points out that according to Victorian laws "Margaret's marriage vows will transfer all legal control of her property and capital to Thornton" (330). But the legal contract protects Margaret's interests (at least the £18,057 she lends him) and serves as a sort of "prenuptial agreement" (330).

17. Knowles sees it as his right to intrude on the lives of the poor and gaze upon them, almost as if they are animals in a zoo rather than human beings with basic rights. In "'The Right to Be Let Alone': Mary Wilkins Freeman and the Right to a 'Private Share,'" Debra Bernardi notes that "for poor people in want of the aid of charity organization societies, there was no fundamental right to domestic privacy" (137). Knowles seeks to erode this privacy further by having the poor move into his communist fraternity, where they will undoubtedly be under constant surveillance, scrutiny, and control.

18. Davis also introduces race with the character of Dr. Knowles, who is a quarter Creek Indian. We are told that he has the "blood of a despised race" and carries in his veins "their pain and hunger" (50).

19. While I see Margaret as assuming a masculine role, thus blurring the lines be-

tween feminine and masculine, I do not agree with Felicia Bonaparte's rather far-fetched argument that this scene renders Margaret "a man" (192). Bonaparte goes on to claim that the business partnership at the end of the novel is the only way that Margaret can "maintain her identity as an independent, male, woman" (193). Like Harman, I believe that "[t]o assign male status to Margaret is to diminish rather than to highlight the transgressive quality of her activity" (195).

20. In her study *Gendered Interventions: Narrative Discourse in the Victorian Novel,* Robyn Warhol discusses the rhetorical value of the "engaging narrator" prevalent in many nineteenth-century novels, especially reform novels. For instance, in *Uncle Tom's Cabin,* Stowe employs a narrator who directly addresses the audience, pulling at their heartstrings and revealing the common humanity of whites and enslaved blacks. The last chapter of the novel contains her most passionate entreaty, directed specifically at mothers:

> And you, mothers of America—you who have learned, by the cradles of your own children, to love and feel for all mankind . . . —I beseech you, pity the mother who has all your affections, and not one legal right to protect, guide, or educate the child of her bosom! By the sick hour of your child; by those dying eyes, which you can never forget; by those last cries, that wrung your heart when you could neither help nor salve; by the desolation of that empty cradle, that silent nursery,—I beseech you, pity those mothers that are constantly made childless by the American slave-trade! And say, mothers of America, is this a thing to be defended, sympathized with, passed over in silence? (384)

Works Cited

Alcott, Louisa May. *Louisa May Alcott: Her Life, Letters, and Journals.* Ed. Ednah D. Cheney. Boston: Little, Brown, 1898.

Anderson, Benedict. *Imagined Communities: Reflections on the Origin and Spread of Nationalism.* London: Verso, 1991.

Austin, James C. "Success and Failure of Rebecca Harding Davis." *Midcontinent American Studies Journal* 3 (1962): 44–49.

Baym, Nina. *Woman's Fiction: A Guide to Novels by and about Women in America, 1820–70.* 2nd ed. Urbana: U of Illinois P, 1993.

Bodenheimer, Rosemarie. *The Politics of Story in Victorian Social Fiction.* Ithaca: Cornell UP, 1988.

Bonaparte, Felicia. *The Gypsy-Bachelor of Manchester: The Life of Mrs. Gaskell's Demon.* Charlottesville: U of Virginia P, 1992.

Coultrap-McQuinn, Susan. *Doing Literary Business: American Women Writers in the Nineteenth Century.* Chapel Hill: U of North Carolina P, 1990.

Davis, Rebecca Harding. *Bits of Gossip.* Boston: Houghton, Mifflin, 1904.

———. "Life in the Iron-Mills." 1861. New York: Feminist Press, 1982.

———. *Margret Howth: A Story of To-Day.* 1861–62. New York: Feminist Press, 1990.

Dickens, Charles. *Bleak House.* 1853. New York: Bantam, 1985.

Easson, Angus, ed. *Elizabeth Gaskell: The Critical Heritage.* London: Routledge, 1991.

Feuchtwanger, Edgar. *Disraeli.* New York: Oxford UP, 2000.

Fisch, Audrey. *American Slaves in Victorian England: Abolitionist Politics in American Popular Literature and Culture.* Cambridge: Cambridge UP, 2000.

Gallagher, Catherine. *The Industrial Reformation of English Fiction: Social Discourse and Narrative Form, 1832–1867.* Chicago: U of Chicago P, 1985.

Gaskell, Elizabeth. *Mary Barton: A Tale of Manchester Life.* 1848. New York: Penguin, 1970.

———. *North and South.* 1854–55. London: Penguin, 1986.

Ginzberg, Lori D. *Women and the Work of Benevolence: Morality, Politics, and Class in the Nineteenth-Century United States.* New Haven: Yale UP, 1990.

Gravil, Richard. *Romantic Dialogues: Anglo-American Continuities, 1776–1862.* New York: St. Martin's, 2000.

Grosz, Elizabeth A. *Volatile Bodies: Toward a Corporeal Feminism.* Bloomington: Indiana UP, 1994.

Hadley, Elaine. *Melodramatic Tactics: Theatricalized Dissent in England's Marketplace, 1800–1885.* Stanford: Stanford UP, 1995.

Harman, Barbara Leah. *The Feminine Political Novel in Victorian England.* Charlottesville: U of Virginia P, 1998.

Harris, Sharon M. *Rebecca Harding Davis and American Realism.* Philadelphia: U of Pennsylvania P, 1991.

Harsh, Constance D. *Subversive Heroines: Feminist Resolutions of Social Crisis in the Condition-of-England Novel.* Ann Arbor: U of Michigan P, 1994.

Hawthorne, Nathaniel. *The Blithedale Romance.* 1852. New York: Penguin, 1986.

Hedrick, Joan D. *Harriet Beecher Stowe: A Life.* New York: Oxford UP, 1994.

Kaufman, Will, and Heidi Macpherson. *Transatlantic Studies.* Lanham: UP of America, 2000.

Kestner, Joseph. *Protest and Reform: The British Social Narrative by Women, 1827–1862.* Madison: U of Wisconsin P, 1985.

Langford, Gerald. *The Richard Harding Davis Years: A Biography of Mother and Son.* New York: Holt, Rinehart, and Winston, 1961.

Lasseter, Janice Milner, and Sharon M. Harris, eds. *Rebecca Harding Davis: Writing Cultural Autobiography.* Nashville: Vanderbilt UP, 2001.

Long, Lisa A. "Imprisoned in/at Home: Criminal Culture in Rebecca Harding Davis' *Margret Howth: A Story of To-day.*" *Arizona Quarterly* 54.2 (1998): 65–98.

Olsen, Tillie. "Biographical Interpretation." *Life in the Iron Mills and Other Stories.* New York: Feminist Press, 1972. 69–174.

Parker, Pamela Corpron. "Fictional Philanthropy in Elizabeth Gaskell's *Mary Barton* and *North and South.*" *Victorian Literature and Culture* 25 (1997): 321–31.

Pfaelzer, Jean. *Parlor Radical: Rebecca Harding Davis and the Origins of American Social Realism.* Pittsburgh: U of Pittsburgh P, 1996.

Poovey, Mary. *Uneven Developments: The Ideological Work of Gender in Mid-Victorian England.* Chicago: U of Chicago P, 1988.

Rose, Jane Atteridge. "A Bibliography of Fiction and Non-Fiction by Rebecca Harding Davis." *American Literary Realism* 22 (1990): 67–86.

———. *Rebecca Harding Davis.* New York: Twayne, 1993.

Sizer, Lyde Cullen. *The Political Work of Northern Women Writers and the Civil War, 1850–1872.* Chapel Hill: U of North Carolina P, 2000.

Stowe, Harriet Beecher. Introduction. *The Works of Charlotte Elizabeth.* 2nd ed. New York: M. W. Todd, 1845.

———. Letter to Elizabeth Gaskell. July 10, 1860. Hartford: The Harriet Beecher Stowe Center and Library.

———. *Uncle Tom's Cabin.* 1851–52. New York: Norton, 1994.

Thomas, Helen. *Romanticism and Slave Narratives: Transatlantic Testimonies.* Cambridge: Cambridge UP, 2000.

Thomson, Rosemarie Garland. "Benevolent Maternalism and Physically Disabled Figures: Dilemmas and Female Embodiment in Stowe, Davis, and Phelps." *American Literature* 68 (1996): 555–86.

Tichi, Cecelia, ed. *Life in the Iron-Mills.* Boston: Bedford Cultural Editions, 1998.

Warhol, Robyn. *Gendered Interventions: Narrative Discourse in the Victorian Novel.* New Brunswick: Rutgers UP, 1989.

Yellin, Jean Fagan. Afterword. *Margret Howth: A Story of To-Day.* New York: Feminist Press, 1990. 271–302.

Yeazell, Ruth Bernard. "Why Political Novels Have Heroines: *Sybil, Mary Barton,* and *Felix Holt.*" *Novel* 18.2 (1985): 126–44.

PART II
Negotiating the Female American Self through Benevolence

5

"The Right to Be Let Alone"

Mary Wilkins Freeman and the Right to a "Private Share"

Debra Bernardi

"Nobody knew how frugal Betsey Dole's suppers and breakfasts were. . . . She scarcely ate more than her canary bird. . . . Her income was almost infinitesimal" (191). This description of the main character in Mary Wilkins Freeman's story "A Poetess" (1891) is only one of many in Freeman's work that highlight her interest in the poor at the end of the nineteenth century. Freeman herself had experienced economic reversals as a young woman, and as Mary Reichardt has pointed out, "the poor house was never far from [her] imagination" (Introduction ix).

Early responses to Freeman's stories of poor women commend the writer for her "accurate portrayal of New England life, especially in its physical and spiritual decline" (Reichardt, "Mary Wilkins Freeman" 77). Later critics have focused on the gendered aspects of Freeman's work. For example, in her well-known study of "local color writers," Josephine Donovan understands Freeman's stories of unmarried, impoverished women to be about the decay of a "woman-centered matriarchal world" (119). In her literary biography, Leah Blatt Glasser argues that Freeman asserts a radical critique of the domestic lives of these women (215). Glasser writes, "At best Freeman's fiction explores and indirectly bemoans the experiences of those [Charlotte Perkins] Gilman described as 'house slaves' in *Women and Economics*" (217). While such contemporary critics understand women's struggles in Freeman's narratives in various ways,[1] most apprehend her as a writer who chronicled the harsh difficulties of women's private lives in New England.

This is not to belittle such private concerns or to suggest that they are in any way "narrow." As Judith Fetterley and Marjorie Pryse have shown in their study of regionalism, writers such as Mary Wilkins Freeman, while focusing on the insignificant, the marginalized, the "tiny" (167; 259), challenge assumptions of dominant discourses, including assumptions about masculinity and femininity and "the projects of nation and empire" (222). Sandra Zagarell also has argued that Freeman's work challenges cultural assumptions about rural life in the nation. I, too, situate Freeman's local concerns within national discourses. Specifically, I read her work as addressing the pressing public issues of poverty and poverty relief at the turn of the century. In this way, Freeman's work moves beyond its undeniable interest in women's personal lives and enters into national debates as to how a growing industrial society should help the poor. I hope such readings will continue to widen our understandings of the significance of Freeman's work. Maybe they would have even helped Sylvia Townsend Warner, who wanted to be more outspoken about Freeman's importance. In a 1966 essay originally published in *The New Yorker,* Warner writes, "If I had had the courage of my convictions downstairs, when everyone was talking about Joyce and Pound and melting pots, I would have said, 'Why don't you think more of Mary Wilkins?'" (120).

Freeman wrote much of her work during the last few decades of the nineteenth century, when poverty was becoming an increasingly visible problem in the United States. The depression of 1873 was the worst in American history. Class segregation became more apparent as factories and businesses grew larger in Northern cities and capitalist agriculture spread in the South. And the new workforce was subject to irregular, seasonal, and often badly paid work. As Michael Katz has noted, the word "tramp" is a good example of the disturbing evidence of poverty; the term entered into widespread use in the 1870s as a label with which to denigrate the soaring numbers of young men roaming the nation in search of jobs (95).

As has been noted elsewhere in this volume, in the face of such obvious economic need, civic leaders turned to the principles of scientific charity to help the poor. Central to the concept of charity organization societies was the need to study the poor within their own homes in order to extend aid. By entering the households of the poor, society agents, it was hoped, would rid the streets of beggars and eliminate indiscriminate aid to people who didn't really need it. For their part, the poor were obliged to welcome agents into their homes if they wanted to eat or keep warm (Katz 70). For poor people in want of the aid of charity organization societies, there was no fundamental right to domestic privacy.

It is within the theories of scientific charity that I situate much of the work of Mary Wilkins Freeman. Freeman needs to be understood as a writer involved with a central political question of the late nineteenth and early twentieth centuries: what rights of privacy does the poor individual have if she or he requires aid? In her major story collections, *A Humble Romance and Other Stories* (1887), *A New England Nun* (1901), and *The Best Stories of Mary E. Wilkins* (1927), and her novel *Pembroke* (1894), frequently considered her finest book-length work, Freeman asserts a fundamental right for her characters: the right for everyone—even those who need charity—to have a private space in which to live the way they choose. But, significantly, Freeman does not call for the right to private property; rather, Freeman's stories acknowledge that in the face of growing poverty, private ownership actually contradicts the right of every individual to her or his "private share." For her, the right to privacy can only be realized if all individuals share what they own.

Many of Freeman's stories of poverty were published contemporaneously with the theories of charity organization societies, which argued against simply giving the poor financial assistance. Josephine Shaw Lowell was one such major theorist of poverty relief, writing *Public Relief and Private Charity* in 1884. Reminiscent of the ideas of American romantic writers, here she asserts the threats of public relief to individual integrity: "people very soon after commencing to receive public aid lose their energy and self-respect" (55). Further, for Lowell there is also the danger that public charity will give the "idle, improvident, and even vicious man . . . the right to live in idleness and vice upon the proceeds of the labor of his industrious and virtuous fellow-citizen" (67).

Rather than this sort of public aid for the poor who want to remain in their own homes (Lowell supported institutionalizing those who couldn't stay at home), Lowell advocates a "Friendly Society," which would regain the intimacy of small-town benevolence. In small towns, people could just "step into the house of a poor friend and give him the help he requires" (97). Lowell writes,

> The only way [to help the poor] is to regain by some means the advantage that the small community had without effort. The same intimate knowledge of those who have to be helped must be got in some way.
>
> A small association of men and women should be formed and a special territory assigned to each so that he may become thoroughly acquainted with all who live within its limits. (98)

By employing this small-town model, a Friendly Society would improve the morals and lifestyles of those they visit; they would, in Lowell's words "raise the standard of decency, cleanliness, providence, and morality" among the poor through "personal influence" (111). That is, the member of the Friendly Society must keep a "constant continued intercourse" among the poor—to show their "high standard" of living to "those who have it not" (111). This would be a relief system that insures moral guidance, discipline, and education for the poor—"a distinct moral and physical improvement on the part of all those who are forced to have recourse to it" (67).

Central to this "improvement" was instruction in creating a proper middle-class home—one that was carefully managed and cleaned. Humphreys Gurteen, in his *Handbook of Charity Organizations*, 1882, asserted his concerns for the private homes of the poor. "It is a fact, a terrible fact," he writes, "that among the poor, in our large cities especially, the idea of 'home' is all but unknown. . . . The effect of pauperism, wherever it exists, is to disintegrate the family, to destroy the home, to sever the social tie, to demoralize the parents, and to send the children forth ignorant of the full meaning of the sacred name of home, ignorant of its sweet memories" (37–38).

In order to help this domestic education, Gurteen, like Lowell, recommended that relief workers become friends to those in need. He writes, "Success in dealing with pauperism can be had through the personal intercourse of the wealthier citizens with the poor at their homes, in other words, the bringing together the extremes of society in a spirit of honest friendship" (113). Gurteen stresses that these "Friendly Visitors" must enter the homes of the poor. "Each cluster of families is committed to the care of an intelligent visitor, who spends a part of his or her leisure time in going in and out among them as a friend. . . . Once let the visitor become the acknowledged friend of a poor family (not the doler out of charity), she would be a power in the home. In a very short time the house would be clean and kept clean for her reception. Her advice would be sought voluntarily on matters of household economy. . . . All avoidable pauperism would soon be a thing of the past" (113; 117). Gurteen approvingly quotes Octavia Hill, an English philanthropic worker, who gave these suggestions to American charity volunteers: "You want to know them—to enter into their lives, their thoughts; to let them enter into some of your brightness, so as to make their lives a littler fuller, a little gladder" (114). The poor were to be permanently uplifted, then, by personal relationships with relief workers who came into their private lives.

Mary Richmond's 1899 handbook for charity workers details how Friendly Visitors should effect change in all matters of private behavior. On one level, she urges that benevolence workers should take some things slowly. For example, "In urging changes in diet upon poor families, it is first necessary to become well acquainted with the families and, even then, to introduce any innovations slowly, one thing at a time" (67). Regarding taste, Richmond writes, "We may find a preference for cheap finery very exasperating, but our own example is far more likely to be followed in the long run if we do not insist on it too much at first" (68). As for addressing the notorious problem of cleanliness, Richmond recommends visitors use "great tact" (69).

Richmond's manual shows the tension between the desire to help the poor, to enter into their homes and literally change their lives, and a regard for their privacy. She cautions against "meddlesomeness" (181), but then details all the aspects of life into which Friendly Visitors should inquire. She writes that if there is a baby in the house, visitors should observe "whether the child is nursed too many months and too often" (78). Visitors should talk to doctors, employers, friends, pastors, former employers; they should investigate the poor's social history (e.g., birthplaces; marriage information; names, addresses, and condition of relatives and friends), medical history, and work history; they should also know the "hopes and plans" of the family (186–88). Richmond explains that the "seemingly inquisitorial features are justified by the fact that it is not made with any purpose of finding people out, but with the sole purpose of finding out how to help them" (189).

Richmond further recommends that visitors take action when the poor are not behaving in appropriate ways. For example, she writes approvingly of a Baltimore visitor who "cured one tired woman of scolding her husband in season and out of season by diverting her attention to other things and by seeking her cooperation in plans for improving the man's habits" (72). Even more aggressively, Richmond suggests that if the husband of a household does not support his family (or moves out), the visitor should have him punished by the courts (52).

Cautioning against "meddlesomeness" while promoting active disruptions of homes, Richmond's work reveals the problems with Friendly Visiting. While visitors were told to get close to the poor, to become their friends, this closeness came at a price: the price of privacy. Linda Gordon notes how child protective workers in the late nineteenth century visited homes of the poor late at night or early in the morning. If they were unable to gain entry, they actually climbed in windows (48).

Such strategies of philanthropic aid became increasingly problematic as the century drew closer to its end and American culture engaged in debates over rights of privacy. As Robert E. Mensel has noted in his essay on photography and privacy rights, up until the last decades of the nineteenth century, the protection of privacy had been a social propriety, a matter of etiquette, rather than law. In an 1890 essay in *Scribner's Magazine,* E. L. Godkin, editor of the *Nation,* writes that privacy was still not yet fully a matter of legal protection: "There still lingers in the minds of the public, even in this country and in England, where the duel has died out, the notion that, though one ought to rely exclusively on the police and the courts for the protection of one's goods and chattels, yet there is certain peculiar fitness in protecting reputation or privacy against libel or intrusion by the cudgel or the horsewhip" (61).

The legal system, however, was beginning to get involved. The earliest case in the United States to claim a "right to privacy," was the case of *DeMay v. Roberts,* heard by the Michigan Supreme Court in 1881. In it, the court found in favor of Alvira Roberts, a poor white woman living in rural Michigan: Roberts sued a doctor who had brought a friend along to watch while she was giving birth (Danielson 1). The court found that the "plaintiff had a legal right to the privacy of her apartment at such a time" (*DeMay v. Roberts* qtd. in Danielson 1). *DeMay* serves as evidence that "the legal maxim and popular proverb that 'a man's house is his castle' had wide application in the nineteenth century" ("Right to Privacy in Nineteenth-Century America" 1894). Other cases addressed sanctions against eavesdroppers and "peeping Toms." As stated in a contemporary *Harvard Law Review* note, "By the late nineteenth-century, the law had erected high walls around the family home by extending criminal penalties for and civil remedies against intrusion by strangers" ("Right to Privacy in Nineteenth-Century America" 1896).

Several prominent court cases in the early 1890s expanded the discussion of privacy beyond the home to other areas of personal rights. A number of cases addressed an individual's right to keep her physical image from being reproduced in media such as photographs and statues. For example, in *Schuyler v. Custis* (1891), the family of deceased philanthropist Mrs. Hamilton Schuyler sought to prevent a statue of their relative from being exhibited. The plaintiffs asserted that exhibition of the statue was an invasion of privacy. The Judge granted the injunction on the grounds that Schuyler was a private character and had a right to privacy that was entitled to protection ("Right," *Green Bag* 1894, 498). Similarly, in the case of *Marion Manola v. Stevens and Myers* (1890), given extensive coverage in the *New York Times*, the complainant alleged that while she was playing in a Broadway theater she was photographed without consent and therefore sought an injunction against use of the photo. The judge issued a preliminary injunction (Warren and Brandeis 195). Further, letters began to be understood as private documents, which retained certain rights for the sender. Public opinion began to regard the "'sanctity of the mails' in the same way it esteemed the inviolability of the home" ("Right to Privacy in Nineteenth-Century America 1899).

While the courts were beginning to act on an expanded right of privacy, most historians assert that the modern concept of a legal right to privacy first came into popular thought with an 1890 article by Samuel Warren and Louis Brandeis, which claims that privacy rights have moved beyond material issues. While they note that the "common law has always recognized a man's house as his castle, impregnable" (220), they argue that these rights should be extended into intangible realms such as "the right to enjoy life;—the right to be let alone" (193). Legal protection of property for them includes "every form of possession—intangible as well as tangible" (193), including the "right to an inviolate personality" (211). They continue: "The design of the law must be . . . to protect all persons, whatsoever; their position or station, from having matters they may properly prefer to keep private, made public against their will" (214–15). Spurring their concerns were the threats to privacy brought about through "recent inventions and business methods" (Warren and Brandeis 195): these included sensational journalism and, as Mensel has detailed, the easy-to-use Kodak cameras.[2]

The Warren and Brandeis article and the court cases surrounding it inspired a series of debates in the popular press, which rehearsed before the American public the expanding privileges of Americans in this arena. For example, in 1891, the journal the *Green Bag* reprints the judicial opinion of the *Schuyler* case and parts of the Warren and Brandeis article. Again in 1894 the *Green Bag* notes that rights to privacy were being extended "beyond the body of the individual to his reputation. Thoughts, emotions, and sensations have acquired legal recognition in certain respects" ("The Right to Privacy" 498). The *Atlantic Monthly* questions this expansion of rights, bringing up issues of freedom of the press, asking if the press should not have the right "to describe the peculiarities, depravities, and deformities of [an individual] and of his household" ("The Right to Be Let Alone" 429). An 1896 article in the *North American Review* affirms the newly established rights: "I believe that the definite establishment of this right of privacy is at this time of the greatest possible moment; for, without such a right and easy enforcement of it, civilization must deteriorate" (Speed 64). The essay quotes Judge Cooley, who asserted, like Warren and Brandeis, that the right of privacy is the "right to be let alone" (64). The *North American Review* continues, "As man comes into the world alone, goes out of it alone, and is alone accountable for his life, so may he be presumed to have by the law of his nature full right to live alone when, to what extent, and as long as he pleases. . . . The modesty of good and common nature sets between him and the modern inquisition the protecting shield of that knightly order whose motto has been aptly termed the eleventh commandment—'Mind your own business'" (65).[3]

With Friendly Visitors inserting themselves into the lives of the poor, these expanding rights to privacy could not help but affect perceptions of charity relief. By 1896, even Josephine Shaw Lowell came to understand that relief work infringed on personal lives. She argues that there is no "excuse for trespassing upon the privacy of other human beings, for trying to learn facts in their lives which they prefer should not be known" (qtd. in Bremner 82). In his early-twentieth-century novel, *Crimes of Charity* (1917), Konrad Bercovici tells the tale of a relief worker horrified by his inability to help the poor within the structure of a charity organization. Among the many troubling aspects of charity that the narrator details is the violation of privacy. The narrator states, "One of the greatest injustices to the poor is the right that the charities arrogate to themselves to visit them whenever they choose. Once you depend upon charity all privacy is gone. The sanctity of the home is destroyed. It is as though the family were living in some one else's—in the charity's—home. The investigator comes into the house unannounced any time of the day or night, questions anybody she finds in the house, criticises the meals, the curtains" (101). In his introduction to Berkovici's book, John Reed echoes a similar sentiment: "[Charity] is made the excuse for lowering the recipients' standard of living, of depriving them of privacy and independence" (n.p.).

Similarly, while the motivations behind the photography of Jacob Riis may have been charitable, the poor also understood his efforts as intrusions into their private lives. A supporter of Josephine Shaw Lowell, Riis went to Boston to "see the humane way in which [she] was dealing with their homeless there" (252). He took his well-known photographs of the urban poor for his exposé *How the Other Half Lives* in 1890, just as the court cases about an individual's control over his or her image were garnering public interest. When Riis photographed his subjects, with the intent to expose the horrors of poverty and generate social action on behalf of the indigent, he rarely asked permission to enter the homes he was photographing. He notes in his 1901 memoir *The Making of an American,* "Our party carried terror wherever it went. The spectacle of strange men invading a house in the midnight hours armed with [flash] pistols which they shot off recklessly was hardly reassuring, however sugary our speech, and it was not to be wondered at if the tenants bolted through windows and down fire-escapes wherever we went. . . . Months after I found our visits hanging over a Stanton Street block like a nightmare" (268–69). At times the intended subjects of the photos pelted Riis and his associates with rocks. In an analysis of one of the Riis' photos, "A Black and Tan Dive on Broome Street," historian David Shi has noted how one of the women in the photo turns her back to the camera and drapes a shawl over her head in order to protect her privacy (192). Inherent, then, in Riis's philanthropic work was an invasive action that engendered resistance in those it was attempting to aid.

A *Harper's* story by George Madden Martin at the turn of the century, titled, significantly, "Rights of Man," takes up the issue of charitable invasions of privacy and efforts of the poor to resist these invasions. In Martin's story, Old Jim avoids the middle-class female charity worker who is "upliftin' us by idols [ideals]" (415). Miss Sidney brings in a woman to clean Jim's cabin, along with pictures for his walls and flowers for his table, violating both his space and his taste—his basic "right to be let alone." Jim complains, "Now she keeps comin' over all times I ain't lookin' for her, to see if I'm keepin' things straight. An' I ask you if that sort of uneasiness ain't upsettin' to any man?" (416). Disturbed by Miss Sidney's attempts to change him, Jim prefers the handouts of Mrs. Carter because "she don't have no strings tied to what she gives" (420). Finally, Miss Sidney goes too far when she tries to force Jim to take a bath. He escapes the disruption of his life in the isolated comfort of a root cellar, asserting that "Ev'ey man's jestified to his quiet place" (421).

Within these discussions of charity and privacy, Freeman's stories become more than tales about individual women in New England. Even two of her best-known stories take on particular political significance when read as part of the debates surrounding privacy. For example, when Mrs. Penn demands her own house in "The Revolt of 'Mother'" (1891), eventually commandeering her husband's barn, the act can be apprehended as a woman's right to her "own castle, impregnable" (to reiterate Warren and Brandeis's words). In "A New England Nun" (1891), Louisa is so reluctant to share her fastidious home with her long-time suitor that she eventually refuses to marry, again underscoring a woman's right to a space of her own.

While these two stories do not specifically address the poor, the same interest in privacy pervades Freeman's stories about the impoverished. However, Freeman is not just interested in the privacy of material space.

She also reveals the needs for the more intangible rights of private life that Warren and Brandeis talked about—for example, in their words, the rights of all people "whatsoever; their position or station, from having matters which they may properly prefer to keep private, made public against their will" (214–15). Freeman's tales specifically address an individual's need to keep her financial situation from public comment. In the 1894 novel *Pembroke,* Sylvia Crane makes every effort to keep her poverty a secret. When she must ask for help from the town selectmen, "she stole around to the back door of Squire Payne's house by night, she conducted herself as if it were a guilty intrigue, all to keep her poverty hid as long as may be" (207). Similarly in "A Gala Dress" (1891), the elderly Babcock sisters go to extraordinary lengths to hide their penury: They "guarded nothing more jealously than the privacy of their meals. . . . It was certain that the old women regarded intrusion at their meals as an insult, but it was doubtful if they would not have done so had their table been set out with all the luxuries of the season instead of scanty bread and butter and no sauce" (148–49). The entire story revolves around the efforts the two women make to avoid letting others in town know they only have one good dress between them.

Melissa McFarland Pennell argues that Freeman's stories about the poor show the shame of poverty that is derived from a Calvinist tradition, which considers indigence as divine judgment ("Liberating Will" 207–8). But Freeman's stories are not just about the cultural shame of poverty; they are also about the legal rights of the poor. While her stories argue for the right of each man *and* woman to have her or his own "quiet place"—going beyond Old Jim's assertion of man's rights in the *Harper's* story—she also asserts an inextricable connection between the private space of the home and the "intangible" rights of privacy—including, in Warren and Brandeis's words, "the right to enjoy life;—the right to be let alone." And while her stories represent the invasive problems of charity relief, they also picture the possibility that the poor might demand their rights and resist such invasions.

Freeman's 1903 story "The Last Gift" (originally appearing in the same issue of *Harper's* as Martin's "Rights of Man") traces the problems with benevolence from the perspective of the charity giver. It tells the story of the minister Robinson Carnes, whose "unselfish love for his kind . . . laudable in itself, had become in time like a flower run wild until it was a weed. His love of giving amounted to a pure and innocent but unruly passion. It had at one time assumed such proportions that it barely escaped being recognized as actual mania. As it was, people, even those who had benefited by his reckless generosity, spoke of him as a mild idiot" (103). His congregation, uncomfortable with his outlandish generosity, eventually asks him to leave their church.

However, while Carnes's obsessions create problems for himself, Freeman is actually tracing the distinction between his honest (if obsessive) generosity and the charity of typical relief workers. Carnes is contrasted with another minister who says "that one's first duty was to oneself, and unjustified giving was pauperizing to the giver and the recipient" (106). Echoing the concerns of Josephine Shaw Lowell, who feared aid could be detrimental to the poor, this other minister is cold and unkind to those who need assistance.

When he meets a destitute family on the road, Carnes knows that he, himself, has nothing to share with the family (he's given away everything he owns). As he considers how to best extend aid, Carnes considers the typical methods of philanthropy: "It became evident to him in a flash what the outside view of the situation would be: that the only course for a man of ordinary sense and reason was to . . . notify the authorities . . . that it was his duty for the sake of the helpless children [in the poor family] to have them cared for by force, if there was no other way" (112). But he realizes immediately the problems that would arise if he were to extend this kind of benevolence: "It seemed an infringement upon all the poor souls had left in the world—their individual freedom" (113). Eventually Carnes finds some money and aids the family financially while leaving their privacy intact.

In "Cinnamon Roses" (1887), Freeman looks at tangible privacy rights from the perspective of the indigent. Elsie's brother and sister-in-law take her in when poverty forces her to leave her home. The result is the discomfort of losing her own space, even though her brother "gave her a front chamber in his large, square white house, and furnished it with her own things to make it seem like home" (171). He can't imagine why she "shouldn't be as happy as a queen" (171). But Elsie sits "forlornly at her chamber window, her elbows on the sill, her sharp chin in her hands, for many an hour" staring at her old house (172). The narrator continues, "It is sad work looking at things that were once one's own, when they have not been given away for love, and one still wants them" (172).

In her story "A Mistaken Charity" (1887), Freeman continues her commentary on the needs of the poor for their "castle, impregnable," but goes further, showing how the poor can resist efforts to deprive them of their rights, both the tangible rights of the private home and the more intangible rights of taste, personality, and private happiness. The story opens with two old, poor sisters living on the edges of material ruin. Their home is so rickety that "rain and snow had filtered through its roof, mosses had grown over it, worms had eaten it, and birds built their nests under its eaves" (43). Harriet and Charlotte rely on the kindness of neighbors for survival. The story reveals that such generosity—like that of Miss Sidney in George Martin's story "Rights of Man"—often ignores the personality and tastes of the recipients: the sisters' neighbor Mrs. Simonds "was a smart, energetic person, bent on doing good, and she did a great deal. To be sure, she always did it in her own way. If she chose to give hot doughnuts, she gave hot doughnuts; it made not the slightest difference to her if the recipients of her charity would infinitely have preferred ginger cookies" (49). As such, Mrs. Simonds's efforts affect the intangible privacy rights—"the right to enjoy life"—that Warren and Brandeis articulate.

Eventually Mrs. Simonds's charitable efforts impinge on the tangible space of the home. She arranges for the sisters to live in the "Old Ladies' Home" in a neighboring city. Freeman emphasizes the fact that this home is "not an almshouse under another name . . . it was comfortable, and in some respects luxurious. . . . The fare was of a finer, more delicate variety than [the sisters] had been accustomed to" (50–51). However, the widow who runs the home encourages a particular style of dress—white lace caps and delicate neckerchiefs—further invading the corporeal lives of the sisters, as well as their rights to their own tastes, their own "inviolable personalit[ies]." The sisters are miserable. "O Lord, Harriet," Charlotte exclaims, "let us go home. I can't stay here no ways in this world. I don't like their vittles, an' I don't like to wear a cap; I want to go home and do different" (52).

Similar to Riis's photographic subjects, the sisters resist these charitable efforts. They decide to leave the Old Ladies' Home: "And they went. With a grim humor Harriet hung the new white lace caps with which she and Charlotte had been so pestered, one on each post at the head of the bedstead, so they would meet the eyes of the first person who opened the door" (53). Their act is a bold move to regain "their private share of the great wealth of nature" (45). Once again in their own rickety home they are happy, finally allowed their own home, their own tastes, their own personality, their "right to be let alone."[4]

While frequently understood as a challenge to ideas of gendered separate spheres (Glasser 49; Fetterley and Pryse 14), Freeman's tale "A Church Mouse" (1891) also argues for a right to private space and private life. Hetty finds herself homeless after the people she's lived with move away. She curtains off a small living space for herself within the local church, where she assumes the duties of the sexton. This move disquiets the congregation, who are uncomfortable with the idea of a woman sexton, not to mention the idea of a woman "pitching her tent in the Lord's house" (282). Thus the community finds a home for her with a neighbor.

But, despite her neediness, Hetty, like Charlotte and Harriet, resists charity that impinges on her personal rights of space, taste, and happiness. "I don't like Susan Radway," she says about the woman with whom she is expected to live, "hain't never liked her, and I ain't goin' to live with her" (285). When the congregation attempts to force her to leave, she locks herself in the church and asserts her rights to live alone and maintain her own "inviolate personality": Hetty says, "[Mis Radway's] used to havin' her own way, and I've been livin' all my life with them that was, an' I've had to fight to keep a footin' on the earth, an' now I'm gittn' too old for't" (290). For Hetty, keeping a "footin' on the earth" means being able to have her own way in her own private space. "I'd 'nough sight rather be alone than have comp'ny, any day" (285), she says. In the end, the townspeople allow her to remain in her little space in the church, and she is fully satisfied when left "with no one to molest or disturb her" (291).

For Freeman, then, every individual—poor as well as moneyed—has a right to her private space and happiness. But, significantly Freeman's stories do not assert the rights of privately owned property. Instead, Freeman's stories assert that each person can only have her "private share" if people share their property, allowing the poor and propertyless the chance to have a space of their own. For Freeman, space needs to be understood as communal; paradoxically, it is the communal nature of space that allows for the privacy that is a fundamental right of the American citizen.

This aspect of Freeman's work can be understood within other theories of poverty relief circulating during the period. For example, as mentioned elsewhere in this book, in 1877 Henry George began his study *Progress and Poverty,* which argued that the unequal distribution of wealth could only be solved by making land common property. As George puts it, "The widespreading social evils which everywhere oppress men amid an advancing civilization spring from a great primary wrong—the appropriation, as the exclusive property of some men, of the land on which and from which all must live" (340). For George, "Wherever there is light to guide us, we may everywhere see that in their first perceptions all peoples have recognized the common ownership in land, and that private property in land is an usurpation, a creation of force and fraud. . . . The equal right of all men to the use of land is as clear as their equal right to breathe the air" (338). While there is no certainty that Freeman read George, her stories show a remarkable parallel to his ideas. For her, this "right of all men" is a right of all men *and* women to claim their private share of communal property. In this reading, Freeman fits a characteristic of regionalism noted by Fetterley and Pryse. They contend that regionalism disrupts the connection between place and property and can be seen to represent a world prior to capitalism (277). Or, as I would put it, Freeman attempts to reimagine property ownership in a noncapitalist way in order to locate private space for all.

Private ownership is often the root of the problem for Freeman's characters. In "Cinnamon Roses," Elsie must leave her beloved home because a new owner forecloses on it. While Nancy is allowed to remain in her family home in "Old Lady Pingree" (1887), "down in the depths of her proud old heart rankled the knowledge that an outsider owned the home of her fathers" (153).

In the face of problems of private ownership, Freeman's stories assert a vision of communal property as a way to help the poor and maintain their legal rights of privacy. In "A Mistaken Charity," the sisters return to a home that they do not actually own. A wealthy man "held a mortgage on the little house in which they had been born and lived all their lives." But he gave them "the use of it, rent and interest free" (42). Freeman asserts that private ownership of the house is ludicrous; it is a part of nature and should be open to the sisters as a tree would be to the insects and birds that inhabit it. The actual owner, the story states, "might as well have taken credit to himself for not charging a squirrel for his tenement in some old decaying tree in the woods. . . . There was as much fitness in a mortgage on the little house . . . as there would have been on a rotten old apple-tree" (42; 44). The propertied in the community, then, by renouncing their rights to personal ownership allow the sisters their "private share" (45). When the sisters return to their own space from the Old Ladies' Home, they are joyous. Harriet draws her key "triumphantly from her pocket" (56), and "everything [in the house] was just as they had left it" (56).

Similarly, in "A Church Mouse," Hetty struggles with her community to be allowed to stay in the meeting house. In an act that Fetterley and Pryse understand as female resistance to male authority (250–51), two women "defiantly" allow her to stay ("Church Mouse" 290) and even provide her with a little room in the church rather than the curtained-off area she had arranged for herself. The end of the story underscores the privacy that this sharing of community space can provide: "Established in that small, lofty room, with her bed and her stove, with gifts of a rocking-chair and a table, and goodly store of food, with no one to molest or disturb her, she had nothing to wish for on earth" (291).

In "Old Lady Pingree," Nancy Pingree may not own her home, but when a widow and her daughter need a place to stay she gives them their own room upstairs and refuses any money for it. Here, in another example of how communal property might work, Jenny and her mother get material aid and are able to have private space for themselves.

These stories set out Freeman's ideals for poverty relief: shared space can mean private space. However, this is not to say that she has no other visions of aid to the poor. In several of her stories, poor women gain economic relief through marriage. For example, in *Pembroke,* Sylvia's long-recalcitrant suitor, Richard, witnesses her trip to the poorhouse. He is moved to save her by finally marrying her. In "Cinnamon Roses," Elsie is rescued from her unhappy life in her brother's house when the man who owns her old home declares he has long loved her. He marries her and consequently she returns to her home, which her new husband shares with her.

But while marriage may alleviate poverty, will it allow a woman the privacy that is her right? Marriage in Freeman's stories is often a troubling institution that negates privacy. Remember, for example, that Louisa in "A New England Nun" releases her suitor in order to retain her home. The result is that she feels "like a queen who, after fearing lest her domain be wrested away from her, sees it firmly insured in her possession" (124). In a similar manner, Mrs. Penn must rebel against her husband in "The Revolt of 'Mother'" in order to get her own house.

So it would seem that marriage may not be a satisfactory solution to the problems of female poverty and privacy. While Glasser reads the marriages in *Pembroke* as a celebration and acknowledgment of feminine values (124), I agree with Deborah Lambert that the marriages in *Pembroke* happen only when women are at their weakest. "In *Pembroke*," Lambert asserts, "men choose to marry when their women have suffered a significant loss of power or status" (204). Unlike the resisting poor in "A Church Mouse" and "A Mistaken Charity," who find happiness in resisting benevolence, Sylvia succumbs to Richard's aid when she is at her weakest—on her way to the poorhouse. Marriage (and the resulting relief from poverty) is not a triumph here; rather, it is a sign of defeat.

Elsie does marry William Havers at the end of "Cinnamon Roses," but here, too, there is something unsettling about this method of benevolence. Near the end of the story, Havers, the owner of Elsie's house, proclaims that he has been in love with her his entire life, and will happily give her old home back to her. But Elsie says she is uncomfortable with this act of charity. Then in the very next sentence, she offers to marry William. While her poverty and the lack of privacy she experienced living in her brother's home are alleviated by marriage, the union seems only a way to hold on to the house she loves—perhaps more than she loves the man who comes with it. In fact, Elsie shows more emotion over the house than she ever does over William. When forced to leave her home at the opening of the story, she is "disfigured by grief" (168); by contrast the only words she says to William before their wedding are, "Well, it don't seem as if thar would be much sense in my gittin' married now, anyway" (179). He talks her into it, but as a method of benevolence, marriage again seems unsatisfactory.

Certainly Freeman longed for privacy in her own married life. Living with her family until the age of thirty, she found that being single "granted her the liberty of solitude" (Glasser 10). Later supervising the construction of a new house during her marriage, she writes in a 1907 letter, "Sometimes I wish I could have a little toy house, in which I could do just as I please, cook a meal if I wanted to, and fuss around generally. . . . If I had my little toy house nobody could say anything" (qtd. in Meese 165). Here Freeman again shows the relationship between private space (the "toy house") and the "right to be let alone" ("I could do just as I please").

I need to note that two stories of Freeman's appear as jarring contradictions to her interest in privacy for the poor. In "A Solitary" (1891), Stephen is a complete misanthrope until the poor, ill Nicholas turns up on his doorstep, determined to avoid the poorhouse to which his sister intends to send him. Nicholas finds paradise on a cot in Stephen's home: the "poor cot in the warm room seemed to him like a couch under the balsam-dropping cedars of Lebanon, and all at once he felt that divine rest which comes from leaning upon the will of another" (233). In "An Independent Thinker" (1897), Esther wants Lavinia Dodge to come live with her. At first Lavinia resists (because Esther works on the Sabbath—an activity of which Lavinia heartily disapproves). But finally Lavinia agrees to the move when, after three months in the almshouse, her rheumatism intensifies so that she becomes nearly helpless. In both cases, then, privacy does not seem an issue in benevolence. But the difference here, perhaps, is that these poor are ill. Freeman makes this point in "An Independent Thinker." Esther realizes that Lavinia's illness means she needs constant aid. When she hears about how debilitating the rheumatism has become, Esther "dropped her knitting and stared radiantly" (310). Her neighbor even comments, "Why Esther Gay, you look real tickled cause she's sick" (310). Freeman asserts strongly the need for the poor to have their own spaces and their own lives; only when stricken by illness does the undeniable need for help supersede the need for a private home.

In most of Freeman's work, then, private space and the intangible rights to one's own tastes and pleasure—that is, the "right to be let alone"—are not just luxuries property owners can afford; they are necessary to survival—in Hetty's words, necessary to "keep a footin' on this earth." In this way Freeman's stories are remarkably current. In the face of twenty-first-century technology, the likes of which Warren and Brandeis never imagined, the rights of privacy have become all the more endangered for everyone, poor or not. As John Gilliom notes in his book on the poor and privacy rights,

> Over the past few decades, there have been dramatic expansions in the quality, the breadth, and the intensity of programs that use new generations of technology for gathering, storing, sharing, and using information. Indeed, if we add up the frequently overlapping profiles encompassing medical records, academic and professional performance, credit ratings, consumer behavior, insurance records, driving records, law enforcement data, welfare agency information, child support enforcement programs, Internet communications, and other information systems, it is safe to say that much of the significant activity of our lives is now subject to systematic observation and analysis. (2)

Gilliom reminds us that this observation and analysis—through technology today as through Friendly Visiting in the nineteenth century—is an expression and an instrument of power. Echoing Michel Foucault's analysis of the Panopticon, he writes, "Surveillance of human behavior is in place to control human behavior" (3).

The poor have long borne an especially heavy burden of surveillance and lost privacy. Gilliom's work notes that "from the sixteenth-century surveys of the poor to the comprehensive computer-based Client Information Systems that most states now use, welfare administration has been inextricably a process of struggling to 'know' the poor; to measure, depict, and examine them. . . . Scientific charity . . . gradually produce[d] . . . the contemporary regimes of welfare surveillance" (22–24). But Gilliom, like Freeman, also notes that there are ways to resist this power. In his study of welfare mothers in Appalachian Ohio in the 1990s, he finds that these women are engaged in "practices of every resistance and evasion to beat, as best they could the powers of surveillance" (6).

Mary Wilkins Freeman's stories reveal underpinnings of current fears about privacy—especially the vulnerability of the poor to those who would help them at the expense of their fundamental rights of happiness. Rather than scientific charity and Friendly Visiting, Freeman's preferred method of benevolence employs a vision of communal property, which allows the poor to maintain privacy in all its diverse nineteenth-century forms. Through her focus on New England women's private lives, Freeman examines the local repercussions of major issues of her day. In these early-twenty-first-century days of John Ashcroft, the Patriot Act, and Homeland Security, the significance of her work remains.

Notes

1. For example, in her introduction to *The Selected Stories of Mary E. Wilkins Freeman,* Marjorie Pryse argues that Freeman emphasizes stigmatized women who often find strength and power in their social exclusion (x–xi). In one essay, Melissa McFarland Pennell traces Freeman's relationship to Nathaniel Hawthorne, arguing that Freeman depicts women "who choose to stand on their own, who accept their marginal lives and meager finances as a means of preserving an uncompromised self" ("Unfortunate Fall" 196). Elsewhere, Pennell reads Freeman's work as an examination of female choices; she asserts that Freeman's characters, with all their difficulties, gain a "degree of freedom to reject social codes and expectations" ("Liberating Will" 208). Susan Allen Toth similarly sees Freeman's characters as struggling "with courageous spirit towards self-expression and independence" (123).

2. Mary Wilkins Freeman, too, had her personal suspicions about public use of images of herself. Sandra Zagarell claims that Freeman resisted editors' and publishers' requests for recent photographs. However, like many authors, she found she could "neither prevent the reuse of images already circulating nor the creation of new ones" (xiv).

3. These weren't the only popular writings on such issues. For instance, the *New York Times* also entered the debates surrounding the right of privacy in 1902, discussing a New York State case and the "amazing opinion" of Judge Parker of the Court of Appeals that the "right to privacy is not a right which in the state of New York anybody is bound to respect" ("The Right of Privacy," August 23, 1902, 8). The *Times* argues that if such a law does not exist, "then the decent people will say that it is high time that there is such a law" ("The Right of Privacy" 8).

4. Glasser argues that this story reflects the fear that aging can undermine female autonomy (209–10). I can't disagree with her point, though all these stories when apprehended together suggest that Freeman was as interested in the autonomy of the poor as she was in the independence of elders.

Works Cited

Bercovici, Konrad. *Crimes of Charity.* New York: Knopf, 1917.

Bremner, Robert. *American Philanthropy.* Chicago: U of Chicago P, 1960.

Danielson, Caroline. "The Gender of Privacy and the Embodied Self: Examining the

Origins of the Right of Privacy in U.S. Law." *Feminist Studies* 25.2 (Summer 1999): 311–44.

Donovan, Josephine. *New England Local Color Literature: A Woman's Tradition.* New York: Frederick Ungar, 1983.

Fetterley, Judith, and Marjorie Pryse. *Writing out of Place: Regionalism, Women, and American Literary Culture.* Urbana: U of Illinois P, 2003.

Freeman, Mary E. Wilkins. "A Church Mouse." 1891. Pryse 273–92.

———. "Cinnamon Roses." *A Humble Romance and Other Stories.* New York: Harper, 1887. 164–79.

———. "A Gala Dress." 1891. Pryse 145–61.

———. "An Independent Thinker." *A Humble Romance and Other Stories.* New York: Harper, 1887. 296–314.

———. "The Last Gift." 1903. *The Best Stories of Mary E. Wilkins.* Ed. Henry Wysham Lanier. New York: Harper, 1927. 102–19.

———. "A Mistaken Charity." 1887. Pryse 41–56.

———. "A New England Nun." 1891. Pryse 109–25.

———. "Old Lady Pingree." *A Humble Romance and Other Stories.* New York: Harper, 1887. 148–63.

———. *Pembroke.* 1894. New Haven: College and University P, 1971.

———. "A Poetess." 1891. Pryse 180–99.

———. "The Revolt of 'Mother.'" 1891. Pryse 293–313.

———. "A Solitary." 1891. Pryse 218–36.

George, Henry. *Progress and Poverty.* 1879. New York: Robert Schalkenbach Foundation, 1955.

Gilliom, John. *Overseers of the Poor: Surveillance, Resistance, and the Limits of Privacy.* Chicago: U of Chicago P, 2001.

Glasser, Leah Blatt. *In a Closet Hidden: The Life and Work of Mary E. Wilkins Freeman.* Amherst: U of Massachusetts P, 1996.

Godkin, E. L. "The Rights of the Citizen to His Own Reputation." *Scribner's Magazine* (July 1890): 58–67.

Gordon, Linda. *Heroes of Their Own Lives: The Politics and History of Family Violence, Boston 1800–1960.* New York: Penguin, 1989.

Gurteen, Humphreys. *A Handbook of Charity Organizations.* Buffalo: Published by the author, 1882.

Katz, Michael B. *In the Shadow of the Poorhouse: A Social History of Welfare in America.* New York: Basic Books, 1986.

Lambert, Deborah G. "Rereading Mary Wilkins Freeman: Autonomy and Sexuality in *Pembroke*." Marchalonis 197–206.

Lowell, Josephine Shaw. *Public Relief and Private Charity.* 1884. New York: Arno Press, 1971.

Marchalonis, Shirley, ed. *Critical Essays on Mary Wilkins Freeman.* Boston: G. K. Hall, 1991.

Martin, George Madden. "Rights of Man." *Harper's Monthly Magazine* 106.633 (February 1903): 416–33.

Meese, Elizabeth. "Signs of Undecidabililty: Reconsidering the Stories of Mary Wilkins Freeman." Marchalonis 157–76.

Mensel, Robert E. "'Kodakers Lying in Wait': Amateur Photography and the Right of Privacy in New York, 1855–1915." *American Quarterly* 43.1 (March 1991): 24–45.

Pennell, Melissa McFarland. "The Liberating Will: Freedom of Choice in the Fiction of Mary Wilkins Freeman." Marchalonis 207–21.

———. "The Unfortunate Fall." In *Hawthorne and Women: Engendering and Expanding the Hawthorne Tradition.* Ed. John L. Idol, Jr., and Melinda M. Ponder. Amherst: U of Massachusetts P, 1999. 191–203.

Pryse, Marjorie. Introduction. Pryse vii–xix.

———, ed. *Selected Stories of Mary E. Wilkins Freeman.* New York: Norton, 1983.

Reed, John. Introduction. *Crimes of Charity.* By Konrad Bercovici. New York: Knopf, 1917.

Reichardt, Mary R. Introduction. *A Mary Wilkins Freeman Reader.* Ed. Mary R. Reichardt. Lincoln: U of Nebraska P, 1997.

———. "Mary Wilkins Freeman: One Hundred Years of Criticism." 1987. Marchalonis 73–89.

Richmond, Mary E. *Friendly Visiting among the Poor: A Handbook for Charity Workers.* 1899. Montclair: Patterson Smith, 1969.

"The Right of Privacy." *New York Times,* August 3, 1902, 8.

"The Right to Be Let Alone." *Atlantic Monthly* 67.401 (March 1891): 428–29.

"The Right to Privacy." *Green Bag* 3 (1891): 524–26.

"The Right to Privacy." *Green Bag* 6 (1894): 498–501.

"The Right to Privacy in Nineteenth Century America." *Harvard Law Review* 94 (June 1981): 1892–910.

Riis, Jacob. A. *The Making of an American.* New York: Macmillan, 1901.

Shi, David E. *Facing Facts: Realism in American Thought and Culture, 1850–1920.* New York: Oxford UP, 1995.

Speed, John Gilmer. "The Right of Privacy." *North American Review* 163 (1896): 64–74.

Toth, Susan Allen. "Defiant Light: A Positive View of Mary Wilkins Freeman." 1973. Marchalonis 123–31.

Warner, Sylvia Townsend. "Item, One Empty House." 1966. Marchalonis 118–31.

Warren, Samuel D., and Louis D. Brandeis. "The Right to Privacy." *Harvard Law Review* 4.5 (December 15, 1890): 193–220.

Zagarell, Sandra. Introduction. *Mary E. Wilkins Freeman: A New England Nun and Other Stories.* Ed. Sandra Zagarell. New York: Penguin, 2000.

6

Women's Charity vs. Scientific Philanthropy in Sarah Orne Jewett

Monika Elbert

> Women's greater involvement in gift-giving today is not simply an effect of their immediate experiences in the household. Rather, it is a consequence of their participation in a discourse of relationships. Through that discourse the present generation of women, and their predecessors, have created their own relational cultures. . . . The dominant social definitions of the gift economy today are derived from a feminized ideology of love.
>
> —David Cheal, *The Gift Economy* (183)

> "Women are, in all ordinary cases, by far the best visitors of the poor. A true woman carries with her an atmosphere of influence which makes itself felt. She can go, without offence [*sic*], where men would not be welcome."
>
> —Rev. R. E. Thompson, *Manual for Visitors among the Poor* (176)

In many of Sarah Orne Jewett's stories, women express their interconnectedness through gift-giving, and the gift becomes a symbol that looms large in the pastoral settings of Jewett's landscapes. One should not consider the exchange of gifts a simple and inane nostalgic activity, but rather a gesture that reflects a type of moral economy prevalent among Jewett's feminine communities. In his extended study about "gift economy" (see epigraph above), David Cheal, drawing from anthropological studies by Claude Lévi-Strauss and Marcel Mauss, concludes that men and women have always "given" differently—that men are involved in a notion of "political economy" because of their outside/public employment, whereas women, through their domestic roles, are more familiar with "the discourse of moral economy" (183). Cheal maintains that in modern times, even with women's changing roles, women still equate gift-giving with intimacy, and certainly, the "predecessors" of the present generation he talks about are those women who have an intimate connection to the home and to the household, women like those who inhabit Jewett's New England settings. Focusing on several well-known stories by Jewett, namely "The Flight of Betsey Lane," "The Town Poor," "Going to Shrewsbury," "Aunt Cynthy Dallett," and "Martha's Lady," and several uncollected works, one can explore the ramifications of Jewett's female-centered and communal (or extended family type of) charity. In these stories, there are often attempts by the larger male community or bureaucratic, patriarchal institution (the selectmen, or the town council, or a greedy male relative) to suppress a woman's individuality by having her sequestered in an almshouse or claustrophobic small space, or by making her move from her ancestral home to smaller quarters or shared lodging. However, with the help of more benevolent women in the community, the poor, homeless woman is able to transcend the limited and sparse vision of life, at least momentarily, and to indulge in a quest that would grant her dignity—ironically enough, by her own ability to give. Thus the image of the "gift" takes on profound significance in the Jewett woman's quest for self-respect and self-reliance, as it also shows the need for women to bond and to enjoy the intimacy of sharing.

An understanding of contemporaneous philanthropic practices is essential for a proper understanding of Jewett's revolutionary women, who resisted the urge to bureaucratize giving and loving. It is true, as recent Jewett critics like Alison Easton and Sarah Way Sherman have pointed out, that Jewett was not able to overcome fully all her prejudices (in her fiction) against women born of a lower class than she.[1] But Jewett did try to show the higher moral ground as that of being charitable to women of even the most modest means, and the benefactresses who help women of the underclass are exalted in her fiction. This attitude was in contradistinction to two movements at the end of the nineteenth century that succeeded in dehumanizing, even demonizing, the poor, and in distancing the financially solvent individual (the upper or middle class) from the poverty-stricken individual. Social Darwinism, which grew out of Herbert Spencer's notion of the "survival of the fittest" (indeed, he coined the term), suggested that the poor deserved what they received as their lot in life and attributed the poor's misfortune to physical sloth or moral lassitude. Applying Darwin's theories of evolution to the structure of society, the British sociologist Spencer facilitated laissez-faire capitalist thinking in economics, which was welcomed by many in the United States. Based on Darwin's ideas of natural selection, Spencer argued against poor laws and government aid to the poor, insisting that the poor needed to be weeded out because they were unfit: "The whole effort of nature is to get rid of such, to clear the world of them, and make room for better" (Hofstadter 41). An ardent disciple of Spencer, William Graham Sumner became the most influential social Darwinist in the United States. In his famous treatise, *What Social Classes Owe to Each Other*, he reiterates quite often and emphatically that self-interest is best for society: "Every man and woman in society has one big duty. That is, to take care of his or her own self. This is a social duty" (98). Very dispassionately, he describes the natural plight of the poor: "Nature's remedies against vice are terrible. She removes the victims without pity. A drunkard in the gutter is just where he ought to be, according to the fitness and tendency of things" (114).

Sumner also feels that the poor often latch on to others because the system of charity condones it. He states that he has no complaint about the man who raises himself above poverty "by his own effort," but he does condemn "The man who has done nothing to raise himself above poverty" and who "finds that the social doctors flock about him, bringing the capital which they have collected from the other class, and promising him the aid of the State to give him what the other had to work for" (21). Thus he perceives the poor as cheats preying on the moral and hard-working American: "Under the names of the poor and the weak, the negligent, shiftless, inefficient, silly, and imprudent are fastened upon the industrious and prudent as a responsibility and a duty" (20). Sumner encourages teaching a man to help himself, so that he can contribute to the good of the community: "If alms are given, or if we 'make work' for a man, or 'give him employment,' or 'protect' him, we simply take a product from one and give it to another" (143). Even the compassionate Charles Loring Brace, who founded the Children's Aid Society of New York in 1853, felt that "this trade of alms and dependence on charities ought to be checked" (385). He is stunned by "the number of poor people who enjoy a comfortable living, derived from a long study and experience of those various agencies of benevolence" (384).

He describes their dependence on charities, which he sees as deceptive and deleterious to their own growth: "They pass from one to the other; knowing exactly their conditions of assistance and meeting their requirements, and live thus by a sort of science of alms" (384). Brace's antidote was kinder than that of social Darwinists; his religious background made him believe that Christianity and an inculcation of morals would break the cycle of poverty and allow the poor to free themselves of alms and crime (23).[2]

As one proponent of social Darwinism proclaimed in the *Nation* in 1894, there was only one way to eradicate poverty—simply put, that was "nature's remedy—work or starve" (Trattner 91). According to Walter I. Trattner in *From Poor Law to Welfare State: A History of Social Welfare in America,* "The idea that distress was an individual moral matter was not only revived but strengthened as the wounds of the Civil War were healed and the nation grew and prospered. The poor were held in contempt in an acquisitive society in which wealth became almost an end in itself" (90). It was a common sentiment among leaders of late-nineteenth-century charitable organizations that "To solve the problem of poverty, character flaws and moral illnesses of the poor had to be weeded out and replaced with virtue, industry, and thrift" (Tice 21). Thus the poor were seen as degenerate and responsible for their plight.

The second drastic change in poverty relief was the attempt to centralize and organize the many individual and disparate charity societies under a concept known as "scientific charity" or "philanthroplogy." Charitable organizations became more and more corporate as they dealt less with human interactions and more with bureaucratic fact-finding, data-collecting, and record-keeping about those who would be on the receiving end. This new type of charity work based on supposed scientific and corporate principles that called for efficiency was perhaps a way to absolve the individual and the community of responsibility and guilt.[3] At the end of the nineteenth century, the so-called Friendly Visiting among the poor was conducted by volunteers only and those paid were the staff members who worked in institutional (often government) offices. The rift became greater and the roles reversed in the early twentieth century as the staff workers became the volunteers and the field workers became professional, paid workers, if they accepted the authority of the charity agency.[4] Proponents of scientific charity were impressed that "the charitable instinct was being disciplined, the head was triumphing over the heart, the 'machinery of benevolence' was coming to be understood and usefully operated" (Bremner 86). Moreover, "Advocates of the charity organization society movement attacked traditional practices of charity and almsgiving as being sentimental and indiscriminate" (Tice 20). Thus, old-fashioned charity was seen as feminine in the worse way (sentimental)—and as conducive to creating more poverty.

There were apologists for gift-giving, if done under the proper circumstances, usually as part of a personal transaction that ennobled the benefactor.[5] Herbert Spencer in his later writings tried to soften his earlier brutal diatribes against the poor: "Spencer was compelled to insist over and over again that he was not opposed to voluntary private charity to the unfit, since it had an elevating effect on the character of the donors and hastened the development of altruism" (Hofstadter 41). But he did persist in attacking "compulsory poor laws and other state measures" (41). Brace distrusted outdoor relief because it forced recipients to manipulate the charity societies, but he sometimes condones private acts of giving: "private alms, though more indiscriminately bestowed, and often on entirely unworthy objects, do not . . . leave the same evil effect as public" (392). There was something in the apparently personal connection of gift-giving that Brace finds preferable and more ennobling: "The influence of the giver's character may sometimes elevate the debased nature of an unworthy dependent on charity. The personal connection of a poor creature and a fine lady, is not so bad as that of a pauper to the State" (392). Still, Brace felt that alms were abused and that one should be less eager to give alms than to prevent the "demand for alms" (393). His objective was to foster independence and productivity among the poor, "to take [from the poor], rather than give," by granting the poor an education and employment (397).

There was a real distinction between giving from the heart or giving from moral duty, and giving because one was required to as part of a large bureaucracy, where so many strings are attached that the emotional values of giving are forgotten. Moreover, the institutionalization of charity began to grind away at woman's and man's dignity. Local and national debates about indoor versus outdoor relief were held; public outdoor relief, or helping poor individuals or families at home, was often seen as preferable to the indoor relief (which ultimately was considerably higher in funding) where individuals would be shut away in poorhouses.[6] Whereas in the past each citizen or townsperson would be responsible for his neighbor's welfare, the big business of charity would make giving less personal, and the pauper's plight less immediate, his suffering more immediate. Some proponents of the new scientific charity movement, with its use of experts in the field rather than volunteer Friendly Visitors, were astute enough to realize that there was a real difference between the old-fashioned style of "Friendly Visit" to the poor (done by volunteers) and the new more mechanical type of visit (done by paid workers). For example, Rev. D. O. Kellogg, likening charity organizations to industrial organizations (a comparison he found positive and progressive), did, nonetheless, detect the danger in using the new highly skilled visitors: "There may seem a danger in thus placing benevolent exertion under law. . . . The individual may be in danger of passing from sight, and machine-like processes may take the place of sympathetic action" (175).

However, many leaders of charitable organizations felt the same way Josephine Shaw Lowell, founder of the N.Y. Charity Society, felt; in her words, "Human nature is so constituted that no [working] man can receive as a gift what he should earn by his own labor without a moral deterioration" (97). Although often seen as a progressive organizer of charities, she shared the same underlying bias about the poor—that they would suffer morally if they received alms. Significantly, her comment shows that there is no gender preference for good charitable works; those who became enmeshed in the hierarchy of institutionalized charity were adversely affected, no matter the gender. Sounding like Ralph Waldo Emerson with his notion of withholding the wicked dollar that would unman the giver and dehumanize the poverty-stricken receiver (in "Self-Reliance"), Josephine Lowell also felt that "No human being . . . will work to provide the means of living for himself if he can get a living in any other manner agreeable to himself" (Trattner 97).[7] Thus there was a basic distrust of and contempt for the individual who found himself or herself in desperate financial need. Even liberal thinkers on charity, such as Lowell with her positive attitudes toward "Friendly Visiting" (though in the context of scientific charity) felt ambivalent about the underlying causes of poverty—often attributing poverty to sloth or immorality. As one proponent of organized charity suggested, the charity worker should be an "expert" at ascertaining whether and to what extent "his alms will do good" (Bonaparte 190). The Protestant work ethic that equated sloth with indigence was partly to blame for this type of skewed thinking.

Emerson had put a transcendental spin on the meaning of work and charity earlier in the century, and although his views vacillate, they reflect attitudes toward charity in the late nineteenth century. His idea is that "some degradation" is wrought when he "rejoice[s] or grieve[s]" at a gift; he feels his independence being "invaded" (537). He feels that the individual who has the means or the power to give ultimately insults the person who is receiving the gift, and that the indignation (and feeling of indebtedness) of the latter might lead to a counterattack: "It is not the office of a man to receive gifts. How dare you give them? We wish to be self-sustained. We do not quite forgive a giver. The hand that feeds us is in some danger of being bitten" (536). But Emerson does believe in an egalitarian type of giving and receiving: "The gift, to be true, must be the flowing of the giver unto me, correspondent to my flowing into him. When the waters are at level, then my goods pass to him, and his to me. All his are mine, all mine his" (537). He also feels that the economy of giving should be based on love, and not on power inequities: "We can receive anything from love, for that is a way of receiving it from ourselves; but not from any one who assumes to bestow" (536). This misguided feeling of one who "assumes to *bestow*" (emphasis mine) is common to those charity workers who would inflict their gift, in terms of dollars or food, onto the impoverished. Emerson, who had great disdain for commercial values, would have felt an antibusiness ethic toward the corporatization of charity. In the sense that charity was a personal gift, his views of charity would accord with women's emotional sense of moral obligation, as expressed by Cheal in the introductory epigraph. Even the vacillating Josephine Shaw Lowell, whom I discuss above, was correct in thinking that something beyond physical relief was needed for the poor: "the real condemnation of relief-giving is that it is material, that it seeks material ends by material means, and therefore must fail . . . even to attain its own ends" (225). Instead, Lowell advocates a regard for the spiritual component of charity and of man, "For man is a spiritual being, and, if he is to be helped, it must be by spiritual means" (225). This latter view may seem reactionary and a means by which the big business of charity could further withhold alms from the poor, but it does foster an earlier transcendental ethos and vision of giving, but more than that, it resonates with the earlier spiritual meaning given to charitable giving in Puritan times.[8]

Although Emerson would have upheld the patriarchal withholding aspect of any kind of philanthropy, he would have had real problems with the dehumanizing aspects of measuring and evaluating the plight of the poor—the practices fostered by scientific charity. He would have agreed with Lowell that material gift-giving would never be man's salvation (neither for the giver or the receiver). Perhaps the distinction between male and female views of charity could be perceived in preconceived notions about male and female social responsibilities: "Benevolence figured in the building of a man's career . . . but it was rarely his central concern or source of identity. Women's benevolent societies by contrast *were* their 'careers,' an accepted extension of their defined roles as wives and mothers" (Scott 24). Female benevolent societies, especially in antebellum America, thrived on the nurturing aspect of "community institutions" like orphan asylums, homes for fallen women, and homes for aging women (Scott 25) and thus were in contradistinction to the bureaucratic male organized charities. However, in postbellum America, the gendered nature of philanthropy changed, and as Lori Ginzberg demonstrates, postwar benevolence changed its focus from gender to class: postbellum reformers were less concerned about morality (which was the domain of antebellum women's benevolent work) and more focused on the need "to control the poor and 'vagrant' " (5). In some ways, then, the discourse of scientific charity infiltrated the earlier female practices of philanthropy, so that the current emphasis was on "business skills and on an unsentimental analysis of social ills" (Ginzberg 10). In some ways, women were becoming more like men as they became more emancipated and took on the jobs of scientific philanthropy. There was a distinct tension between the "business principles" of scientific charity and "the older ideal of the feminine task of redemption," which the newer generation of benevolent women rejected (10). Late-nineteenth-century reform movements among women also gave rise to a certain kind of sisterhood, one detectable in Sarah Orne Jewett's works. Women forged strong bonds with each other in crusading for others and participating in local charity organizations—and their own lots were improved by their sense of mission (Sander 42). But at the end of the nineteenth century, when the business of charity was being "masculinized," women moved away from the discourse of nurturing and "increasingly tempered feminine rhetoric to include male-oriented values of commercialism and entrepreneurship to their organizations" (Tice 42).

Dissenting feminine voices (in the late nineteenth century) to the bureaucratic charitable institutions included Jane Addams, founder of Hull-House at Chicago, who felt that charity organizations built on their "pseudoscientific" calculations and evaluations were cold, impersonal, and withholding, and that their philosophy of giving was not very effective as it dealt with bestowing advice in the form of moral rhetoric and "don'ts." Her protest was against their authoritarian type of advising, not against alms-giving.

A most interesting combination of balanced notions of charity could be found in the late-nineteenth-century philosopher Marietta Kies (1853–1899), one of American's first women Idealists and one of the first American women to achieve a Ph.D. (1891, University of Michigan) (Rogers 1). Kies is able to strike a balance between two contending ideas, between "justice," which she associates with strong individualism, and "grace," which she associates with charity. As Dorothy Rogers notes, "Kies' theory matches current feminist 'ethics of care' or other feminist theories that try to reconcile individualism and communitarianism" (1). When describing "justice," Kies sounds very much like a social Darwinist as she describes the importance of individual right and self-determination (justice) and as she compares "survival of the fittest" among lower forms of life to grace among humans: "the individual shall give up his life for the larger life of the species" (4). Ultimately, she feels that justice and grace are complementary:

> Man, in seeing the effects of his own deeds upon himself, learns to measure justice to another; and in his struggle with evil in his own soul, and in his moments of repentance and humiliation, and in his attempts at helpfulness to others, he learns true charity. (Kies 6–7)

Kies does not condone self-sacrifice for the sake of martyrdom, yet she does feel that humans, being superior to animals, can gain by giving,

"Because of the free will of man, the return of his own deeds upon him is a mark of respect to his dignity, while the return of its own deed upon a lower animal might annihilate it" (7). Kies did not believe that charity or altruism was gender based, but rather she felt that it was "a principle applicable to men and women alike, and . . . not limited to the private sphere, but to be implemented in the public realm" (Rogers 2).

Another dissenting voice that sought to reconcile private and public belonged to Sarah Orne Jewett, who, though not a crusader for the impoverished in any political way, was clearly sympathetic to the plight of the poor, especially of impoverished women, alone in society. Her fiction offers a counter-proposal to the harsh measures suggested by the charity societies, as Jewett formulates a new way to think about gifts and gift-giving, one that perhaps harked back to early New England days, when the Puritan sense of communal sharing was the ideal, and also to earlier nineteenth-century practices of benevolence. Her thinking about charity may also have been influenced by her close friendship with Annie Fields, who, besides being a mentor to female writers, including Sarah Orne Jewett, was an active reformer interested in the welfare of the poor. With Mrs. James Lodge, Annie Fields established in 1875 the "cooperative Society of Visitors among the Poor" (Sherman, *Sarah Orne Jewett* 77–78). Moreover, Fields continued to work for charitable causes: in 1879, at the time Jewett was writing many of her early stories about charity, Fields helped establish the "Associated Charities of Boston, which she directed until 1894"; Fields wrote an important work on economics and social welfare, titled *How to Help the Poor* (1883); and when Fields died in 1915, she left $40,000 to the Associated Charities of Boston (Sherman, *Sarah Orne Jewett* 78).[9] Sarah Way Sherman points out the similarities between Fields's notion of charity and Jewett's concept of charity. Apparently, Fields followed the principles of British social worker Octavia Hill, who emphasized Friendly Visits as well as self-reliance for the poor through their own labor (Sherman 78). Sherman asserts that the ideas Fields adopts would later be obvious in Jewett's fiction: "Individual purpose and firsthand acquaintance would later be important principles in Sarah Jewett's attitude toward country life and working-class people" (78). Indeed, that Octavia Hill was a role model for Fields (and indirectly for Jewett) is significant as Hill preached equality between the classes and asked that the middle class not see the poor "as a different class" but rather as "members of households" and families, "as we are ourselves" (Woodroofe 49). In her essay, "The Organization of Charity" (1870), Hill advises social workers to treat the poor with dignity: "In the deep souls of those who appear the worst . . . there is a spark of nobleness" (Woodroofe 51). In Jewett's world of women, this attitude translates into compassion and regard for those suffering women, a perspective that allows the giver to develop as well as the receiver. In her essay, "Our Dealings with the Poor," Hill looks back to a simpler time where the ideal was to "promote the happy, natural intercourse of neighbours" (Woodroofe 52). Her description of Friendly Visits among the poor sounds much like the backdrop of the setting for Jewett's rustic women, with their intimate bonding. As Octavia Hill writes, "Only when face meets face, and heart meets heart; only in the settled link with those who are old friends . . . is (there) more opportunity . . . to grow and to shine" (Woodroofe 52).

In contrast to the bureaucratic practices of providing for the poor, as promoted by the scientific school of philanthropy, are the simple and humane "giving" practices of Sarah Orne Jewett's country women. Although Jewett is writing during the period of literary realism, with the ornate backdrop of the Gilded Age, in which material objects take on profound meaning as ends in themselves for the greedy consumer,[10] Jewett depicts a more sacred and more symbolic vision of the material goods that women create, purchase, or exchange. Far from the world of Charlotte Perkins Gilman's diatribe on women as parasitic consumers rather than producers in *Women and Economics*,[11] we find women, even the poorest of women, who know the value of work and of sharing their scant material resources. Truly, Jewett's vision of communal charity and of individual acts of charity reminds us of an earlier era in New England history when the idea prevailed that we are all our brothers' keepers (in Jewett's case, our sisters' keepers).[12]

In Jewett's "The Flight of Betsey Lane" (1893), Betsey has visions of attending the Philadelphia Centennial, a veritable temple of material objects. She sees it as her mission to be the representative woman of the poorhouse to attend the exhibition and to bring back some souvenirs (fetishized images of the consumer culture she and others long for) to the inmates of the poorhouse. This exhibition hall is in stark contrast to the Byfleet Poorhouse in which Betsey lives. Her mission to attend the

Centennial is not for any personal gain but to share the events and the gifts she procures for her two best friends living with her in the poorhouse. It is compelling to view Betsey as a representative member of a female benevolent society who tries to help her poorer sisters. Jewett's use of the Centennial Exhibition is telling, and helps us understand the story on a deeper level. The 1876 Centennial Exhibition in Philadelphia highlighted more than any other event the progress in "woman's work, lot, and outlook" (Sander 43). It became a showcase for women's economic independence as "Women representing voluntary groups from coast to coast gathered in the city where the Exchange idea had started four decades earlier to show the strength of their numbers and collective force" (43). These outreach programs and societies, in which women helped other women fallen on hard times produce and sell handiwork on consignment, granted women a degree of independence not generally granted them. "The Centennial was a watershed" in that women could see quite clearly how they could "use the voluntary sector to their economic advantage" and also raise the level of respect for home production, an earlier art and economic form that had fallen into disfavor (43). It is no wonder Betsey feels driven to attend the Centennial, as participation in the exhibition symbolizes in many ways her independence from the atmosphere of the poorhouse, a setting so oppressive to the women inmates.

The quest for economic independence, in Jewett's fiction, to step outside the narrow constraints (spiritually and materially) imposed by indigence, is always initiated by a woman in power—a woman with money. In this way, the woman, whether it is Betsey, the new gift-giver (with the money received from Mrs. Strafford), or Mrs. Strafford, the original gift-giver, is like the typical woman in a voluntary organization. The gift becomes the bond of sisterhood. It has the potential to raise the level of the giver and the recipient. In terms of the "woman's voluntarism" movement, both benefited: it could "promote not only charitable self-help for the needy but also self-improvement among all women," rich and poor alike (Sander 43). In Betsey's case, Mrs. Strafford, a daughter of a grateful former employer, wants to reward Betsey for her kindness and loyalty when she was in the family's employ, and so rewards her with a monetary gift. With this money, Betsey travels to Philadelphia and purchases artifacts of beauty (such as a shawl) for the forlorn women in the poorhouse. This vision of beauty, even though its source is the great Exhibition (an appropriate symbol of the Gilded Age with its excessiveness), becomes far more than a consumer bauble in the hands of Betsey and her sister paupers. Indeed, it becomes a holy relic of sorts, which symbolizes an exchange of all that is most valuable in life. Although not the quest for the Holy Grail, it is a spiritual quest that will allow Betsey to transcend her surroundings (and also one that will culminate, symbolically, with her myopic friend's improved vision). Betsey's socialist philosophy, from start to finish, is, as she proclaims to her friends Lavina Dow and Peggy Bond, "What's for the good o' one's for the good of all" (92). In fact, one of the reasons Betsey ventures forth so courageously to the Centennial in Philadelphia is to procure spectacles for her very myopic friend, Peggy Bond (though the doctor she meets assures her that Peggy needs more than glasses because of her cataract condition and promises to pay a visit to the poorhouse). She is motivated primarily by the needs of others, and her altruistic intentions revolve around restoring her inmate's vision, or perhaps restoring hope in humanity. As Betsey tells her friends when she arrives with her sack of presents, "I felt sure that somebody ought to go from the neighborhood, if it was only for the good o' the rest; and I thought I'd better be the one" (192). Her resolve reflects her growing self-reliance and her developing self-esteem and disdain of those in power at the poorhouse, "I wa'nt goin' to ask the selec'men neither" (192). Compared to Mary W. Freeman's Louisa in "One Good Time," who wants to splurge selfishly in the department stores of New York, Betsey is on a mission: she "wanted to have a real good time" (as she puts it) in order to "collect small presents for almost everybody she knew at home" (188). She squanders money—but only for the pleasures of others ("I fetched ye all a little somethin'," she says [192]), and so, she continues the cycle of generosity the charitable granddaughter of her former employer had started.

Jewett clearly shows that the Byfleet Poorhouse inmates are not at fault for their poverty (and thus inherently critiques the bias of her era)—that their residence in the poorhouse was sometimes only seasonal, in the winter: "old age had impoverished most of them by limiting their power of endurance; but far from lamenting the fact that they were town charges, they rather liked the change and excitement of a winter residence on the poor-farm" (172).[13] Peggy Bond has fallen on hard times because of her failing eyesight; Lavina Dow is afflicted with crippling rheumatism. These are not "types" of sloth and immorality that the typical charitable organizations would point to in cautionary tales about individuals who contributed to their own descent into poverty. Betsey Lane, too, is not one of the stereotypical poor. The narrator exonerates her as well for mismanaging her money and sometimes for being too generous, "by sad misfortune and lavish generosity everything had been scattered [her savings/legacies], and after much illness, which ended in a stiffened arm and more uncertainty, the good soul had sensibly decided that it was easier for the whole town to support her than for a part of it" (174). If generosity is partly to blame for her current indigence, generosity is also the way she regains her stature.

The entire story hinges on a cycle of giving and generosity. Even before the arrival of Mrs. Strafford, the descendant of her old employer from England, Betsey notes the generosity of the aristocratic family whom she cared for, and who, while they were still alive, made sure she was comfortable in her old age. She brags to her inmates, "While there was any of Mis' Gen'ral Thornton's folks left, I wa'nt without visits from the gentry" (177). Mrs. Strafford carries on the tradition of the "visit" and rewards Betsey for having served her family so well. One could point to the class hierarchy in this instance and maintain that the Thorntons/Straffords have an unequal share of power, but Jewett makes it clear that the current generation of Thorntons, in the shape of Mrs. Strafford, feels genuine affection toward Betsey and even treats her as family, promising to send her photos of her family. Tellingly, Betsey asks Mrs. Strafford to send her a small mirror as a favor (and she agrees), since Betsey has not been able to see herself in the mirror since her departure from her household employ at the Thorntons. This small token of affection, the mirror, symbolically would give Betsey a greater sense of self and a new vision.[14] After receiving the "gift" of money from Mrs. Strafford, Betsey is able to get to Philadelphia and find free board through her own good nature and practical ability. In exchange for a free train ride to Philadelphia, Betsey "sews on a couple of buttons" for the trainman. And another compassionate traveler on the train advises her to stay with his distant family relation once she embarks in Philadelphia. It is not as if Jewett is suggesting that one should receive charity for nothing, but rather like Emerson, she fosters a type of dignity that would continue the free flow or cycle of giving. Even the trainman who supposedly offers Betsey "a free ride" asks for the sewing favor in return. And early on, the women at the poorhouse are depicted as picking "a bushel of beans"—as if they are heeding Henry David Thoreau's advice on self-reliance and economy. Finally, the cycle of gift-giving and generosity comes full circle as Betsey returns with her gifts for the poorhouse inmates. There is a final vision of hope and of splendor as we hear the returning Betsey and her two best friends, "set forth *triumphant* toward the poorhouse" (193, emphasis mine). In this way, all the negative associations with the poorhouse have been removed as Betsey has been able to subvert the meaning of poverty.

This dynamic—a sacred exchange of love and of goods—occurs in other Jewett stories, so that consumerism, charity, and poverty are not stigmatized and not antithetical; they come from a common desire to love and to be loved, in the purest sense of the word love, or Christian "caritas," as it connotes charity. In "The Town Poor" (1890), for example, two well-meaning and benevolent women galvanize the townspeople to take responsibility for two elderly sisters, who have lost their property and been turned out of their ancestral home. These poor women, in turn, are granted the opportunity to retrieve their dignity by offering a most humble (but lovingly prepared) meal to the charitable donors, and so, the cycle of giving is perpetuated. In "The Town Poor," Jewett does point an accusing finger at those townspeople who are, initially at least, remiss in their moral obligations to the poor. Mrs. Trimble, who has inherited a modest income from her deceased husband, becomes an "active business woman . . . [who] looked after her own affairs herself, in all weathers" (278). With her warm heart and generosity, she "play[s] the part of Lady Bountiful in the town of Hampden" (179). But she postpones her visit to her lame friend, Rebecca Wright, for too long and chastises herself, "I should have be'n more considerate about fetchin' of you over" (280). More significantly, the two women have postponed their social duty, or "Friendly Visit," as the charitable visit to the poor was called, to the Bray sisters, for too long, and they realize their error when they actually pay their visit. The worst of Rebecca Wright's fears are confirmed when they appear at the Abel Jane household, where the Bray sisters have been "taken in." Jewett condemns the manner in which the impoverished are randomly "taken in" by or assigned to community members' homes. As Rebecca Wright recalls, "I just sat down an' cried good when I found Abel Janes' folks had got hold of them. They always had the name of bein' slack an' poor-spirited, an' they did it just for what they got out o' the town" (280). Thus, it seems as if households take in the poor—not for any genuine charitable reason—but as a way to get an added income.

The real culprit in "The Town Poor" seems to be the governing body that makes these random and mismatched living arrangements. Rebecca Wright places the blame accurately: "The selectmen this last year ain't what we have had" (280). Jewett finds fault with the patriarchal management of charity, as organized by the selectmen and the minister. Indeed, in some ways, she knows intuitively that women are better at being charitable. Like a page from a contemporaneous handbook on Friendly Visiting, this story illustrates a popular notion about women's superiority as visitors of the poor, as indicated in my introductory epigraph: "Women are, in all ordinary cases, by far the best visitors of the poor. A true woman carries with her an atmosphere of influence which makes itself felt" (Thompson 177). Mrs. Trimble and Rebecca Wright, as outside "visitors," can immediately detect the squalor and depression that have befallen the Bray sisters, who have basically forfeited their rights as human beings (being shipped off like cattle) in accepting the verdict of the selectmen: "They give their consent to goin' on the town because they knew they'd got to be dependent, an' so they felt 't would come easier for all than for a few to help 'em. They acted real dignified an' right-minded, *contrary to what most do in such cases,* but they was dreadful anxious to see who would bid 'em off, town-meeting day" (280, emphasis mine). Essentially, this "bidding off" renders the Bray sisters as helpless as slaves. It is telling that Rebecca Wright comments that most paupers do not allow themselves to be removed in as "dignified" a way as the Bray sisters have; certainly, some of Jewett's class biases are apparent in this instance, as Rebecca suggests that the impoverished lack dignity and ought not to resist being removed from their homes. But the living conditions at the Abel Jane household are atrocious, which makes Mrs. Trimble respond "with resentment and the shame of personal responsibility" (285). She makes the resolution that "The girls shall be well settled in the village before another winter, if I pay their board myself"

(285). Governed by this truly charitable impulse, Mrs. Trimble is finally absolved of her guilt in the matter by her final decision to make a political statement—to rebuke the minister with his customary laissez-faire lecture, on "What's everybody's business is nobody's business" (286). She learns to realize that the town poor are everyone's business, not in terms of an economic obligation but rather as a moral obligation (to borrow the terms from David Cheal's introductory epigraph). Moreover, as more than Lady Bountiful, now with a new reformer zeal, Mrs. Trimble decides to take on the entire board of selectmen on her own the next day and to restore the home and its furnishings to the Bray sisters. Like Betsey Lane, Mrs. Trimble redeems herself through her charity.

In "Going to Shrewsbury" (1889) and "Aunt Cynthy Dallett" (1896),[15] Jewett likewise reveals the consequences of unfortunate business practices or deals for the impoverished women who finally must resort to living with family relations. In these stories, this proves to be a viable solution as it leads to a symbiotic relationship between the poor relation and her more economically secure relatives. Both stories act as cautionary tales to show women how to economize or how to be less naïve in economic dealings with those they trust. In "Going to Shrewsbury," Mrs. Peet is forced to sell her farm and to join her nieces because her nephew, "a prosperous money-lender," swindled her out of her farm. Although her nieces treat her well, it is traumatizing for Mrs. Peet; as the narrator describes her fate, "Mrs. Peet was too old . . . to be suddenly transplanted from her native soil" (209). Not long after taking up residence, within a year's time, Mrs. Peet dies. Jewett clearly shows her sympathy toward the displaced, elderly poor woman.

In "Aunt Cynthy Dallett," another displaced woman fares a bit better because of her age. Miss Abby Pendexter represents the woman who has fallen on hard times; again, the depiction resists the conservative view of the poor as deserving of their situation because of bad morals or sloth. Abby loses her job, is forced to sell her chickens, and finally is unable to pay her rent. But a charitable gesture saves the day: delivering mince-pies to her kindhearted but elderly and lonely Aunt Cynthy for the New Year, she discovers that Aunt Cynthy could use a roommate. Actually, it is a case of reverse charity, as her aunt realizes Abby's desperate condition: " . . . she's gittin' along in years . . . she begins to look sort o' set and dried up. . . . She oughtn't to live all alone; she's one that needs company" (317). Once again, the gift generates rewards for the giver and the recipient, as they participate in a flowing circuit, as Emerson would see charity in the most positive sense of the word. And the idea of reflexive charity upholds the principles about charity preached by liberals of the time: "The enlightened benevolence of the present age . . . bids us give the poor 'not alms but a friend.' I would ask rather for both: alms are needed; but alms, to do real and lasting good, must come, and be known and felt to come, from a friend" (Bonaparte 190).[16]

The centrality of the "gift" cannot be overlooked in the Jewett canon. Even the gift of charity is seen as a personal business, and as a two-way street; both giver and recipient must be aware of their common bond. One contemporaneous essay written by a female advocate of Friendly Visiting gave this advice to potential visitors: "We do personal work among the poor, we say; but do we make the poor people feel that it is personal to them? We can make it so by really giving ourselves, not merely our thought and care in their affairs, but telling them from the first something of our own" (Smith, "Education" 206). This attitude of "giving of oneself" is able to help Jewett's female protagonists reach out to the poor as well as to the underclass. Jewett's "Martha's Lady" (1897) can be perceived as a rather dark story in its treatment of the servant class as somehow seeming to be the property of the moneyed class. But one might read the story as entertaining two possibilities—that of an inherent upper-class snobbery (as embodied in Miss Harriet Pyne) and that of an emerging egalitarian relationship between classes (as embodied in the youthful cousin, Helena Vernon).[17] Martha, the servant of the rather ascetic New Englander, Miss Pyne, is overjoyed when Pyne's youthful cousin from Boston arrives, a veritable breath of fresh air in the old stuffy ancestral mansion. The relationship between Martha and Helena blossoms to the point where Martha is almost infatuated by Helena because of her vivacity and generosity. Indeed, Helena does appear to be Martha's "lady," not in any servant-lady relationship, but more as a medieval ideal in chivalry (though that still smacks of class biases with its feudalism). Nonetheless, Helena does seem genuinely fond of the servant Martha and tries to foster that relationship, even at the approach of her wedding, when she wants to invite Martha to the occasion, but the more staid and traditional cousin Harriet reinforces the class boundaries: she feels that "Martha would be out of her element; it was most imprudent and girlish to have thought of such a thing" (255). As Helena embarks for England with her husband the day after the wedding, she disregards any class boundaries by having Harriet take a present back to Martha. It consists of a piece of the wedding cake, and while the other womenfolk around her are hurrying her to leave, Helena still thinks of the servant Martha and wraps up a few tokens in one of the wedding gift boxes: "she still lingered and ran to take one or two trifles from her dressing-table, a little mirror and some scissors that Martha would remember, and one of the pretty handkerchiefs marked with her maiden name" (256).

Although one might argue that these gifts are trifles, they have sentimental value (a nexus of female bonding), and the mirror especially has symbolic value for Martha's developing sense of self.[18] Helena had taught her to feel more proud of herself and to forget about her awkwardness, and so Martha continues to try to catch a semblance of that proud self when she gazes at the mirror Helena has bestowed upon her: "When she looked in the little keepsake mirror she always hoped to see some faint reflection of Helena Vernon, but there was only her own brown old New England face to look back at her wonderingly" (257). Martha never realizes her own self-worth because she feels eclipsed by the magnanimous Helena; she cannot even join the local church because she does not feel worthy. But Helena has taught her a lesson in charity and generosity, and Martha's life takes on new meaning. She follows the traditions Helena has taught her—she adorns her mistress's house with the flowers that so appealed to Helena, she uses the good china and does not save it for holidays, she brings freshly picked cherries to the minister (a practice started on one of Helena's good-natured whims), and on the day of Helena's return, she has decorated the house with lilies and other flowers and proffers the best strawberries she has picked to the returning Helena. Only at the end of the story are all class boundaries crossed with Martha's horrifying epiphany that "Miss Helena is an old woman like me!" (261) and with the good-night kiss that dispenses with all class proprieties. One critic, Glenda Hobbs, has termed the relationship between Martha and Helena as a natural type of Thoreauvian friendship, where both are seen as equal. Further, Hobbs asserts that Helena is truly charitable: "Helena is not motivated by a do-gooding Christianity, an intentional good will; her actions are the natural outgrowth of her affection for Martha rather than expressions of pity" (100).

Just as the wealthy are reminded to throw crumbs to the have-nots on special happy occasions to absolve themselves of guilt (as could be construed in "Martha's Lady" if Helena weren't so genuine), so on Christmas, people of all classes are reminded to think of those less fortunate, those who are lonely and suffering. Jewett's many Christmas and holiday stories that she wrote for women's periodicals are especially telling in the context of charitable giving. In this manner she follows the tradition of the Christmas story as "culture-text," best exemplified by Charles Dickens's *A Christmas Carol.* Paul Davis, who has written extensively about the lasting appeal of Dickens's famous tale, has pointed to its pivotal role as "culture-text" in evoking sympathy for London's urban poor.[19] After reading a parliamentary report on the plight of the city's poor children and women in 1843, Dickens started writing his famous Christmas story, which he hoped would have the effect of a sledgehammer on his audience; Davis views Dickens's tale as the "sledgehammer for the poor" though "wielded with . . . gentleness" (47). Scrooge is redeemed by his charity; in helping others, "he will achieve a kind of immortal life within this life, an immortality of charity" (81); it corresponded in the late Victorian period with "an image of human interdependence and sharing" (83). Jewett's depiction of giving is, similarly, not obligatory but rather symbiotic and beneficial to both the giver and the recipient. We have already seen this is the case in "Aunt Cynthy Dallett," which was called in its earliest publication, "The New-Year Guests." In a holiday story with a similar plot line, "An Empty Purse," Miss Debby Gaines finds herself depressed at Christmas time because she has lost the money she saved for her Christmas gift money.[20] Nonetheless, she keeps the spirit of Christmas alive by mending her old clothes and giving them to the needy; for example, she is mending one of her old petticoats to give to "Old Mrs. Bean, at the poorhouse" (236). In contrast to Miss Debby is the wealthy Mrs. Rivers, who spends her time refurbishing and decorating her house for the holidays. In contrast to Miss Debby who likes to give away Christmas presents, Mrs. Rivers "always found Christmas a melancholy season. She did not like the trouble of giving presents then, or at any other time" (237). Miss Debby knows the art of gift-giving, as she explains, "Presents aren't nothing unless the heart goes with them" (237). She also gets to the parsimonious nature of many New Englanders by saying, "Tis a day when we New England folks can seem to speak right out to each other, and that does us some good" (237).

Miss Debby gives equally to the poor and to the wealthy, even without having money to spend; she baby-sits for a poor widowed woman, so that she might go out and buy presents for her children. She pays a visit to the well-to-do elderly Mrs. Wallis, whose granddaughters have abandoned her for the evening to attend more scintillating Christmas events. Mrs. Wallis concludes that "There are all my pretty presents on the table. . . . Somehow they haven't been very good company; this is the first Christmas in all my life that I have happened to spend quite alone" (240). Miss Debby's visit to the minister is appreciated more than gifts, as we hear that the discouraged minister just needed some kind words from his congregation. And the final good that comes out of the relationship between Miss Debby and Mrs. Rivers on Christmas is that Miss Debby discovers Mrs. Rivers's essential loneliness in her big house and Mrs. Rivers learns to despise her lack of generosity. Mrs. Rivers sends along some presents to Miss Debby with a note about her transformation: after her talk with Miss Debby about Christmas presents, Mrs. Rivers recants her ways, and announces in her note, "I am going right to work to try to make as many people happy as I can. And you must feel that my heart goes with these presents that I send you first. They are some of my own things that I liked, and I send them with love" (240–41). The lesson here is that true presents are given in a sacrificial manner, and that they must come from the heart.

In yet another holiday story, "Mrs. Parkins's Christmas Eve," the stingy woman, Mrs. Parkins, a widow left with a large inheritance from her husband, is admonished for her uncharitable ways. When the minister and his family essentially save her from freezing to death in a snowstorm on Christmas Eve, Mrs. Parkins, by witnessing the Christmas singing, celebration, and gift-exchange by the minister's family, realizes the folly of her miserly ways. By New Year's Day, Mrs. Parkins is a changed woman; she gives freely of herself and her money. She pays a friendly visit to her poor cousin Faber, brings her back to her house for a visit, and even gives her a wagon full of supplies for future provisions. She gives her neighbor, Lucy Deems, a basketful of butternuts.

And most importantly, she gives the minister enough money to take his ailing son to a brilliant surgeon in New York for a "restoration of his health" (156). Although earlier in the story, young Lucy Deems, the child of Parkins's neighbor, has referred to Mrs. Parkins in a compassionate tone, "Isn't Mrs. Parkins real poor, mother" (148), by the end of the story, Mrs. Parkins has discovered the true meaning of Christmas and of Christian giving: "She could no longer live in a mean, narrow world of her own making; she must try to take the world as it is, and make the most of her life" (156). Mrs. Parkins also learns to treat herself compassionately; she starts wearing her best winter bonnet and gives up her practice of wearing the somber felt gray-and-black bonnet she had worn after her husband's death. Significantly, she loses that old hat in the winter storm, and the minister's daughters, finding it in the spring, appropriately decorate the parsonage scarecrow with the rusty hat in the fall.

Examples of such moments of self-transformation abound in many of Jewett's holiday stories. In another Christmas story, "The Becket Girls' Tree," two well-meaning children of a rather middle-class family are left home alone when their parents need to pay a visit to an ailing aunt. Jess, the daughter, is disappointed for she had already crocheted various gifts for her parents, and both she and her brother John were looking forward to decorating the finest Christmas tree for them. But charitable as they are, John and Jess get the fine idea of bringing the tree to the Becket girls, who are actually not girls at all, but two older sisters who have not fared so well in life. The parents return in time to give Christmas presents to the children, a sled for the boy, and gloves and a hood for the girl, as well as some candy. The children, who had earned money from berrying and lobstering, give each other treasures they had been yearning for: John gives Jess a paint-box, and Jess gives her brother a foot-rule. Most importantly, the children learn the real meaning of giving, as they give their beloved tree to the Becket women. They are disappointed that their parents did not see the pleasure on the Becket women's faces, but the mother is aware of the larger gift they have given her, as she tells them about the lesson of giving, "You will find out better the older you grow that the way to have a good time yourself is to make somebody else have one" (99).

Good deeds are usually repaid in manifold ways in Jewett's holiday stories about charity. For example, in "In a Country Practice," the Ashurst family is trying to be generous on Thanksgiving after the recent death of Dr. Ashurst, the father, and with that, their recent impoverishment. The mother exclaims, on seeing the two poor Dent sisters approaching their household, "I wish we had something—I really don't know how to be poor at Thanksgiving time. . . . They shall have a pie at any rate" (217). Immediately after the mother makes this observation, the daughter, Nelly, opens a letter from an unknown benefactor from Cuba, whom the father had helped by lending him a coat and giving him advice. The benefactor leaves a legacy of $50,000 to the Ashurst family. Again, the moral of the story is that good acts are repaid many times over. The doctor was known to always perform charitable acts, "but the fact remained that one heart that seemed at the moment to forget his kindness, has really remembered, and was grateful for years of health and activity, which he had ceased to expect. Out of his wealth he had made return, not only for himself, but for many another beside" (217). The Ashurst family continues to be beneficent and to share their wealth with others, the ex-patients of the father and the neighborhood poor.

Jewett is also aware of misplaced charity, which might be evident in acts of communal or (on a larger-scale) national kindness. In "The Growtown 'Bugle,'" Miss Prudence Fellows is convinced by an ad in a local newspaper that she should give money for a new development in Kansas, a town out West to be called "Growtown." In the process, she will be able to make a fortune of her own. Pleased with her success at helping to found a new town and to become wealthy at the same time, she is not aware, until the end, how poor in spirit she has become. By neglecting the local poor, she does not realize that alms were in order for her closest of neighbors, and so Mrs. Peck dies along with the little girl, Lizzie, whom she was romanticizing about adopting. Miss Prudence Fellows realizes her guilt as she faints: "Her neighbors had starved within the sound of her voice, while she made money and took thought of those at a distance. She never felt so poor in her life as when she came to herself again" (131). Two schools of charitable thinking are critiqued here: the idea that charities were more aware of the plight of the poor in distant parts of the country or of the world (the minister in the story even thought of trying to get Miss Prudence to invest in a missionary cause) and the belief that it was ethical to remove poor children from their natural parents and real homes. In a recent critique of such charitable practices, Stephen O'Connor exposes the story of the minister Charles Loring Brace, mentioned previously as the founder of the Children's Aid Society (1853), which sponsored the "Newsboys' Lodging House" (1854) and the "Girls' Lodging House" (1862). For the "good" of impoverished children, he advocated for the program to remove them from their parental homes and send them on "orphan trains" to be resettled in families in the West and Midwest; this "orphan train" campaign continued between 1854 and 1929. Astute critics during Jewett's time knew the shortcomings of such practices, and R. E. Thompson asserts in his manual for visits to the poor that "the unnecessary separation of children from their parents is always to be avoided" (179).[21] Jewett does present the proper way of caring for those far away and also for unfortunate children in the story, "A Garden Story," where the protagonist, Miss Ann Dunning, who has proven to have a veritable green thumb and who has shared her delightful flowers with the rest of her community, decides to take in a poor city girl for a week. Poor Peggy McAllister is a true orphan, with no living relative in Boston, but she so benefits from her visit in the country with Miss Dunning that the church authorities allow her to be adopted by Miss Dunning. At first, Miss Dunning sees this as a potentially heavy burden, but they become fast friends as "house-mates." Miss Dunning learns that she can raise children as well as she had raised flowers. Little Peggy learns the lessons from the heart by also giving to the community, as she convinces old Miss Dunning to send her unwanted flowers and plants (as seedlings) to the poor people in the city hospital. Ultimately, Miss Dunning's gardening seems sacred, as she is able to give life as unstintingly to the abandoned girl, who comes to love her as a relative. Again, the symbiotic relationship between the giver and the recipient is perpetuated.

In this context of Jewett's gift-giving, it is helpful to look at anthropologist Marcel Mauss's "moral conclusions," as he calls them on the modern practice of gift-giving. Studying gift-giving in primitive societies, he deduces that "The theme of the gift, of freedom and obligation in the gift, of generosity and self-interest in giving, reappear in our own society like the resurrection of a dominant motif long forgotten" (66). He suggests that just as courtesies need to be repaid, so do gifts, though they might not be of the material kind. Like the social worker and reformer Zephra Smith (see above) who believed that we can only make an imprint on the poor person's life by sharing our common experiences and acting from personal and not meddlesome love, Mauss believes in a reciprocal relationship between the giver and the recipient:

> Much of our everyday morality is concerned with the question of obligation and spontaneity in the gift. It is our good fortune that all is not yet couched in terms of purchase and sale. Things have higher values which are *emotional as well as material; indeed in some cases the values are entirely emotional.* Our morality is not so commercial. We still have people and classes who uphold past customs and we bow to them on special occasions and at certain periods of the year. (63, emphasis mine)

This type of sacred exchange of a gift is important to Jewett's country women, and especially, as Mauss points out, on "special occasions," the holidays that reinforce our connection to others. Mauss, too, believes that individuals cannot be happy or at peace unless they join the common cycle of giving, unless their wealth is redistributed (81). In this manner he feels that economy is intrinsically allied with morality and with aesthetics.

Charity is a secret hiding place or refuge for Jewett's female characters in an increasingly materialistic world. The gift becomes more than just a material object; it becomes a public or communal expression of charitable feelings. For example, in *The Country of the Pointed Firs,* the gift of love from Nathan Todd, initially meant for "poor" Joanna, is circulated—the exotic coral brooch moves from Mrs. Todd to Joanna, back to Mrs. Todd, and finally, the pin is given to the narrator. With this gift exchange, the women are united in the isolation the brooch represents. Captain Todd, in his wanderings around the world, bequeaths the symbolic legacy of isolation to Mrs. Todd and poor Joanna, who are also stranded on distant shores. And the narrator becomes part of that isolation, as she receives the brooch upon leaving.[22] Nevertheless, their acts of charity allow them to rise above their isolation and give them some sense of connectedness. The destiny of all Jewett women is bound together in the gift (whether material or emotional) or in a simple shared meal—uniting all classes, from the benefactress to the impoverished and homeless. Truly, in Jewett's works, with few exceptions, the poor are not the victims, but rather, those poor in spirit become the victims and the outsiders.

Notes

1. Recently, Jewett critics have focused on the dark side of women's lack of bonding in Jewett's fiction. Whereas earlier feminist critics, like Josephine Donovan (in *New England Local Color Literature*) and the early Sandra Zagarell (in "Narrative of Community"), praised Jewett for establishing beneficial communities of women, more recent critics look at class boundaries in her work that limit women's connection to each other.

Sarah Way Sherman, in her recent essay on Jewett, "Party Out of Bounds," suggests that the distance between the classes can never be reconciled. And Alison Easton, in "Negotiating Class in Jewett," shows how class differences are more powerful than "gender commonalities" and that "class boundaries are not transcended" in most of the work of Jewett (209; 211). Indeed, in her analysis of "Martha's Lady," which I discuss later, Easton points out how upper-class and working-class women are brought together artificially, "in a structure that reinforced unbridgeable distinctions even when it expected servants to create a home (which was not theirs) by standards which were not theirs" (118). In "The Gray Mills of Farley" (1898), which Easton also discusses in terms of the working-class background of the town, I see the small orphan girl, Maggie, as being a victim of the large industrial machine of labor. Maggie lives at the "mercy of her neighbors" (268), and she seems to be always scrounging for lodging.

Sandra Zagarell, in her recent essay on Jewett, recants her early position on the beneficence of Jewett's women by showing their xenophobia in *Country*. Cynthia J. Davis seems to revise the early positive assessment of Jewett's community of women by showing how "The Foreigner" portrays "the possibility of an outside, of a world where ethnic differences evaporate through the transformative, homogenizing, homoerotic power of women's love, even as it constitutes that outside as marginal, ephemeral, and as already imperiled . . . 'by the world of men's activities'" (105). I see this positive unifying homoerotic bond that rejects class distinctions in "Martha's Lady" as well.

In her most recent essay, Josephine Donovan undercuts a classist reading of Jewett, the kind recently espoused by critics.

2. Brace is discussed later in my essay as well. Although of a kinder disposition than others, he does condone visits by charity bureaus to ascertain whether the poor are worthy to receive aid: "Cases of poverty and misfortune might be visited and examined by experts in charity, and the truth ascertained, where ordinary individuals, inquiring, would be certain to be deceived" (386).

3. Earlier in Puritan times as well as in early New England days, almsgiving was actually done by the greater community, who claimed responsibility for the impoverished individuals. See Trattner's chapter on charity in colonial America, 16–29; "Most communities attacked the problem of poverty with a high degree of civic responsibility" (28). As Trattner also points out, during the height of the "scientific charity" movement

in the late nineteenth century, "voluntarism," which was "viewed earlier as a civic duty," "became, instead, a privilege granted by agencies to those who accepted their authority and discipline" (105).

Some social critics and reformers of Jewett's time also felt that charity in the country was preferable to the system of charity in the city, for, among other things, "Country people can give employment, friendship, membership in the family, hospitality" (Smith, "Country Help for City Charities" 215). Jewett probably would have agreed with this assessment of rural charity.

Wenocur and Reisch point out the problems of the growing professionalization of social work, and with that the decline of true voluntarism. In the 1890s, "the importance of volunteers in social work, especially friendly visitors, rapidly declined" (36). By the early years of the twentieth century, "more than 50% of the major COS [charitable organization societies] had abandoned the use of friendly visitors entirely. . . . Soon volunteers were restricted to carefully defined and supervised activities and, in many cities, did little more than office work" (36).

4. For studies about nineteenth-century scientific philanthropy and about the debates on indoor versus outdoor relief, as well as about narrow-minded and biased views of judging the poor as immoral or degenerate, see Katz (90–156); Leiby (90–135); Trattner (79–139); Warner (115–262); Wenocur and Reisch (30–91); Woodroofe (77–117).

5. In a study of earlier practices of charity, Mary Templin's analysis of women's benevolence in panic fiction (in this volume) shows how the middle-class woman could sometimes retrieve her fallen status by lording it over the poorer women—by participating in acts of charity.

6. For a view of the poorhouse, in terms of positive or negative connotations, as "panoptic" or "sentimental," see Karen Tracey's essay in this volume. For the often-invasive character of public relief, see Debra Bernardi's essay in this volume.

7. Cf. Sumner, who concludes quite similarly about the ill effects of charity on the slothful man—and of inequities in giving: "A free man in a free democracy derogates from his rank if he takes a favor for which he does not render an equivalent" (34).

8. See my notes three and twelve for a discussion of charitable giving in Puritan times. Cf. Thoreau's more altruistic and romantic view of charity to Emerson's begrudging view: "The town's poor seem to me often to live the most independent lives of any. May be they are simply great enough to receive without misgiving" (*Walden* 328).

9. See Paula Blanchard's biography of Jewett, where she maintains that Annie Fields perceived her charity work "from the vantage point of her own class prejudices" (which at times saw the vices of the poor as the cause of their destitution) (130–31). Like Easton, who focuses on *Deephaven* in her analysis of class tensions, Blanchard asserts that Fields's "mixture of condescension and compassion is typical of women of her class and time and is reminiscent of Kate Lancaster of *Deephaven,* who was based on one or several of Sarah's earlier friends" (131). Blanchard concludes, though, that Fields "genuinely sympathized with the poor and labored to help them break free of the cycle of despair" (131). I feel that Jewett also maintained this attitude of respect and compassion toward the poor.

10. For the importance of the material object as fetish in this Gilded Age era, see my essay on fetishism in Mary Wilkins Freeman.

11. Charlotte Perkins Gilman is dismayed by the growing consumerism of modern women and laments their lack of productivity in *Women and Economics*. Indeed, unlike Jewett, Gilman sees the women as takers, and not as givers. She comments that women's parasitism wears away at men's strength. She describes women's inertia in not being able to produce and to give: "We have made for ourselves this endless array of 'horse-leech's daughters, crying, Give! give!' To consume food, to consume clothes, to consume houses and furniture and decorations and ornaments and amusements, to take and take and take forever,—from one man if they are virtuous, from many if they are vicious, but always to take and never to think of giving anything in return except their womanhood" (118–19). Gilman is quite strong in her indictment of women "as the priestess of the temple of consumption, as the limitless demander of things to use up" (120). Jewett feels that women, as givers, are more empowered in their economic influence.

12. Moral obligation was the underlying motivation behind charitable practices in colonial New England (for both genders) and for women in the early nineteenth century. (See also note three, above.) For a discussion of women's charitable work in antebellum America, see Ginzberg's study, which I cite in the text. In Puritan New England, the community felt compelled to do good works and to care for the town poor. As David Rothman asserts, "The poor [in colonial times] were usually spared the animosity and suspicion as well as the ameliorative effects of their neighbors" (156). Trattner also demonstrates that the colonists "accepted responsibility for so many of their indigent; they did not allocate blame for poverty, nor, for the most part, did they blame or isolate the needy" (27). There was a religious obligation felt by community members to take care of the indigent, provided that the individuals were part of the community, and not outsiders (Jones 153–65; Rothman 3–19; Trattner 16–31; Wright 14–23). Needy members of society, whether they were aging parents, single mothers, or ailing widows would be cared for by the community at large; the individual was taken in by a relative or circulated through various townspeople's homes during the year. Civic responsibility was the protocol, and communal wealth was to be shared. Jewett's small-town women seem to hark back to this earlier period of New England benevolence, whereas the power structures that oppress the impoverished women reflect the late-nineteenth-century practices of organized, scientific charity. However, one could detect the tensions that would continue to haunt American practices of benevolence in the attitudes of some Puritan New England leaders. Even though common sentiment among Puritans showed their "special obligation to bring the duty of neighborly and brotherly love, everywhere professed, into 'familiar and constant practice'" (Bremner 9), sometimes moral leaders, like Cotton Mather, feared "that an excess of benevolence might nourish and confirm the idle in their evil ways" (Bremner 14). The idea, according to Mather, was to give, but to give wisely.

13. Jewett seems to know intuitively that public or outdoor charity, where charity is given to the poor at home, is preferable to private charity, where poor are removed from home and put into an almshouse. The happiest Jewett paupers find relief with

their family or through public relief in their own homes; the almshouse is acceptable only, as in the case of "The Flight of Betsey Lane," when the residence is temporary and seasonal, such as in the winter. Great controversy in two types of relief, outdoor (to the poor living in their own homes) and indoor (institutional support, in terms of almshouses), was generated in national debates by various charitable organizations. Franklin B. Sanborn, chair of the NCCC (National Conference of Charities and Correction) in 1890, maintained that is was dangerous to break up families, and he called for "household aid" for families in distress (220).

14. Vision, in terms of the spectacles and of the mirror that Betsey asks for, plays a significant role in this story. In "Martha's Lady," discussed later, the mirror as a present from the mistress to her maid is also relevant. See Jenijoy LaBelle's study of the mirror as "a tool of self-exploration and self-discovery" in women's fiction (185).

15. "Aunt Cynthy Dallett" was first published as "The New-Year Guests" in *Harper's Bazaar* (January 11, 1896).

16. Charles J. Bonaparte, the grandnephew of Napoleon, was a distinguished citizen (and attorney) in Baltimore society and even presided over the Charity Organization Society of Baltimore for many years (Pumphrey 187n).

17. See Margaret Roman, in her gender study of Jewett. Roman asserts that in Jewett, "the aristocratic, or upper-class women are removed from the natural landscape" and are thus as limited as the paralyzed men who have "subscribed to the patriarchal system" (81).

18. See note fourteen above on the significance of the mirror in women's writing.

19. Paul Davis's book is a reception study of Dickens's *A Christmas Carol,* from its publication to the modern day. Interestingly, in the 1840s, during the period it was published, the tale was perceived as exemplifying the popular mythology that conceived "the country as the place of simple innocence and the city as the seat of corruption and vanity" (36). By the time Jewett was writing, these distinctions between city and country no longer held, as poverty seemed universal, especially in the small deteriorating shipping communities in Maine that Jewett knew too well. Although the redemptive bond in Dickens seems to be a patriarchal bond—between father and son (Bob and Tim representing the "patriarchal Victorian ideal" [Davis 83])—for Jewett, that bond is maternal—as witnessed by the givers and recipients in her Christmas stories. Note also Sarah Way Sherman's discussion of Jewett's "The Christmas Ghosts," an unpublished story, where the protagonist is redeemed by the visit of her dead mother; the bond between daughter and deceased mother makes the gift-giving of the season seem extraneous (*Sarah Orne Jewett* 60–63). For more on the maternal bond to charity, see Jill Bergman's essay in this volume.

20. The next several stories I discuss are from Richard Cary's edition of Jewett's uncollected stories. Here I would like to mention the original dates and places of publication: "An Empty Purse," *Boston Evening Transcript,* December 21, 1895; "Mrs. Parkins's Christmas Eve," *Ladies' Home Journal* 8 (December 1890); "The Becket Girls' Tree," *The Independent* 36 (January 3, 1884); "In a Country Practice," *Philadelphia Press,* November 27, 1894; "The Growtown 'Bugle,'" *Harper's Weekly* 32 (August 18, 1888); "A Garden

Story," *The Independent* 38 (July 22, 1886). Indeed, there are many stories of the Christmas genre in which women or children learn the meaning of charity. See, also, for example, "A Christmas Guest," *Wide Awake* 24 (January 1887), where a young child gives shelter unwittingly to a general, who later pays her back generously with money as well as a visit from his family. The young girl and his daughter become fast friends.

21. For another perspective, see the report by the Massachusetts Board of State Charities (in 1868), which seemed to view the business of farming out orphan and friendless children to real homes as positive, especially over their being sequestered in almshouses. The report maintains that visitors are making sure that the children are properly placed in good homes and so "Cases of injustice and abuse are the exception" (155).

22. The passing down of the brooch, like the hopelessness of Bartleby's dead letters that haunts the lawyer-narrator in Melville's story about charity, "Bartleby the Scrivener," also is an indication of Jewett's contention that we must be our sisters' keepers.

Interestingly, Derrida shows the impossibility of true gift-giving in the context of an earthly economy—and he discusses the Christian notion of sacrifice and death as the pinnacle of giving.

Works Cited

Blanchard, Paula. *Sarah Orne Jewett: Her World and Her Work.* Radcliffe Biography Series. Reading: Addison-Wesley, 1994.

Bonaparte, Charles. "The Ethics of Organized Charity." Pumphrey and Muriel 188–191.

Brace, Charles Loring. *The Dangerous Classes of New York, and Twenty Years among Them.* 1872. Washington, D.C.: National Association of Social Workers Classic Series, 1973.

Bremner, Robert H. *American Philanthropy.* 2nd ed. Chicago: U of Chicago P, 1988.

Cary, Richard, ed. *The Uncollected Short Stories of Sarah Orne Jewett.* Waterville: Colby College P, 1971.

Cather, Willa, ed. *"The Country of the Pointed Firs" and Other Stories.* New York: Doubleday, 1989.

Cheal, David. *The Gift Economy.* New York: Routledge, 1988.

Davis, Cynthia J. "Making the Strange(r) Familiar: Sarah Orne Jewett's 'The Foreigner.'" *Breaking Boundaries: New Perspectives on Women's Regional Writing.* Ed. Sherrie A. Inness and Diana Royer. Iowa City: U of Iowa P, 1997. 88–108.

Davis, Paul. *The Lives and Times of Ebenezer Scrooge.* New Haven: Yale UP, 1990.

Derrida, Jacques. *The Gift of Death.* Trans. David Wills. Chicago: U of Chicago P, 1992.

Donovan, Josephine. "Jewett on Race, Class, Ethnicity, and Imperialism: A Reply to Her Critics." *Colby Quarterly* 38.4 (December 2002): 403–16.

———. *New England Local Color Literature: A Woman's Tradition.* New York: Ungar, 1983.

Easton, Alison. "'How Clearly the Gradations of Society were Defined': Negotiating

Class in Sarah Orne Jewett." *Jewett and Her Contemporaries: Reshaping the Canon.* Ed. Karen Kilcup and Thomas S. Edwards. Gainesville: UP of Florida, 1999. 207–22.

Elbert, Monika. "The Displacement of Desire: Fetishism and Consumerism in Mary Wilkins Freeman." *Legacy: A Journal of American Women Writers* 19.2 (2002): 192–215.

Emerson, Ralph Waldo. "Gifts." *Essays and Lectures.* Ed. Joel Porte. New York: Library of America, 1983. 535–38.

Gilman, Charlotte Perkins. *Women and Economics.* 1898. New York: Harper and Row, 1966.

Ginzberg, Lori D. *Women and the Work of Benevolence: Morality, Politics, and Class in the Nineteenth-Century United States.* New Haven: Yale UP, 1990.

Hobbs, Glenda. "Pure and Passionate: Female Friendship in Sarah Orne Jewett's 'Martha's Lady.'" *Critical Essays on Sarah Orne Jewett.* Ed. Gwen L. Nagel. Boston: G. K. Hall, 107–18.

Hofstadter, Richard. *Social Darwinism in American Thought.* Boston: Beacon, 1944.

"Homes for Orphan and Friendless Children." Pumphrey and Muriel 155–56.

Jewett, Sarah Orne. "Aunt Cynthy Dallett." 1896. Cather 306–20.

———. "The Becket Girls' Tree." 1884. Cary 90–91.

———. "An Empty Purse." 1895. Cary 236–41.

———. "The Flight of Betsey Lane." 1893. Cather 172–93.

———. "A Garden Story." 1886. Cary 106–10.

———. "Going to Shrewsbury." 1889. Cather 208–17.

———. "The Growtown 'Bugle.'" 1888. Cary 124–31.

———. "In a Country Practice." 1894. Cary 212–18.

———. "Martha's Lady." 1897. Cather 244–61.

———. "Mrs. Parkins's Christmas Eve." 1880. Cary 146–57.

———. "The Town Poor." 1890. Cather 278–89.

Jones, Douglas Lamar. "The Transformation of the Law of Poverty in Eighteenth-Century Massachusetts." *Law in Colonial Massachusetts, 1630–1900.* Ed. Frederick S. Allis, Jr. Boston: Colonial Society of Massachusetts, 1984. 153–90.

Katz, Michael B. *Poverty and Policy in American History.* New York: Academic Press, 1983.

Kellogg, Rev. D. O. "The Principle and Advantage of Association in Charities." Pumphrey and Muriel 174–76.

Kies, Marietta. *Institutional Ethics.* 1894. Ed. Dorothy G. Rogers. London: Thoemmes Press, 2003.

LaBelle, Jenijoy. *Herself Beheld: The Literature of the Looking Glass.* Ithaca: Cornell UP, 1988.

Leiby, James. *A History of Social Welfare and Social Work in the United States.* New York: Columbia UP, 1978.

Lowell, Josephine Shaw. "The Economic and Moral Effects of Public Outdoor Relief." *Proceedings of National Conference of Charities and Corrections.* 1890. Pumphrey and Muriel 221–26.

Mauss, Marcel. *The Gift: Forms and Functions of Exchange in Archaic Societies.* New York: Norton, 1967.

O'Connor, Stephen. *Orphan Trains: The Story of Charles Loring Brace and the Children He Saved and Failed.* Boston: Houghton Mifflin, 2001.

Pumphrey, Ralph E., and W. Muriel, eds. *The History of American Social Work: Readings in Its Philosophical and Institutional Development.* New York: Columbia UP, 1961.

Rogers, Dorothy. "Private Virtue in Public Life: Marietta Kies's Challenge to Hegel." New Jersey Regional Philosophy Association. April 21, 2001. 13 pp. Online. Montclair State University, March 30, 2004. <http://www.american-philosophy.org/>.

Roman, Margaret. *Sarah Orne Jewett: Reconstructing Gender.* Tuscaloosa: U of Alabama P, 1992.

Rothman, David J. *The Discovery of the Asylum: Social Order and Disorder in the New Republic.* Boston: Little, Brown, 1971.

Sanborn, Franklin. "Indoor and Outdoor Relief." Report of the Standing Committee, National Conference of Charities and Correction. 1890. Pumphrey and Muriel 219–21.

Sander, Kathleen Waters. *The Business of Charity: The Woman's Exchange Movement, 1832–1900.* Urbana: U of Illinois P, 1998.

Scott, Anne Firor. *Natural Allies: Women's Associations in American History.* Urbana: U of Illinois P, 1993.

Sherman, Sarah Way. "Party Out of Bounds: Gender and Class in Jewett's 'The Best China Saucer.'" *Jewett and Her Contemporaries: Reshaping the Canon.* Ed. Karen Kilcup and Thomas S. Edwards. Gainesville: UP of Florida, 1999. 223–50.

———. *Sarah Orne Jewett: An American Persephone.* Hanover: UP of New England, 1989.

Smith, Zilpha. "Country Help for City Charities." 1888. Pumphrey and Muriel 214–18.

———. "The Education of the Friendly Visitor." *Proceedings: National Conference of Charities and Corrections.* 1892. Pumphrey and Muriel 203–7.

Sumner, William Graham. *What Social Classes Owe to Each Other.* 1883. Caldwell: Caxton, 1989.

Thompson, Rev. R. E. *Manual for Visitors among the Poor.* 1879. Pumphrey and Muriel 176–81.

Thoreau, Henry David. *The Illustrated Walden.* Ed. J. Lyndon Shanley. Princeton: Princeton UP, 1973.

Tice, Karen W. *Tales of Wayward Girls and Immoral Women: Case Records and the Professionalization of Social Work.* Urbana: U of Illinois P, 1998.

Trattner, Walter I. *From Poor Law to Welfare State: A History of Social Welfare in America.* New York: The Free Press, 1994.

Warner, Amos G. *American Charities: A Study in Philanthropy and Economics.* New Brunswick: Transaction, 1989.

Wenocur, Stanley, and Michael Reisch. *From Charity to Enterprise: The Development of American Social Work in a Market Economy.* Urbana: U of Illinois P, 1989.

Woodroofe, Kathleen. *From Charity to Social Work in England and the United States.* London: Routledge and Kegan Paul, 1968.

Wright, Conrad Edick. *The Transformation of Charity in Postrevolutionary New England.* Boston: Northeastern UP, 1992.

Zagarell, Sandra A. "*Country's* Portrayal of Community and the Exclusion of Difference." *New Essays on* The Country of the Pointed Firs. Ed. June Howard. New York: Cambridge UP, 1994. 39–60.

———. "Narrative of Community: The Identification of a Genre." *Signs* 13.21 (Spring 1988): 498–527.

7

"Oh the Poor Women!"

Elizabeth Stuart Phelps's Motherly Benevolence

Jill Bergman

> It is certain that I very early had the conviction that a mother was a being of power and importance to the world.
>
> —Elizabeth Stuart Phelps, *Chapters from a Life*

Elizabeth Stuart Phelps (1844–1911), the prolific and popular nineteenth-century writer, was deeply interested in benevolence, and many of her novels deal with it. One of her earliest stories, "The Tenth of January" published in the *Atlantic Monthly* in 1868, described the 1860 collapse of the Pemberton mill in Lawrence, Massachusetts, an accident that resulted in the deaths of many of the 750 mill employees. Phelps, who had been sixteen years old when the accident occurred just a few miles from her home in Andover, credits this event with heightening her awareness of the working classes. In her autobiography, she explains:

> Upon the map of our young fancy the great mills were sketched in lightly; we looked up from the restaurant ice-cream to see the "hands" pour out for dinner, a dark and restless, but a patient throng. . . .
>
> Sometimes we counted the great mills as we drove up Essex Street . . . but this was an idle, aesthetic pleasure. We did not think about the mill-people; . . . One January we were forced to think about the mills with curdling horror, which no one living in that locality when the tragedy happened will forget. (88–89)

Her engagement with this event intensified several years later:

> At the time this tragedy occurred, I felt my share of its horror, like other people; but no more than that. My brother, being of the privileged sex, was sent over to see the scene; but I was not allowed to go.

> Years after, I cannot say just how many, the half-effaced negative came back to form under the chemical of some new perception of the significance of human tragedy.
>
> It occurred to me to use the event as the basis of a story. (91)

In this multilayered event—combining the mill's collapse from which she was barred as a woman, her later reflection upon it, and her use of the event to write a story—coalesce Phelps's interest in human suffering, her awareness of "the peculiar needs of women as a class" (*Chapters* 99), and her commitment to writing, a joining that would inform her literary theory for the next forty years. Defending her status as a realistic writer in the face of William Dean Howells's criticism of writers who "still helplessly pointed the moral in all they did" (*Chapters* 260), Phelps vehemently asserted that a great writer could not lose sight of morality: "In any highly-formed or fully-formed creative power, the 'ethical' as well as the 'aesthetical sense' is developed. Where 'the taste' is developed at the expense of 'the conscience,' the artist is incomplete" (*Chapters* 262).

Following her conscience, Phelps constructed the act of writing as an avenue for benevolence—both as a way of comforting suffering readers and of offering instruction in benevolent behavior—and in this way, she claimed for herself a benevolent role as a writer. She theorized and dramatized benevolence as a personal, familial reform particularly available to women and indebted to the antebellum ethos of domesticity. Moreover, she cast this motherly benevolence as distinct from—and superior to—religiously oriented reform models of the antebellum era as well as the institutionalized and formal postbellum reform models. This maternal model gave rise to contradictions in her work, however. While Phelps's maternal metaphor holds promise for a feminist and socialist vision, calling for a close and affectionate connection between benefactor and recipient of care, the model does have limitations. Her motherly position allows her as an author—and her middle-class readers as potential reformers—to solidify her middle-class status by maintaining a position of superiority over the "children" of the model. Phelps's notion of motherly benevolence, then, is a double-edged sword that encourages benevolent behavior and grants authority to middle-class women but undermines the possibility of sisterhood across class lines.

The Motherly Writer

As she reflected on her life in her autobiography, *Chapters from a Life* (1896), Phelps conceived of the act of writing as a form of and site for benevolence, and she described her writing as a distinctly feminine endeavor, an act she linked closely to mothering. The subject of mothering and motherlessness became very real to Phelps at the age of eight, when her mother died in childbirth. Her mother's life and death had a profound impact on the young Phelps who took her name (she had been christened Mary Gray)[1] and followed in her footsteps as a writer (her mother had been a popular author as well). She describes herself wearing her mother's old fur cape as she wrote, and while she initially donned the cape for warmth in the attic where she used to write, the symbolic import of invoking her mother's spirit through the garment is hard to overlook.[2]

Her very popular first novel, *The Gates Ajar* (1868), depicts the suffering of women who had lost loved ones in the Civil War and gives some insight into the theory of comfort that would come to inform Phelps's ideas about benevolence. Here Phelps lays the groundwork for her alignment with the sentimentalism popular before the Civil War. The novel's central conflict is between the two forces that attempt to help the protagonist Mary through her grief over her brother. On the one hand, the religious establishment—represented by male characters in the novel—preaches to Mary and condemns her grief as a sign that she loved her brother too much—to the point of idolatry—and casts her grief as the sin of questioning God's ways. Phelps critiques this model as anti-sentimental, deriving from an abstract, disembodied notion of personhood. In contrast, Mary's aunt, Winifred Forceythe, represents a motherly, sympathetic response expressed in physical closeness.[3] Upon her arrival, although Winifred offers to withhold her kiss because she is wet from the rain, Mary is drawn to her comforting presence: "I don't know what possessed me, whether it was the sudden, sweet feeling of kinship with something alive, or whether it was her face or her voice, or all together, but I said:—'I don't think you are too wet to be kissed,' and threw my arms about her neck" (23). Understanding and accepting Mary's grief, Winifred comforts Mary and helps her develop a view of heaven as a domestic haven, complete with pianos, front porches, and—

significantly—physical bodies, where she can imagine her brother being quite comfortable, and can look forward to her reunion with him there.[4]

According to Phelps's account in her autobiography, her purpose in writing *The Gates Ajar* resembled Aunt Winifred's dealing with Mary: Phelps sought to comfort suffering women. She saw her message as conflicting directly with religious leaders who tried to address mourning women's needs through religion and doctrine:

> For it came to seem to me, as I pondered these things in my own heart, that even the best and kindest forms of our prevailing beliefs had nothing to say to an afflicted woman that could help her much. Creeds and commentaries and sermons were made by men. What tenderest of men knows how to comfort his own daughter when her heart is broken? (98)

With her mention of the father's inadequacy, Phelps invokes the mother, whom she credits with a natural facility for comforting. The motherly comfort she modeled through the character of Winifred Forceythe gave Phelps the opportunity to mother the many readers who wrote to her in what she describes as a "New England snowstorm" of letters (*Chapters* 122). Both men and women wrote to her, but as she explains, she felt a closer bond to the women: "But the women—oh, the poor women! I felt less afraid to answer them. Their misery seemed to cry in my arms like a child who must be comforted. I wrote to them—I wrote without wisdom or caution or skill, only with the power of being sorry for them, and the wish to say so" (127). Describing her readers as children to be comforted, Phelps metaphorically embodies a mother—clad in her own mother's fur cape—physically comforting the heartbroken in her arms. Significantly, this act of comforting arises not out of training but out of natural inclination and the spontaneity of emotional, physical response, a distinction that would become important to her theory of benevolence.

In this self-portrait, as well as in her fiction, Phelps distinguishes her theory of benevolence from two schools prevalent in the nineteenth century United States: evangelical, moral reform and institutionalized benevolence.[5] As Lori Ginzberg points out, much of the benevolent reform work of the antebellum era was inextricably connected to evangelical reform.[6] Jane Tompkins describes the work of the New York City

Tract Society as exemplary of this movement. This organization sought to bring a religious tract to each poor family once a month, a practice that grew out of the belief that "the only real help one could offer another person, rich or poor, was not material but spiritual" (594). As Tompkins explains, this belief informed the sentimental genre prominent at this time, in which the important arena for action was not the world but was the human heart. As a result, when the Tract Society's annual report depicts a benevolent visitor's attendance upon a woman dying of consumption, there is virtually no mention of physical needs met. Instead, the visitor attends to the spiritual needs of the woman facing death (Tompkins 594–95). Phelps criticized this type of reform in *The Gates Ajar* and, as we shall see, in her 1870 novel *Hedged In.* Historians have noted that in the latter half of the nineteenth century, benevolent work shifted its focus "from the religious to the secular," seeking to provide material aid (Sáez 164–65). With this shift, the work also became increasingly organized and professionalized.[7] Phelps participated in the temperance movement for several years and apparently found some value in this type of reform effort. However, as her work indicates, she prefers the spontaneous and personal nature of her motherly benevolence over such organized reform, which she describes as requiring training and preparation.

Phelps provides an example of her notion of motherly benevolence with a scene from her own life. One evening in Gloucester (the seaside town where she spent her summers) a murder took place in a local saloon as the result of a drunken brawl. She overhears locals discussing the event and stops to get the particulars. Learning that one man has been stabbed to death by another, Phelps asks after the widow; specifically, she wonders if "any woman [has] gone to her" yet (*Chapters* 203). Receiving a negative answer, she "turned [her] horse and drove straight to the smitten family" (203). When Phelps arrives at the home of the widow, she waits a moment to observe and determine how she should proceed. As she looks on, a neighbor responds, a "big, red woman," by Phelps's description. This woman tells the new widow to "Be still . . . and have the patience of God." Phelps does not find this a satisfactory act of comfort, so she steps in:

> In point of fact, nothing and nobody quieted the woman; and so I went up, saying no words at all, and took her in my arms.

> For a little her wailing continued steadily; then I saw, at last, that her eyes had fallen upon my gloves. They were white, like the rest of my dress; the room was heavy with the advancing dusk, and I suppose they made a spot of light, by which her frenzied sight was arrested. Her sobbing broke; she turned, and looked up into my face. Still I did not speak, but only held her quietly. (*Chapters* 204–5)

Phelps responds to this situation in a decidedly physical, familiar, and instinctual manner. She counters the distanced, religious comfort offered by the "big, red woman" with her own motherly comfort that looks first to the widow's emotional needs. Taking the woman into her arms, Phelps emphasizes connection between herself and the widow over separation and individualism. Marianne Noble has made a similar observation in her treatment of *Uncle Tom's Cabin:*

> Stowe idealizes bodily activities—feeding, sitting on laps and touching faces, dancing and rolling on the floor together, tickling one another or pulling one another's toes—as physical means by which individuals construct intersubjective, non-individuated identities. When, in the opening of the novel, Chloe alternately feeds her baby and herself, and when the baby subsequently buries her fat hands in Tom's hair, Stowe offers visual images of the way bodies serve as a means *not* of separating the "me" from the "not-me," but of extending the "me" to the "not-me." (295–96)

According to Noble, Stowe and writers like her used this construction of nonindividuated identities to bring feeling into dominant ways of thinking and reasoning. They sought to "pierce through anaesthetizing abstractions and make readers think through the subjective responses of intuition, imagination, and sympathetic extensions to others" (295).

Phelps participates in a similar project in her benevolence literature. Characterizing her reformer as a maternal figure facilitates physical affection between the giver and receiver of benevolence. More, with this relationship, she establishes the interconnectedness of individuals and emphasizes the possibility of a relational identity. With her story of comforting the widow, Phelps shows her credentials to promote benevolent behavior among her readers. Indeed, she seems to feel somewhat defensive about her own benevolent activity. Anxious to cast her writing as a site of motherly benevolence, Phelps defends what might be considered her secondhand benevolence through authorship as an acceptable means of doing "some honest, hard work of my own in the World Beautiful, and for it" (*Chapters* 66). As a witness, she invokes "Mrs. Livermore," probably Mary Ashton Livermore (1820–1905), a well-known activist in the temperance and woman suffrage movements and the founder and editor of the *Agitator* and the *Woman's Journal,* to come to her defense. In response to pressure from "some unknown agitator" that Phelps be more active in women's causes, Livermore answered, "Do not trouble her. She works in another way from ours" (*Chapters* 253).

If motherly benevolence through writing was the "work" Livermore had in mind, then Phelps was hard working indeed. In much of her fiction, she foregrounded the need for benevolence toward victims of poverty. Her "honest, hard work" for the world takes the form of modeling, through her fictional characters, her ideal of motherly benevolence toward the poor and working classes. Following the lead of the antebellum domestic fiction that used the motherlessness of the protagonist as a sign of the chaos needing to be set right in the course of the novel, Phelps casts the problems experienced by her working-class characters in terms of motherlessness as well, making motherly benevolence a fitting and effective response. In her descriptions of city and factory settings she portrays the toll taken on families—particularly on mothers and children—by poverty. Her notion of motherly benevolence, not surprisingly, shares many of the characteristics that domestic ideology attributed to mothering. It takes the form of caring and nurturing. It is instinctual; women are naturally equipped for it. It is personal and often emotional as well as physical. Just as Phelps's characters mother members of the lower classes in these novels, Phelps herself mothers her readers through instruction. By telling them the truth as she understands it about the lower classes, she teaches them, as a mother should her children, about the world around them and provides moral instruction. She carries out the work of motherly benevolence and the reproduction of motherly benevolence, exhorting her readers to do the same.

Motherly Benevolence in *Hedged In*

In *Hedged In* Phelps criticizes middle-class reformers for their class bias, for their tendency to put their own family needs before the needs of the larger family of society, and for their interest in spiritual reform without physical care. As a contrast, she depicts her ideal of motherly benevolence: a woman's natural outreach to someone—in this case a young woman—in need.

The novel opens with fifteen-year-old Nixy Trent and her two-week-old child. Nixy is recovering from her parturition in a seedy tenement building on Thicket Street—a location that comes to serve metonymically for all poor areas in any big city. With no family to turn to (specifically, no mother) and haunted by the prospect of indoor reform—being taken to an asylum or poorhouse[8]—Nixy sneaks off one night into the suburbs, leaves her baby on a doorstep (as opposed to killing the baby, an alternative chosen by previous Thicket Street women in Nixy's situation), and attempts to find "honest" work. She loses her first job of housekeeping and child care when her employer learns that she has had an illegitimate child. Finally, she is taken in by what she judges to be "God's folks"—Margaret Purcell and her daughter Christina—who, in a commitment to Christian charity and in full knowledge of Nixy's past, make her not a servant, but a member of their family. Four years later, when Nixy has "made good"—she has become a respectable member of society and the local schoolteacher—the rest of the town discovers the secret of her past. The town "fathers" ask her to resign her post as the molder of young minds, but her new family fights for her and demands Christian forgiveness for Nixy. With this redemption, Nixy reclaims her son, who has been in an orphanage, takes over as Margaret's daughter when Christina marries, and begins the task of mothering the poor in Thicket Street. Her own practice of motherly benevolence comes to an abrupt end, however, with her surprising and dramatic death.

Phelps's novel begins in the city slums, a place where domestic ideals cannot flourish because economic conditions replace homes with tenements, housing as many as four families per room. Phelps portrays the details of the novel's setting—the harshness of Nixy's childhood environment—in terms of corrupted family and domestic life. Philosophizing about city streets, she says, "We make over our streets to degradation, like old jackets to the last boy. The big brother always has the new clothes. The little one, overgrown and under-dressed, remains 'the eternal child,'—more simply, (and perhaps to the Father of the ends of the earth none the less tenderly for the economy,) the 'baby of the family'" (1–2). Thus, early in the novel she introduces her vision of the family of humanity, extending the domestic setting to include all of society with God as the father of all, and so laying the groundwork for public motherhood. According to this vision, she portrays the city slums as a place where lack of mothering corrupts the family. Children play in the streets, frequently being injured by "a wheel or a hoof" (2), and "heaps of babies" are indistinct from heaps of garbage in the darkness, suggesting an undervaluing of children (3). Women's bodies are damaged: an old woman wears a "childish leer," and a young woman, "haggard and old, crouche[s] on the pavement, sunning herself like an animal" (4). The site of the domestic family life is rendered gothic by the economic conditions of tenement dwelling:

> The room was full and foul. Babies were numerous and noisy; several women were drunk. The tenement, low and dark, commanded, through dingy and broken windows, a muddy line of harbor, wharves, and a muddy sky. . . . I could see, within, nothing characteristic or familiar. I should except, perhaps, a certain dull stain, which bore a rude resemblance to a spider, over in the eastern corner of the tenement, low upon the wall. A hospitable lady in a red frock, anxious to do the honors of the place, pointed it out.
>
> "*There*'s where a gal murdered her baby; years agone. If 't had n't been so long afore our day, I might have accommodated ye with partikkelars." (5)

Phelps's emphasis on women and children underscores her message of the damaging effects of poverty on the motherhood ideal. In this setting, women cannot mother. At best, they neglect their noisy babies for alcohol; at worst, they kill them.

Nixy experiences a motherless upbringing consistent with the Thicket Street setting. She worked as a street musician with a man whom "she was taught to call" her uncle. This man then "sold" her to a woman, who in turn gave her to another woman who "got drunk every Tuesday, and beat her with the bottle Wednesday mornings." After a stint in an orphan asylum, she found herself "with the Thicket Street babies, hunting for apple-cores in the mud." She finally got a job in a saloon, where she worked until she became pregnant (16–17). The novel suggests that such an upbringing explains Nixy's inability to mother her newborn son. When Lize, a woman in her flat, criticizes her for her lack of motherly attention to the baby, Nixy answers, "Mother? I wish *I* had a mother. To go to now, you know, Lize. To take me in, mebbe, and help bear what folks say, and all that. S'pose she'd be ready and willin'? I wonder if she'd kiss me!" (24). Nixy mourns the absence of a mother as someone to provide for her, to accept her despite her immoral behavior, and to provide her with physical affection. As she lies on her mat near the stain on the wall marking the infanticide of years ago, she imagines that the young woman who committed that murder was also motherless and finds in that lack an explanation for the violence (27).

When Nixy runs away from Thicket Street to the more domestically sound suburbs, she falls victim to the institutionalized reform work so popular among leisure-class women. Phelps demonstrates that such work rarely focuses on truly caring for those in need or providing the mothering they lack but strives instead to effect spiritual and/or moral reform, recalling the conflict in her earlier *The Gates Ajar* between religious reform and true comfort. Phelps demonstrates that as long as Nixy needs mothering herself, she will never be able to "reform," nor will she be able to mother her own child. Rather than fault Nixy for her pregnancy and her lack of maternal feeling, Phelps blames the social circumstances and the thwarted domesticity that have brought Nixy to this point. For many of the women not accounted for in the domestic ideal, motherhood constituted a physical and economic jeopardy, not a blessing. Steeped in the tradition of the cult of motherhood, reformers "had come to see the affection and devotion of the mother to the child as a natural instinct, independent of historical circumstances or the economic conditions in which a woman came to motherhood" (Evans 85). They condemned what could only, in their code of understanding, be called neglect and unnatural behavior. Through Nixy, Phelps demonstrates that economic need undermines maternal instinct. Nixy's economic situation does not allow her to feel the emotions that the ideology of motherhood insists she should have. Poor, unmarried, and too young, Nixy illustrates the unacknowledged fact that, in order to provide for their children according to the standards of the ideal, women must live in material comfort.

Phelps uses Nixy's situation to address the typical model of women's reform, suggesting that well-meaning reformers may actually contribute to the downfall of needy women. Prior to abandoning her baby, Nixy goes from house to house looking for honest work. But she comes to understand that no one with the means to hire servants will be interested in a young, single mother. The repeated reference to *honest* work hints at the availability of *dis*honest work, never specified, but lurking around the edges of this story. Dishonest work, presumably prostitution or theft, appears to be readily available in Thicket Street, and, according to the values of the novel, Nixy exhibits a natural morality in her determination to avoid these occupations in favor of the more difficult route. Phelps will not allow her to be dismissed as simply a bad person; Nixy's lack of maternal feelings is not a failure of morality. And yet Phelps demonstrates that Nixy's impulse for good is discouraged by the very class of people most associated with reform movements: the middle class. Although she lacks loving feelings for her child, she feels a sense of responsibility to him, but cannot see any way to act on that. Having either lost or been turned down for several jobs because of her child, Nixy concludes, "The baby was the mischief of it! Was there, then, no way in which she could be the baby's honest mother?" (55).

Those who attempt to help Nixy set out to reform rather than mother her, and their reform has a distinctly religious emphasis. One conversation between Nixy and a hopeful reformer early in the novel, and prior to Nixy's abandoning of her child, is telling:

> "I suppose you know how wicked you've been," suggested the lady of the house, anxious, in the only way that presented itself to her vivid invention, to "reform" the girl.
>
> "Yes," said Nixy, in her unhappy, unmeaning way. She was wondering where she should spend the night.
>
> "It is a dreadful thing,—you so young!"
>
> "O yes."
>
> "It will be very hard,—with the child."
>
> "Yes."
>
> The lady looked at her, puzzled.
>
> "I doubt if she understands a thing I say."
>
> But she was mistaken. Nixy had perfectly understood and would remember her last remark. She was growing very tired of the child. (52)

This woman attempts to elicit some sense of remorse in Nixy for her sin. Like the other women Nixy has met in her quest for work, this woman speaks only reform rhetoric without giving Nixy the practical, material help she needs. It is important to recognize that as an adherent of nineteenth-century Christian morality, Phelps probably judged Nixy's action of conceiving a child outside marriage as sinful. She recognizes the immediate physical needs of the "sinner," however, to be more pressing than any spiritual needs perceived by her hopeful reformers. In this scene, Nixy cannot ponder the error of her ways when she has no prospects for lodging. The woman's reference to Nixy's spiritual or moral reform can only be read by Nixy in physical terms. So when this woman observes that moral improvement will be difficult for Nixy given how far she's fallen "with the child," Nixy understands her to be referring to the far more immediate difficulty she will have—the difficulty she has already encountered—in getting work and lodging "with the child."

The problem with these reformers' approach, according to Phelps, stems from their failure to extend their family to include Nixy. They turn her away in the name of their private mothering duties, specifically their need to protect their own children against the bad influence Nixy, as a fallen woman, represents. Mrs. Myrtle, the first woman to hire and then to dismiss Nixy, and later, the one who threatens to expose Nixy's past to the rest of the town, justifies her actions in terms of the "superior claims" of her private mothering duties. She explains:

> I could not feel it to be my duty to run the risk, which you, my dear Mrs. Purcell, ran, with this unfortunate girl. My field of usefulness, as the mother of my Fanny, is necessarily so very much in the—what might be called the domestic affections. It was a depressing circumstance that I was obliged to dismiss the girl from my service as I did. (147)

Mrs. Myrtle believes that her duty as a mother requires her to protect her own child from exposure to Nixy's bad influence. Prone to the same abstract thinking Phelps criticized in *The Gates Ajar,* Mrs. Myrtle fails to see a connection between herself and Nixy. Insisting upon individuation, she allows for only the biological tie that exists with her own daughter. "Domestic affections" for Mrs. Myrtle apply strictly within the confines of the home and the body, and cannot be extended; Phelps advances a program of inclusion that would extend the boundaries of home and the body through physical connection.

Margaret Purcell embodies Phelps's ideal of motherly benevolence. Like Mrs. Myrtle, Margaret initially balks when she learns Nixy's story, and she fears the kind of influence Nixy might be on her innocent daughter, Christina. But rather than back away from Nixy's story, she asks to hear it, and then she offers Nixy a home with her. Margaret's decision to take Nixy in resembles Phelps's description of her own turn to motherly benevolence with the widow from Gloucester—not a studied choice, but rather the spontaneous response of a mother to a needy child. Margaret is not an unusually good woman; like Phelps, she has "never headed a 'cause'" nor "had a 'mission'" (81). Indeed, she feels disgust to rival any of her peers when Nixy faints "right on my carpet" (88), and blanches to see the physical connection established when Christina gives Nixy a sisterly kiss (138). But when she learns of Nixy's motherlessness, her conviction to do right according to her Christian beliefs and her motherly tendencies force her to overcome her feelings, and eventually Margaret takes Nixy "into her family" (87). When she describes this process later to a friend, she explains that she "bore with Nixy" at first (124), a phrase likening the process of bringing Nixy into her family to physical childbirth. She does not call Nixy her daughter—when describing their relationship she seems at a loss, calling her "what, exactly, whether pupil, child, friend, or all, or neither, time must prove" (133)—yet, for all practical purposes, Nixy has become her child. Margaret educates her alongside Christina, provides for her—materially, emotionally, and spiritually—protects her from gossip, and loves her.

As part of her project of promoting motherly benevolence and a maternal ethic, Phelps addresses popular notions that class somehow correlates to one's morality; she shows instead that class standing is purely an accident of birth. So doing, she imagines a community of women that transcends class boundaries. Nixy's and Christina's similarities—apart from their upbringing—serve this purpose. As Christina ponders: "'I don't wonder she could n't find work,' continued Christina, lifting her innocent eyes. . . . 'I could n't find work, if I had to earn my living, unless I could make tatting or give music-lessons. I've been thinking all this evening how funny that I should be your daughter, and she should be she, you know'" (98). And Nixy, too, wonders "what kind of a girl she, Nixy Trent, should now be, had she lived all her happy life in a pearly-gray room" like the one Margaret puts her up in. Would she be like Christina? (106). The treatment Nixy has received at the hands of other women—women who "had held her on a slow toasting-fork of curiosity all day" (53)—has given her no reason to hope for a "community." Phelps addresses those women through Margaret, who condemns the tendency to judge Nixy. In a speech to Mrs. Myrtle, Margaret's voice seems only a thin veil for the thoughts of the author: "you and I are women, and her sisters, and her fellow-sinners, Heaven forgive us!" (152).

At the climax of the novel, having been mothered in a material way, Nixy experiences redemption according to the tenets of Christianity and domestic ideology, and her redemption inducts her into the middle class. Nixy's transformation into a new woman has all the earmarks of religious conversion, including confession and repentance. Although "they do not understand in Thicket Street how to be ashamed" (164), she must learn shame in order to be redeemed. Her testimony to Margaret that she "understood what I had never understood before. I understood that I was ashamed—ashamed!" (163), indicates that she has achieved the spiritual insight needed to repent. Nixy's transformation is marked by a new name—appropriate, since, as Margaret points out, the name *Nixy* "must be a corruption of something" (167). Margaret convinces her to go by her christened name, Eunice. The giving of the new name is, to Nixy, now Eunice, "like a baptismal blessing," marking further her redemption (167). Yet the new name carries domestic significance in addition to its spiritual significance. Eunice, in the Bible, was the mother of Timothy (one of Christ's followers) and the apostle Paul commends her for her faithfulness and for raising Timothy well.[9] Thus with the name Eunice, Phelps draws on the tradition of civilizing motherhood that attributed to mothers the power of raising up sons who would be good citizens. Nixy is redeemed, not only as a Christian but as a mother as well. Fittingly, she reclaims her son from the orphanage where he had been placed, and brings him to live with her new family.

Part of Eunice's transformation requires that she leave behind the underclass ways of Nixy and Thicket Street and become middle class, and she succeeds in this venture, at least to some extent. Nixy experiences a thorough transformation: she learns to speak properly, learns not to eat with her knife, learns to dress modestly (she quits wearing the flashy pink hair ribbons that Margaret disapproved of and begins wearing black dresses, in mourning for her lost innocence), joins the church, and rarely, if ever, mentions Thicket Street (146). And, appropriate to her new status, she enjoys a motherly authority over her former Thicket Street acquaintances. When the father of her child comes to see her, they both notice the difference of status between them, a difference that sets Nixy above Dick. Dick explains that he had intended to find Nixy and marry her, but once he has seen her, he recognizes the distance between them, comparing it to his own distance from the moon, for which "there warn't never a ladder in the world made high enough to reach the thing" (244). Far from the nonindividuated identity created through the physical affection of motherly benevolence, here separation is emphasized. Nixy does nothing to bridge that distance; in fact she emphasizes it by talking to Dick as a mother to a child: " 'I know you don't mean to be a bad boy, Dick. I know you didn't mean to give me the—pain—you have given me to-night. But it can't be helped. God led me one way, you another. We are different, Dick,—don't you see?—different now, forever' " (246). Eunice has been invested with motherly authority over Dick by virtue of her new class status.

With this new status Eunice makes a trip to Thicket Street. She explains her motivation for this visit as a desire " 'to pass along into some other hands . . . a little part of all that I have borrowed from you [Margaret],—the long-suffering and the patience, the trust and tenderness; the courage and the watching and the praying and persistence which,' said Eunice, with much emotion, 'would save the world if the world were Thicket Street!' " (292). When she gets to Thicket Street, she finds Moll Manners, a woman who had laughed at her years before, now dying of consumption. Nixy arranges for her to be taken from the gutter, where she finds her, to an asylum so that she can die in a clean, warm bed. The scene of Moll's death replicates Nixy's search for someone to love and care for her rather than to reform her. Mrs. Myrtle, who runs the asylum, tries to read from the prayer book or sing a hymn for Moll, but Moll asks instead for "Nix." Moll's request foregrounds the conflict between reform and mothering:

> "But if you are not prepared for the great change," urged Mrs. Myrtle, looking much distressed.
>
> "Must run my chances," said Moll, doggedly. "I'm too sick to hear religion,—much obleeged to you. That dress of yourn rustles all kind o' through my head. Is that a prayer-book you've laid along down there on my feet? It's awful heavy to me." (278)

When Eunice arrives, Moll asks of her all she needs: "I only wanted you to ask you—if you don't mind—to let me take hold of your hand. There!" She took the hand that Eunice held out to her, and laid it up between her own, against her cheek, and, so lying, slept again" (279). Only after Eunice has provided this loving, physical, and motherly comfort does Moll intimate her interest in "God's folks" as Eunice has described them—people who care for and love the ones everyone else turns away. Only after her need for mothering has been met in some measure can Moll consider her spiritual needs.

Phelps tells a domestic tale about Eunice Trent. A homeless and motherless waif at the beginning of the novel, she overcomes the obstacles she faces with the help of a mothering friend, and successfully enters the middle-class domestic setting and ideology. All's well that ends well, it seems, when motherly benevolence is applied. But all doesn't end well for Eunice in *Hedged In.* Her untimely and highly dramatic death signals Phelps's hesitation to break down class barriers so completely and requires that we take another look at Phelps's motherly benevolence. Closer examination indicates that while motherly benevolence as Phelps imagines it addresses crucial weaknesses in extant reform programs and allows for the construction of a relational self, it has limitations, particularly in the area of class.

Mother Metaphor: Self and Other

Let's return to Phelps's anecdote illustrating her own experience with motherly benevolence toward the Gloucester widow. Early in the scene—

even before reaching the widow's house—Phelps establishes the class of the widow with the fact that she has twelve children and with the uneducated dialect of her husband's friends who report the murder to Phelps. In the tableaulike scene described by Phelps, in which she holds the widow in her arms, Phelps—clad in white dress and gloves—stands out as a ray of light in the otherwise dark room.[10] "I suppose [the gloves] made a spot of light, by which [the widow's] frenzied sight was arrested. Her sobbing broke; she turned, and looked up into my face" (205). Disingenuously, perhaps, Phelps attributes the widow's arrested sight to the contrast of her light gloves in the dark room rather than to the fact that Phelps obviously belongs to another class and her presence in this working-class widow's room is decidedly unexpected. Had the two women been equals, we might call Phelps's visit an act of friendship or sisterliness. But the act becomes maternal in the light of the class distinction between these two women. Mothering assumes a child, or a childlike object to be mothered. Phelps stands in the position of mother, someone who is over her "children" in some way. In this case, her superiority comes through class standing. Thus the connection formed, the nonindividuation as Noble has termed it, becomes complicated by the presence of disparate authority.

The key to understanding this complication comes through Phelps's deployment of the mother metaphor. As Noble explains, Stowe's images of bodies connecting and interacting make it possible to blur the boundary between the self and the Other, or the "me" and the "not me." In the image of the mother, however, this boundary is already broken down. Julia Kristeva explores the blurring of the self in the unique identity of the mother in her powerful essay, "Stabat Mater," locating the explanation for the feminine psyche in the unique nature of the maternal body. As she reflects on her own experience of maternity in the informal and poetic observations that stand in contrast to and alongside the main body of the text, she describes the mother's simultaneous connection to and disconnection from her child:

> My body is no longer mine, it doubles up, suffers, bleeds, catches cold, . . . and it laughs. . . . But the pain, [my child's] pain—it comes from inside, never remains apart, other, it inflames me at once, without a second's re-

> spite. As if that was what I had given birth to and, not willing to part from me, insisted on coming back, dwelled in me permanently." (167)

More than simply an emotional connection, Kristeva claims a physical relationship, through pain, that more than blurs the "me" and the "not me"; this relationship makes the "not me" always part of "me." Disturbed by the vulnerability deriving from the permanent connection to an Other and troubled by "the immeasurable, unconfinable maternal body" (177), Kristeva longs for "someone . . . who might make me be by means of borders, separations, vertigos" (176). She describes the paradox: "A mother is a continuous separation, a division of the very flesh. . . . Then there is this other abyss that opens up between the body and what had been its inside: there is the abyss between the mother and the child. . . . The child, whether *he* or *she* is irremediably an other. . . . I confront the abyss between what was mine and is henceforth but irreparably alien" (178–79). For Kristeva, there is always a connection between mother and child, even, paradoxically, as the child becomes separate. And while Noble finds something liberatory and feminist in the nonindividuation of the self, something "anti-patriarchal" (295), Kristeva indicates a more complicated response to this possibility, acknowledging the conflict between the self who desires "borders" and she who longs for a permanent connection to her child.

Phelps, too, appears to struggle with the blurring of the boundaries of the self—enabled through the physical and sympathetic connection of motherly benevolence. Indeed, her interest in writing was spurred, she reports, from her desire at the age of thirteen "to become an individual" (*Chapters* 19). So, whereas motherly benevolence is an avenue to close connection and nonindividuation, writing is a source of individuation. These conflicting goals, not surprisingly, come into tension in her work.

This conflict becomes manifest in the power disparity invested in Phelps's configuration of motherly benevolence between the "mother" and the "Other," the object of her care. Motherly benevolence served as a way for middle- and upper-class women to fulfill the expectations of the ideology of mothering and to minister to the needs of the poor. But it also enabled them to solidify their class standing and individuality by defining the lower classes as different from (and less powerful than) themselves.[11] As Phelps believed, "a mother was a being of *power* and *importance*" (*Chapters* 14, emphasis mine). This may explain why a philosophy of motherly benevolence would attract a woman like Phelps. Raised in the shadow of powerful and intelligent men—both grandfathers as well as her father were well-known theologians, writers, and scholars—and taught from an early age the doctrine of submission as a necessary trait for women, motherly benevolence allowed her to assert power over—and separation from—those "beneath" her.

Class Complications and the Death of Nixy

It appears, however, that more than simply the opportunity to wield some power, Phelps ultimately must draw a distinction between her middle-class and working-class characters in order to maintain her own middle-class identity.[12] Even the redeemed Eunice cannot fully leave behind her history as Nixy, and while Margaret Purcell may have forgiven her, it appears that Phelps cannot allow this fallen, working-class woman to move entirely into the middle class. Well before its dramatic ending, the novel undermines the redemption of working-class Nixy by showing her to be exceptional—by showing that one doesn't have to dig very deep to find the Eunice in Nixy. Although she comes from Thicket Street, Nixy seems to be marked as an atypical underclass woman with a hidden nature that did not fit her Thicket Street heritage. Even on their first meeting, Margaret is struck by the "curious mingling of rough and elegant grammar in Nixy's language" (*The Gates Ajar* 90). And she reports to her friend, the novel's narrator, after the first year of Nixy's tenure in Margaret's family, "I have not been able to lay my finger upon a thread of coarseness in that girl" (134). Phelps implies that Nixy could be redeemed in a way that others from Thicket Street who are "coarse" could not.

By separating Nixy from most lower-class people, Phelps makes the class unity at the end of the novel between Margaret and Nixy more palatable. And yet her exceptional nature is not enough to justify her full induction into the middle class. Phelps seems unwilling to completely erase class distinction—and Nixy's sexual transgression—or to construct a connection with Nixy by allowing her a permanent place in the middle class as a fellow practitioner of motherly benevolence. Although she occupies the position of daughter when Christina leaves home to marry, as an adult with her own mothering work, she threatens to dissolve the class distinction necessary to Margaret's—and Phelps's—identity.[13] So the novel finds itself in a bind: Nixy and her son cannot happily remain in their new middle-class lives, nor can the plot's trajectory allow the town fathers to cast this single mother and her illegitimate child out of the town and back to a life of poverty. Thus, following the barely mentioned death of Nixy's son from scarlet fever, Phelps substitutes a sentimental and melodramatic death for Nixy in the place of a realistic solution. The bizarre death scene takes place one evening when the narrator is visiting Margaret and Nixy and, therefore, has first-hand access to the episode. A violent storm causes much distress in the two older women; Nixy has retired to her room. The drama of the scene is telling, and should be quoted at length:

> "I don't know but we are all going to perish here! This is horrible!" cried Margaret, groping for her matches. "Do let us die in the light, at least, and together. Eunice! How dark it grows! Eunice, Eunice! She does not hear. We must get to her, or she to us. Hear that!"
>
> As she spoke, such a shock struck the house as made her stagger where she stood in the middle of the room, and the match in her hand went out. She struck another,—it flashed and darkened; another, every match in the room,—every match in the room went out; and it was as blue and ghostly and ugly a sight as ever I saw.
>
> Margaret threw down her match-box, and groped her way, with an exclamation of horror, through the dark to the gray room.
>
> "Eunice—" she pushed open the door; but when Eunice made no answer, she stopped and called me, and we went both of us in together.
>
> When the storm was over, and the stars out, and the lighted house grown still, we could see how quietly she lay,—not struck by the storm, as we had thought, but sunk in her soft white dress, as she had fallen hours ago, at the foot of the great wooden cross, and with her arms around it. (294–95)

In this final scene, Phelps retreats almost entirely from any attempt at realism, giving us instead a scene both gothic and devotional. On this "dark and stormy night," matches do not light and the place has a "ghostly" atmosphere. Margaret's fear of dying as a result of the storm combines with the setting to achieve the exaggerated, eerie tone. And yet Phelps carefully divorces Nixy's death from the eeriness by insisting that she had in fact died peacefully, embracing the wooden cross she had kept in her room since being convinced that "God's folks" had made the difference in her life. Dying at the foot of the cross, Nixy becomes almost allegorical, certainly heroic, elevated through her association with Christ in a gesture reminiscent of Tom's death in *Uncle Tom's Cabin.* By making Nixy both heroic and dead, Phelps manages to preserve her redemption while preventing her from enjoying her middle-class status with impunity, thereby threatening Margaret's class position. More, by elevating her to the level of martyr, she removes her from a place of identity with Margaret.

In *Hedged In,* Phelps explores motherly benevolence as a vehicle for bridging class boundaries. She tries to imagine the life of an underclass girl transposed into a middle-class, domestic setting and connected in a motherly relationship to a middle-class woman. In the end, however, the possibilities of connection, of nonindividuation, across class lines register as threatening to Phelps.[14] Resorting to a sensational conclusion, Phelps eliminates the threat Nixy represents while maintaining her status as redeemed mother.

Notes

1. Precisely when she made this change is uncertain. In her chronology of Phelps's life in the introduction to *The Story of Avis,* Carol Farley Kessler offers 1852 or 1856 as likely dates. For a discussion of the timing, see Kessler (16).

2. Nancy Schnog makes a similar observation in "'The Comfort of My Fancying': Loss and Recuperation in *The Gates Ajar.*"

3. Harriet Beecher Stowe, who was an influence for Phelps, portrayed a similar conflict in *The Minister's Wooing* (1859). As Judith Fetterley explains, "Stowe explores her antipathy toward Calvinism and argues instead for a theology based on alternative feminine values" (376). I am indebted for the formulation of the abstract and disembodied vs. the intersubjective, nonindividuated subjectivity to Marianne Noble's work, "The Ecstasies of Sentimental Wounding in *Uncle Tom's Cabin.*"

4. For further discussion of Phelps's treatment of heaven in *The Gates Ajar,* see Nina Baym's introduction to *Three Spiritualist Novels,* the University of Illinois Press 2000 reprint of this novel.

5. For a discussion of competing forms of benevolence, see Monika Elbert's chapter in this volume.

6. See Ginzberg's chapter two, "Her Strongest Moral Organ," on the focus on morality in women's benevolent work.

7. See Ginzberg (119–21) and Evans (100–101) on the professionalization of reform work after the Civil War.

8. See Elbert's discussion of indoor reform in chapter six. Both Karen Tracey and Debra Bernardi provide insightful discussion of the fears among the poor of asylums and poorhouses.

9. In his letter to Timothy, Paul writes: "I have been reminded of your sincere faith, which first lived in your grandmother Lois and in your mother Eunice and, I am persuaded, now lives in you also" (2 Timothy 1:5). Also Acts 16:1: "He [Paul] came to Derbe and then to Lystra, where a disciple named Timothy lived, whose mother was a Jewess and a believer, but whose father was a Greek." The fact that it is the mother's influence that has prevailed with Timothy over his father's seems to suggest that the biblical Eunice took some responsibility in teaching her son her faith.

10. In this scene, Phelps engages in the rhetorical practice that Ellen Goldner has labeled "arguing with pictures." According to Goldner, Harriet Beecher Stowe sought "'to paint pictures' for her readers because 'there is no arguing with pictures'" (71). Phelps's work is heavily influenced by that of Stowe, and this use of tableaux may be a mark of that influence.

11. Rosemarie Garland Thomson makes a similar observation in "Benevolent Maternalism and Physically Disabled Figures." However, she argues that women define themselves as central against the marginality of people with physical disabilities or deformities. I agree with her claim, but I don't believe it goes far enough. Middle-class women "other" everyone they care for simply by setting themselves up as caregivers.

12. See Mary Templin's essay in this volume for further examples and discussion of the way benevolence assures class standing.

13. Amy Kaplan has argued that, in the context of the changes and upheaval of the late nineteenth century, writers used their fiction as a way to solidify their own middle-class identity against the other of the working classes.

14. Lisa Long arrives at a similar conclusion in her reading of Phelps's other work: "an unbridgeable gap between Phelps's developing sense of self and the 'miserable' people who enable her personal reformation undermines the communal effect of her efforts" (272).

Works Cited

Baym, Nina. Introduction. *Three Spiritualist Novels.* By Elizabeth Stuart Phelps. Urbana: U of Illinois P, 2000. vii–xxiii.

Evans, Sara M. *Born for Liberty: A History of Women in America.* New York: The Free Press, 1989.

Fetterley, Judith. *Provisions: A Reader from 19th-Century American Women.* Bloomington: Indiana UP, 1985.

Ginzberg, Lori D. *Women and the Work of Benevolence: Morality, Politics, and Class in the Nineteenth-Century United States.* New Haven: Yale UP, 1990.

Goldner, Ellen. "Arguing with Pictures: Race, Class, and the Formation of Popular Abolitionism through Uncle Tom's Cabin." *Journal of American and Comparative Cultures* 24.1–2 (Spring–Summer 2001): 71–84.

Kaplan, Amy. *The Social Construction of American Realism.* Chicago: U of Chicago P, 1988.

Kessler, Carol Farley. Introduction. *The Story of Avis.* By Elizabeth Stuart Phelps. New Brunswick: Rutgers UP, 1985. xiii–xxxii.

Kristeva, Julia. "Stabat Mater." *The Kristeva Reader.* Ed. Toril Moi. New York: Columbia UP, 1986. 160–86.

Long, Lisa A. "The Postbellum Reform Writings of Rebecca Harding Davis and Elizabeth Stuart Phelps." *The Cambridge Companion to Nineteenth-Century American Women's Writing.* Ed. Dale M. Bauer and Philip Gould. Cambridge: Cambridge UP, 2001. 262–83.

Noble, Marianne, "The Ecstasies of Sentimental Wounding in *Uncle Tom's Cabin.*" *Yale Journal of Criticism* 10.2 (Fall 1997): 295–320.

Phelps, Elizabeth Stuart. *Chapters from a Life.* Boston: Houghton, Mifflin, 1900.

———. *The Gates Ajar.* 1868. *Three Spiritualist Novels.* Ed. Nina Baym. Urbana: U of Illinois P, 2000. 1–138.

———. *Hedged In.* Boston: Fields, Osgood, 1870.

———. "The Tenth of January." 1868. *The Silent Partner and "The Tenth of January."* New York: Feminist Press, 1983. 305–51.

Sáez, Barbara J. "The Discourse of Philanthropy in Nineteenth-Century America." *American Transcendental Quarterly* 11.3 (September 1997): 163–70.

Schnog, Nancy. "'The Comfort of My Fancying': Loss and Recuperation in *The Gates Ajar.*" *Arizona Quarterly* 49.1 (Spring 1993): 21–47.

Thomson, Rosemarie Garland "Benevolent Maternalism and Physically Disabled Figures: Dilemmas of Female Embodiment in Stowe, Davis, and Phelps." *American Literature* 68.3 (September 1996): 555–61.

Tompkins, Jane. Afterword. *The Wide, Wide World.* By Susan Warner. New York: Feminist Press, 1987. 584–608.

8

Frances Harper's Poverty Relief Mission in the African American Community

Terry D. Novak

Throughout most of her works, especially her novel *Iola Leroy,* Frances E. W. Harper consistently toils to address her concerns over the uplifting of her race. There is no doubt that at the center of this uplifting is the end of poverty and oppression of all kinds. Harper knows that a poor person is a depressed person, one incapable of reaching his or her highest potential. Harper also knows that in order to better the race as a whole, poverty must be eliminated—or, at the very least, significantly altered. Harper herself was a woman with an education and a comfortable upbringing who taught school in her early years and developed into an advocate of many social causes of her day, including abolition, temperance, and the importance of education. She was an active member of many political and social organizations such as the Women's Christian Temperance Union, the American Women's Suffrage Association, and the American Equal Rights Association. She was a good Christian woman who attempted to practice her faith in her daily life. She believed in—and lived by—many of the tenets of the popular Cult of True Womanhood. She was, in other words, in many ways typical of a certain type of privileged woman in nineteenth-century America. Harper was aware of both the privileges that had been allotted her and the struggles that she would continually encounter. She dealt with this dichotomy by channeling her privileges into a deep sense of responsibility toward helping other, less privileged African Americans.

Frances Ellen Watkins Harper was born on September 24, 1825, in Baltimore, Maryland, to free parents who died when Harper was still a toddler. Harper was raised and educated by her uncle, the Reverend William Watkins, who owned and ran the William Watkins Academy for Colored Youth. It was there that Harper was formally educated until she reached the age of thirteen. While many of her white counterparts—that is to say, those women of an upper class within their race—would have found this an absurdly abbreviated formal education, as many of them were able to attend female colleges and seminaries, Harper realized her fortune as a black woman in being able to attain such a high level of education. Harper left school to become a domestic and to train to become a seamstress. She continued her intellectual education informally at the home of her employer, who allowed her free access to the family's extensive library. In 1851 she was hired by Union Seminary, an Ohio school run by the African Methodist Episcopal Church, to teach sewing. Harper left this position within a year's time and moved to another teaching position in Pennsylvania.

Unlike the women Lori Merish discusses at length in her essay on the "Sentimental Seamstress" in this volume, Harper did not become dependent on the economic vagaries of her work as a seamstress or on her teaching of such. Rather, she took an interesting—and necessary—approach to her foray into the world of the seamstress. She first used the skill as a means of support; she then used the skill as a means to help other African American women support themselves; and she then combined the teaching skills and survival skills she had learned with the "book learning" she had been able to acquire to step into the role she felt to be her true calling. When Harper abandoned her second teaching position in 1854, she began to lecture against slavery and to assist with the Underground Railroad movement. This work, which was to set the frame for her life's work, was propelled by the 1853 passage of a law in Harper's home state of Maryland, stating that free blacks who entered the state were subject to enslavement.

Harper's public work was interrupted for a period of four years, while she was married to Fenton Harper. The death of Fenton Harper, while economically disastrous to his wife on many levels, also freed Frances Harper to return to her work, this time with the accompaniment of her young daughter and her three stepchildren, on the lecture circuit. Although Harper surely would consider her lecture work of supreme importance, she was also establishing herself as a popular poet as well as a short story and essay writer even before her marriage to Fenton Harper.

But in all of her work—lecturing and writing alike—Harper consistently focused on what she considered to be her raison d'être: the uplifting and upbuilding of her race, particularly through preparing and encouraging women to become educated, self-sufficient members of the race who could, in turn, raise their children to be the same while also urging their spouses on to greater dignity as fruitful members of society. While this philosophy certainly fit into the major tenets of the nineteenth-century ideals of True Womanhood, it also specifically recognized that the race could in truth count only on itself for real, significant social progress. A critical part of this personal mission of Harper's revolved around her belief that poverty and disadvantage among African Americans could and must be relieved in order for the race to find and sustain true independence and freedom. Harper preached and worked on this mission through her actions, through her speeches, and through her writing, especially focusing on her belief that poverty relief among African Americans should be a primary duty of other, more financially secure and better educated African Americans. Thus Harper's work was unlike that of many of her contemporary African American writers, who generally avoided issues of racial poverty and stereotypes of poor blacks in favor of strict representations of middle-class African Americans, as Jill Bergman and Debra Bernardi point out in the introduction to this volume.

Harper embodies the crux of her poverty relief and social uplifting credo in her 1892 novel, *Iola Leroy, or Shadows Uplifted.* Speaking through the protagonist Iola, Harper makes her belief in the critical need for African Americans to help one another absolutely clear. Harper knew enough of her white counterparts and the ways of white benevolence to realize that if the newly freed African Americans were to make real strides in American society and be able to enjoy full citizenship, it would be up to other, more privileged African Americans (like herself) to see that this was accomplished. Harper's realization of the overwhelming scope of this task becomes evident in her novel as she places Iola in a position very close to the author's own social position. As Frances Smith Foster points out in her introduction to a reprint of *Iola Leroy*,

> Harper was a persuasive and sensitive writer, a popular and articulate speaker, and the friend of some of the best-known political activists, religious leaders, educators, and artists. Her own involvements ranged from the establishment of Sunday schools to the support of John Brown's raid on Harper's Ferry. Harper was a nationally recognized leader in such organizations as the American Association of the Education of Colored Youth, the Women's Christian Temperance Union, the American Woman's Suffrage Association, and the National Council of Women. . . . Long before she attempted her novel, *Iola Leroy* . . . she had gained an international reputation as a writer, lecturer, and political activist. (xxvii–xxviii)

Historians have done an excellent job of teaching the importance of women's work for social reform on a variety of levels in nineteenth-century America, as Bergman and Bernardi discuss. In his book *Christian Volunteerism in Britain and North America,* William H. Brackney tells us that "[a] total of over fifty societies for and by women came into being in North America in the fifteen years before 1890. Women followed the trend of the era toward cooperation . . . and helped to form unions . . . which suggested future paradigms of American volunteerism" (37). Other historians have kept the names of many leaders of the volunteerism movement alive. We know that Elizabeth Cady Stanton and Susan B. Anthony fought for women's suffrage and equality. We know of Frances Willard and her tireless work for the temperance movement. We know of Catharine Beecher's work with education. We know of the women's clubs that worked as vehicles of activism for women stuck between a desire to use their talents and intelligence to ease social ills and a need to remain part of True Womanhood, as defined by their society. We also know of Jane Addams and her Hull-House work on behalf of immigrants. (See both James Salazar's and Sarah Chinn's essays in this volume.) And we know of scores of largely Christian women who worked on behalf of abolition and reconstruction. We also know that, for the most part, these tireless women were generally upper middle class or upper class, had solid educational backgrounds, and were white.

Set next to any of these women, Frances Harper looks strikingly familiar—except that she was African American. Harper's race made all the difference to her social activism. She belonged to the same organizations as her white counterparts, but often as the only African American member. Harper believed that she had the right to be a full part of her society; thus, her answer to being the only black member of an organization was often to run for office and urge other African American women to join as well. Harper saw it as part of her mission in life to attempt to enlighten her white counterparts on the needs of African Americans as well as on the need *for* African Americans in a society that often saw the race as dispensable, couching philosophical discussions on race around the phrase, "the Negro question." Although Harper worked for the race at large, it is true, as Maryemma Graham suggests, that "she was particularly concerned . . . about the impact of slavery and racism on women. For Harper, there could be no fate worse than the moral and human degradation experienced by black women" (xlvii). These were concerns that Harper fought valiantly to bring to the forefront of the organizations with which she was involved; these concerns also predominate the themes of her writing.

Out of all of Frances Harper's literary works, her novel *Iola Leroy* remains the highlight of her career and the best formulation of her social theories. In fact, the novel represents a large part of Harper's life, as she indeed toiled over the text for a good deal of her adult existence, presumably editing and rewriting her work as her social theories jelled into maturity. The novel enjoyed success when it was first published in 1892, but by the time Harper died in 1911, *Iola Leroy* had been largely forgotten by the public. Mention of the novel happens sporadically over the next several decades, especially in the context of African American literature at large. Much of the attention given to the novel in these decades is fleeting and not necessarily complimentary. Robert Bone, for example, writing in *The Negro Novel in America* (1965), criticizes Harper's perceived lack of interest in the traditional mode of protest writing (32). Other critics have dismissed Harper as just another sentimental woman writer of the nineteenth century. More contemporary critics, writing from the 1980s on, have been much more attentive to and appreciative of Harper and her work. Scholars such as Frances Smith Foster have worked tirelessly to give Harper her due. Most contemporary critics have focused on Harper's dedication to her race and on her feminist activities and attitudes. For example, Melba Joyce Boyd writes of *Iola Leroy,* "The novel critiques the concepts of race identity in America and reflects the compounded socioeconomic repression that subjugated nineteenth-century black women . . . it also provides political dialogue that encompasses the ideological dilemmas the black intelligentsia confronted during and after Reconstruction" (17). Boyd points out that, in addition to enlightening the race, Iola and her colleagues encounter the same issues that Harper and her colleagues encountered in real life: "[T]he adverse reactions of lynching, Ku Klux Klan terrorism, corruption in politics and the church, as well as alcoholism, undermine the vision of the future" (184). Other critics, such as Elizabeth Young, see *Iola Leroy* as a historical study of the Civil War, from a particular racial standpoint: "We may take the politics of domesticity in another direction, however, by viewing *Iola Leroy* as a domestic novel about a domestic political crisis: the Civil War" (274).

Looking from the distance of the early twenty-first century, it is easy to see that Harper is writing Iola largely as herself, with all of her mature feminist ideals. Within this context, it is just as easy to see that Harper's novel fits well into the genre of benevolence literature, just as Harper's life itself fit into a very definite mode of benevolence. Both Iola and Harper are dedicated primarily to uplifting the race from the dregs of poverty, depression, confusion, and, oftentimes, hopelessness. Both Iola and Harper realize that in order for this uplifting to be accomplished, a certain amount of social consciousness is going to be necessary and that the brunt of this social work is going to have to be accomplished by those African Americans who have had privileged upbringings: those African Americans like Harper and Iola themselves. Iola realizes, as does Harper, that African Americans cannot look to white society to help them out of their current situation. This becomes an absolutely critical point in Harper's arguments about the uplifting of the race. While there obviously were many Caucasians in need of assistance out of poverty and distress in Harper's day—as the work of the writers referred to in this volume certainly shows—the case of the impoverished among the

African American race was always more compelling and of immediate concern to Harper, for Harper was well aware that of the many social devices in place to help the impoverished, most of those devices were geared toward poor whites. Harper never fooled herself into thinking that anyone but an African American would have to be held responsible for helping her or his own people out of their poverty. The ugly truth was that most whites, even those who volunteered to work in the reconstruction efforts, while sorry for the horrible sins of slavery, still saw any black as a lesser human being. Harper's role in working to eliminate poverty and other social ills from the African American community became critical, then.

Like her creator Frances Harper, Iola Leroy, who for all practical purposes appears white, is unlike her African American brethren in many ways. She has been highly educated, and she has been treated as a member of upper-class society. So ingrained in her has been her upbringing as the privileged daughter of a Southern gentleman of means that she has formed her own prejudices against the "Negro race." When she realizes her new station in life, she almost instantly decides to fully cast her lot with her newfound race, attempting to help her people at every given chance. After being freed from slavery, Iola clings to the race with all her heart and soul and dedicates herself to the uplifting of the race. Like Harper, Iola is educated, refined, and in a position to help those less fortunate than she. Also like Harper, Iola believes strongly that education and industry are key to moving the newly freed race out of the depths of poverty and oppression and into a life of true liberty and happiness. Iola also shares Harper's abhorrence for the use of alcohol, which she considers the ruination of many a person and family. Without alcohol as a hindrance, a person would be more likely to apply himself or herself to both learning and working—the two keys that would help assure a person financial stability.

Harper points out many times in *Iola Leroy* the importance of African Americans working to help one another. She does this most poignantly by illustrating again and again the prejudices against skin color and caste that are held against blacks by whites in the novel. She further illustrates this by impassioning Iola with an absolute dedication to the race, despite the fact that she has been raised white and could pass with little if any trouble as a white woman. Early in the novel, when the white

Dr. Gresham witnesses Iola, whom he thinks is white, tenderly kissing the black Tom on his deathbed, he remarks to the officer, "I can eat with colored people, walk, talk, and fight with them, but kissing them is something I don't hanker after" (57).

Dr. Gresham is smitten with Iola from his first encounter with her. Even when he discovers her "tainted blood," he wishes to marry Iola, thinking that she could—or would—hide her African ancestry from his family and society. During one of their many discussions on race, some telling revelations come to light:

> "But," said Dr. Gresham, "they [African Americans] must learn to struggle, labor, and achieve. By facts, not theories they will be judged in the future. The Anglo-Saxon race is proud, domineering, aggressive, and impatient of a rival, and, as I think, has more capacity for dragging down a weaker race than uplifting it. They have been a conquering and achieving people, marvelous in their triumphs of mind over matter. They have manifested the traits of character which are developed by success and victory."
>
> "And yet," said Iola earnestly, "I believe the time will come when the civilization of the [N]egro will assume a better phase than you Anglo-Saxons possess. You will prove unworthy of your high vantage ground if you only use your superior ability to victimize feebler races and minister to a selfish greed of gold and a love of domination." (116)

Iola is cut off at this point in the novel, but her argument is clear and becomes one of the staying points of the entire story. Iola's mission is to educate and socially uplift the race not only for the immediate means of the alleviation of poverty and other ills but also as a means of setting the stage for members of the race to become future leaders with a strong sense of social ethics that would place them in the center of benevolence activities for all.

Later in the novel the white Dr. Latrobe, unaware that the fair-skinned Dr. Latimer, who is included in his conversation, is indeed African American, boldly asserts his prejudices: "There are niggers [*sic*] who are as white as I am, but the taint of blood is there and we always exclude it" (229). Iola herself is subjected to losing employment when her coworkers discover she is "black." And her fair-skinned Uncle Robert has some difficulty securing lodging for the family once his obviously black mother is seen. Iola makes clear how important complexion is when discussing her brother's new friend, Lucille Delaney, with him. On hearing that Miss Delaney is dark, with "[n]either hair nor complexion show[ing] the least hint of blood admixture," Iola responds, "I am glad of it. . . . Every person of unmixed blood who succeeds in any department of literature, art, or science is a living argument for the capability which is in the race" (199). Such sentiments, coupled with the discussions and evidence of the horrors of lynching, abuse, and denial of rights that are illustrated, show the difficulties that both Harper and Iola faced when attempting to help uplift the race. While there were white people who denied prejudices, and while there were white people who seemingly worked to overturn wrongs, there was also the underlying suspicion of whites that had grown so deeply ingrained in blacks that the simplest and best solution seemed to be for the race to help itself as best it could, strengthening itself sometimes one person at a time. Iola's sense of justice is keen enough to show her that oftentimes human nature dictates that a person work most diligently for his or her own; in this case, characters such as Lucille will ultimately advance the agenda of the social uplifting of the race more than even Iola herself could hope to. It is the Lucilles who are meant to become the true keys to relieving the poverty and oppression of African Americans.

Harper's portrayal of Iola is very much the portrayal of a nineteenth-century feminist. Both Iola and Harper realize that a great deal of poverty and misery can be avoided if women are prepared for and capable of meaningful work. Iola, outside of her brief experience as a slave, always exhibits a great natural need for independence and work of her own, with that work's accompanying pay. She is the educated, intelligent, articulate daughter of a woman who has enjoyed the same privileges that come from being sent to school. When Iola is freed by the army, she works diligently and wholeheartedly as a nurse. Once the war ends, she engages in the profession of teaching, working particularly with freed blacks. When she moves North with her uncle, Iola seeks and finds employment as a store saleswoman, explaining to her uncle: "I have a theory that every woman should have some skill or art which would insure her at least a comfortable support. I believe there would be less unhappy marriages if labor were more honored among women" (205). Iola continues with these matter-of-fact thoughts on women's work throughout the novel and continues to earn her own living, even after her marriage to Dr. Latimer. This belief in a woman's preparation for and engagement in meaningful work would not have been a theory held by a majority of nineteenth-century social leaders, but Harper knew, from her own experience and from that of others, that sometimes things don't work out in the idealistic way that society dictates. If a woman could be economically independent of her husband, should something happen to him, she and her children would not become victims of poverty. There is also the presumption, of course, that this would also mean that a woman would not be at the mercy of a man who has turned out to be a bad choice. Harper shows in her writings many men gone wrong via the path of alcohol; had the women in these stories been capable of easily supporting themselves and their children, the complete tragedies that often occurred could have been averted.

Harper's philosophy of benevolence through the race often shows itself through a belief that education—very specifically, learning to read and write—will make all the difference to the now liberated race. This philosophy becomes an important credo for Harper in all of her work, perhaps especially in *Iola Leroy.* Iola consistently preaches the importance of learning to read and sets about helping others learn this skill. Several times she attempts to convince the elder Aunt Linda that she too should learn to read. Linda, however, sees herself as too old to learn such a thing. Harper's Iola Leroy holds strong ideas on the importance of education for women. Besides her teaching efforts, Iola presents a paper titled "Education of Mothers" to the group of black intellectuals who gather regularly in her home. As part of the discussion that follows this particular meeting, the Reverend Carmicle states,

> I was delighted with my visits to various institutions of learning, and surprised at the desire manifested among the young people to obtain an education. Where toil-worn mothers bent beneath their heavy burdens their more favored daughters are enjoying the privileges of education. . . . [I] saw young ladies who had graduated as doctors. (258)

Once again the presumption is that a highly educated woman will be more useful not only to herself but to society as well. Such a woman can keep herself from poverty and dependence—whether on a husband or on society—but she will also be exceedingly capable of helping others, including her children, gain strength and economic freedom. As Joyce W.

Warren points out, "Harper, who was a middle-class, educated free black woman, devoted her life to writing and activism, working, as she said, to elevate her race; but she refused to buy into the dominant culture's notion that the way to assert men's independence was to enforce the dependence of women" (155).

Along with her portrayal of Iola as a black feminist, Harper also writes Iola as a very spiritual being who is Christ-like in many ways. Religion was important to Harper, as it was to many African Americans in her day. For many, it had been the one stronghold that had helped them survive slavery and that continued to help them try to overcome the social oppression with which they continued to be faced. Harper's own faith was seemingly solid; therefore, it is no surprise when her women characters, Iola Leroy in particular, have similar anchors in Christianity. When Iola chooses to dedicate her life to working for and with the "downtrodden" rather than continuing a climb in upper-class white society, she is following the same mission Christ set for himself in the gospel stories: working with the lowly and shunning the comforts that would have come from joining the ranks of the accepted priests and rabbis. Also Christ-like, Iola has no fear of sharing a meal with the poorest of the poor or of associating with what the highest of society would consider its dregs. She does not possess airs of greatness; like Christ, she humbly accepts everyone—however low on society's ladder—as important and very worth her while. Harper's message here is clear: one must necessarily associate with the poor in order to best help them. Neither Frances Harper nor Iola Leroy is the type of missionary personality who believes in helping from a distance. The modus operandi is clearly the same as was Christ's: respect the poor, know the poor, then help the poor so that they can in turn help themselves.

Iola Leroy's message of poverty relief also appears in a long dialogue on the evils and stupidity of drinking, Aunt Linda says,

> I ain't runnin' down my people. But a fool's a fool, wether he's white or black. And I think de nigger [*sic*] who will spen' his hard-earned money in dese yere new grog-shops is de biggest kine ob a fool, an' I sticks ter dat. You know we didn't hab all dese low places in slave times. An' what is dey fer, but to get the people's money. An' its a shame how dey do sling de licker 'bout 'lection times. (160)

Aunt Linda is aware how much money is being wasted in the saloons, and she is also aware of how many wives and children are suffering because of this wasted money. One of Harper's biggest concerns about the abuse of alcohol was the economic problem. Quite simply, if a man were spending what little money the family had on alcohol, then that was money that could not be used to feed and clothe the family. To Harper—and to Aunt Linda, for that matter—alcohol was an evil, plain and simple.

Harper works tirelessly to illustrate how the race should uplift itself through her writings, through her speeches, and through her own political and social activism. In her 1877 speech, "Coloured Women of America," Harper espouses the glories of social activism:

> The coloured women have not been backward in promoting charities for their own sex and race. . . . By organized effort, coloured women have been enabled to help each other in sickness, and provide respectable funerals for the dead. They have institutions under different names; one of the oldest . . . has been in existence . . . about fifty years. . . . There are also . . . homes for aged coloured women. . . . The city of Philadelphia has also another home for the homeless. . . . The coloured women of Philadelphia have formed a Christian Relief Association, which has opened sewing schools for coloured girls, and which has been enabled, year after year, to lend a hand to some of the more needy of their race . . . and has . . . sustained an employment office for some time. (274–75)

Certainly, charities run by white women were following the same lofty goals and principles, but Harper consistently points out that those charities cared for few if any "colored" folks. It was part of Harper's mission to see to it that her own race was helped with as much fervor, if not more, than were their white counterparts.

Truly Frances Harper practiced what she preached in her own life. Harper's belief in education and work as means of independence and as assurance against poverty was deeply ingrained in her own existence and became a part of her life's mission. As Warren writes,

> All of her life, even during her marriage and as the mother of a young child, Harper worked: she wrote and lectured and taught and organized. She published nine books and numerous poems, essays, and stories in magazines. She donated her own money to the antislavery cause. She or-

> ganized and practiced a boycott of slave-produced goods; she worked actively with the Underground Railroad; she traveled to Canada to meet with and help fugitives. After the Civil War she became active in the Women's Suffrage movement. (155)

While Harper was an absolute believer in the educated and privileged African American's duty to help his or her less fortunate brethren, she was also vigilantly hopeful that her white colleagues in the many women's social organizations to which she belonged would also see that they as well had a duty to help raise the African American out of poverty and social distress. Perhaps this is why some of Harper's most important protagonists, such as Iola Leroy, are women of mixed race who look white. Unfortunately, Harper's hopes seem to have gone without realization. And perhaps *this* is why Harper pens Iola as a character determined to make the *most* of the strength of the African American woman by celebrating jubilantly her own African American heritage and that of others in the novel. (It is worth noting that in the short novel, *Minnie's Sacrifice,* Harper does much the same thing. Minnie—another mixed-race character—discovers she is indeed African American as she embarks upon young womanhood and goes on to embrace her racial heritage.) Harper remained true to her course, knowing without any doubts that she could begin to effect a change just by doing what she had been called to do. She did this not only through her own social activities but also through her writings. The examples of benevolence and active charity that she illustrates in *Iola Leroy* are important to Harper's own canon and to the larger canons of African American literature, American literature, women's literature, and the literature of benevolence. Harper's work continues to act as a beacon for a new generation still seeking to uplift, uphold, and celebrate the race.

Works Cited

Bone, Robert. *The Negro Novel in America.* New Haven: Yale UP, 1965.

Boyd, Melba Joyce. *Discarded Legacy: Politics and Poetics in the Life of Frances E. W. Harper, 1825–1911.* Detroit: Wayne State UP, 1994.

Brackney, William H. *Christian Volunteerism in Britain and North America.* Westport: Greenwood Press, 1995.

Foster, Frances Smith. Introduction. *Iola Leroy, or Shadows Uplifted.* By Frances E. W. Harper. 1853. New York: Oxford UP, 1988. xxvii–xxxviii.

Graham, Maryemma. Introduction. *Complete Poems.* By Frances E. W. Harper. Ed. Maryemma Graham. New York: Oxford UP, 1988. xxxiii–lx.

Harper, Frances E. W. "Coloured Women of America." *A Brighter Coming Day: A Frances Ellen Watkins Harper Reader.* Ed. Frances Smith Foster. New York: Feminist Press, 1990. 271–75.

———. *Iola Leroy, or Shadows Uplifted.* 1892. New York: Oxford UP, 1988.

———. *Minnie's Sacrifice, Sowing and Reaping, Trial and Triumph: Three Rediscovered Novels by Frances E. W. Harper.* Ed. Frances Smith Foster. Boston: Beacon Press, 1994.

Warren, Joyce W. "Fracturing Gender: Woman's Economic Independence." *Nineteenth-Century American Women Writers: A Critical Reader.* Ed. Karen L. Kilcup. Malden, Mass.: Blackwell, 1998. 146–63.

Young, Elizabeth. "Warring Fictions: Iola Leroy and the Color of Gender." *American Literature* 64 (1992): 273–97.

9

"To Reveal the Humble Immigrant Parents to Their Own Children"

Immigrant Women, Their American Daughters, and the Hull-House Labor Museum

Sarah E. Chinn

In 1899, Hilda Satt, the daughter of Jewish immigrants to Chicago, visited Hull-House for the first time. Her father had recently died, and although her mother "faced life with the heroism of the true American pioneer" (Polacheck 44), she was barely scraping by. Hilda hoped that Hull-House, with its low cost cafeteria, activities for immigrant women, men, and children, and focus on neighborhood outreach, would be able to alleviate her family's dire financial and emotional situation. While the initial visit made some impression, it was Hilda's second trip to Jane Addams's settlement house that had the greatest effect on the girl.

Jane Addams took Hilda on a tour of Hull-House, starting off with one of the house's most innovative projects, the Labor Museum. The Museum featured the traditional crafts of the immigrant communities that made up Hull-House's neighborhood, and "showed the evolution of cotton, wool, silk and linen" (Polacheck 64). Next to the textiles were descriptions of how each crop was raised, spun, woven, and dyed. The spectators at the Museum were a mixed crowd: immigrants and their children, well-heeled philanthropists, devotees of the then avant-garde Arts and Crafts movement. The Museum was also fully interactive; when Hilda finished looking around, Mary Hill, the Museum's coordinator "asked me whether I would like to learn to weave something that was typically American. . . . [V]ery soon I was weaving a small Navaho-style blanket" (Polacheck 64).

As Hilda soon learned, the Labor Museum was not simply a showplace for traditional handicrafts. It was also a moneymaking venture: Hull-House sold the products of the people who exhibited their skills in the Museum, and used the money to fund settlement-house projects. However, as Hilda Satt, writing decades later as Hilda Satt Polacheck, pointed out, one of the Museum's primary concerns went beyond consciousness or fundraising. She realized that "Miss Addams found that there was a definite feeling of superiority on the part of children of immigrants towards their parents" who participated in the Museum's exhibits (65). Hilda saw that for these children, mostly in their teens, "the Labor Museum was an eye-opener. When they saw crowds of well-dressed Americans standing around admiring what Italian, Irish, German, and Scandinavian mothers could do, their disdain for their mothers vanished. . . . I am sure the Labor Museum reduced strained feelings on the part of immigrants and their children" (66).

Addams's discovery of this "feeling of superiority" was hardly a surprise to her. She designed the Labor Museum with that result in mind, a fact of which Polacheck, whose memoir, *I Came a Stranger: The Story of a Hull-House Girl,* was dedicated in "humble gratitude to the memory of JANE ADDAMS" (2), could hardly have been unaware. Jane Addams created the Labor Museum as a way to address a problem that obsessed her contemporaries: the attitudes of American-born children of late-nineteenth-century immigrants toward their parents on the one hand, and the United States on the other—what was often thematized as the conflict between the "Old World" and the "New World."[1] This generation of new Americans was entering adolescence as Addams was embarking on what would be a historic philanthropic project, and by 1900, when Hilda Satt was making her way through the Hull-House Labor Museum, they constituted a huge demographic bubble comparable to the baby boom of the 1940s and 1950s.[2]

In this essay I explore how the Labor Museum dealt with the "problem" of American-born teenage children of immigrant parents, particularly the daughters of immigrant women, and how Addams represented that problem in her writing. These children provided a bridge between their parents and the culture of the United States that was often undecipherable to the older generation and also built a wall between themselves and their parents, a wall that popular American culture helped construct and maintain. For a variety of reasons, Jane Addams wanted to demolish that wall and reunite foreign-born parents and U.S.-born children—she had, as she put it, "an overmastering desire to reveal the humble immigrant parents to their own children" (HH 171–72)[3]—and she imagined that the Labor Museum would go some way toward achieving that goal. But she was fighting a powerful cultural trend: the adolescent children of immigrants were in the vanguard of creating and adopting a new and in many ways unique working-class culture, organized around factory labor and the leisure that their incomes made possible. This culture bore many of the hallmarks of what we still imagine are typical of American teenagers, such as a strong investment in mass culture, particularly music and performance; an open and often playful sexuality; a focus on fun as a self-sustaining reason for activity.

In two texts in particular, Addams addressed the issue of American-born children of immigrants. In *Twenty Years at Hull-House* (1910), a memoir of her life up to the point of the founding of Hull-House, and a chronicle of the work and philosophies of the settlement house, and *The Spirit of Youth and the City Streets* (1909), Addams's book-length exploration of the needs of and limitations placed on urban adolescents, Addams embarked on an ambitious project, to reshape public opinion about urban youth, particularly in immigrant communities. Although she did not realize it at the time, Addams was grappling with an issue that concerned (and sometimes even consumed) many of her contemporaries. Debates raged over the proliferation of dance halls, beer gardens, and amusement parks as places that young people spent time in, as well as perceived and actual increases in sexual license and prostitution among young women and drunkenness among women and men. At the same time, these young people thwarted many of the efforts of U.S.-born philanthropists whose attempts to "help" them—that is, not simply lift them out of poverty and the grinding work of sweatshops and department stores, but reform their morals and lead them to middle-class values—they viewed with attitudes ranging from cynical humor to outright contempt.

Addams's project to reconcile immigrant mothers and their American-born daughters derived in part from a desire to restore dignity to the lives of the older women and to the cultures from which they came, but it also resulted from a need to reinstitute the traditional parent-child power relations that had been so formative in her own childhood. Addams's mother died when she was a young child, and she admired her father with an almost violent passion.[4] Like her contemporaries, Addams was alarmed at the dissolution of familial hierarchy among new immigrants, particularly given the spending power many adolescent boys and girls had from their jobs in factories, hotels, department stores, pushcarts, and other employment. These changing social conditions eased into being a new way of looking at these young people poised between childhood and full adult status. Adolescence, or, rather, *the adolescent,* was emerging as a new object of theory and prescription, an identity separate from childhood on the one hand and adulthood on the other.

The advances in union organizing in various industries, the institution of compulsory education, and the exclusion of children under sixteen from the permanent workforce created a new category of worker: the adolescent, not yet an adult, but also legally empowered to leave school and earn a wage. Given the sharp increases in living expenses in major cities as immigrants crowded in, adolescent children represented a significant source of family income. In the first decade of the 1900s in New York, fewer than half of working-class families depended upon the father for sole financial support (Peiss 12). The novels of immigrant life that became increasingly popular in the early decades of the twentieth century—Anzia Yezierska's *Bread Givers,* Abraham Cahan's *The Rise of David Levinsky,* Willa Cather's *O Pioneers!,* to name only a few—invariably featured representations of adolescent children at work to help cover basic family living expenses.

Kathy Peiss's groundbreaking work on young women's leisure activities in New York at the end of the nineteenth century underscores many of the arguments I make here. As she points out, four-fifths of wage-earning women in New York in 1900 were single, and one-third were between the ages of sixteen and twenty (34). Although many young women handed over much or even all of their pay to their parents, many others had access to at least some of their income. Unfettered by children of their own and old enough to desire the pleasures the city had to offer, young women broke away from the leisure activities of their immigrant mothers: visiting with friends and female family members, sharing childcare, gossiping with neighbors (22). A burgeoning adolescent culture organized around leisure and sexuality suffused urban life, marking out a new terrain, "distinct from familial traditions and the customary practices of their ethnic groups, signifying a new identity as wage earners through language, clothing, and social rituals" (Peiss 47).

This identity, I argue, formed at the intersection of adolescent and new American identities: the young women Peiss discusses were, after all, teenagers in a culture in which adolescence was jelling into a meaningful identity category. Unlike the more rigidly gender-segregated lives their parents led, working-class adolescent girls, many of them the children of new immigrants, were creating a heterosocial world for themselves through the flamboyant hats they wore, the dance halls they frequented, the trips to amusement parks and vaudeville, an environment in which, as Peiss argues, "commercialized recreation fostered a youth-oriented, mixed-sex world of pleasure, where female participation was profitable and encouraged" (6).

Or, rather, encouraged by some. As Laura Hapke points out, the lives of young workingwomen were fascinating to their bourgeois contemporaries, and from the 1890s on, "staid publishing houses with a wide middle-class readership brought out numerous tenement tales with sweatshop and box-factory workers, shop girls and cloak models, genteel daughters of failed businessmen reduced to department store work, even former dance hall girls who manage saloons and female stevedores who take men's names" (4). At the same time, however, among reformers and philanthropists, enthusiasm for the ways in which young women were shaping and responding to work and leisure was muted, to say the least.

Part of this concern was intertwined with anxieties about what adolescence as a gendered social category actually meant, and how this new class of people—of workers and participants in the public sphere—would shape the larger theater of American culture. G. Stanley Hall, already a famous (one might even say notorious) psychologist by the end of the nineteenth century, detailed these anxieties in his two-volume study, *Adolescence.* His characterization of adolescent boys and girls as vital yet vulnerable, resilient yet subject to the "shipwrecks" of the "hothouse demands" of a rapidly changing era, was echoed by many of his more progressive contemporaries. Reformers such as Belle Moskowitz in New York and Louise De Koven Bowen in Chicago organized their efforts around the needs of teenage immigrant girls. De Koven Bowen's 1910 study of "department store girls" expressed many of the same concerns as Hall, although with the welfare of the girls, rather than "the race" in mind: "It is evident that the long day of twelve or more hours cripples the human system, dwarfs the mind, gives no time for culture and recreation and shortens life" (n.p.). The average age of the young women working in department stores was nineteen, and almost all were American-born daughters of immigrant parents. Department store girls were poorly paid, "constantly surrounded by the articles which are so dear to the feminine heart," but often unable to afford most of them (n.p.).[5]

What Hall, De Koven Bowen, Moskowitz, and Addams all had in common was a belief that adolescents had an innate desire for pleasure and recreation, but that the commercialization of recreation had transformed a healthy and generative need into a corrupted search for cheap thrills. Debates raging over appropriate recreation for working-class youth, particularly young women, stemmed from a variety of sources. The most vocal was the fear of criminality among boys and prostitution among girls. Not all these fears were unrealistic. The largest proportion of urban prostitutes were U.S.-born daughters of immigrants (Rosen 139); in 1900 over one-third of all girls in the New York State Reformatory were daughters of Jewish immigrants, mostly imprisoned for prostitution and petty theft (Perry, *Belle Moskowitz* 22). More often, prostitution was informal and part of a quid pro quo with young women exchanging a night on the town or a day at the beach for sexual favors with their dates.

Nonetheless, given the explosion of recreations for young people, social commentators felt that they had to respond to the phenomenon. Addams saw recreation among youth as a social good, since "one generation after another has depended upon its young to equip it with gaiety and enthusiasm, to persuade it that living is a pleasure" (*Spirit of Youth* 3–4). Working-class women's desire for "frivolous" finery was a way to make that gaiety and enthusiasm visible; as Addams argued, "through the huge hat, with its wilderness of bedraggled feathers, the girl announces to the world that she is here. She demands attention to the fact of her existence, she states that she is ready to live, to take her place in the world" (8).

Although they saw commercial dance halls as "largely controlled by the brewery, saloon and vice interests," progressive reformers like Addams, De Koven Bowen, and Moskowitz argued that prohibiting dance halls would do more harm than good (De Koven Bowen, *Public Dance Halls* 3).[6] Rather, what young people needed was "a rationally conceived program of regulated and municipalized recreation resources" and, in a telling phrase that brings us back to Addams, the "general motherhood of the commonwealth" (Perry, "Dance Hall Reform" 724–25).

Implicit in these critiques of modern amusement sites was a nostalgia for older, less sexually explicit modes of recreation. Hall hearkened back to dancing's formerly "pristine power to express love, mourning, justice, penalty, fear, anger, consolation, divine service, symbolic and philosophical conceptions, and every industry or characteristic act of life in pantomime and gesture" (214). Instead, the "dance of the modern ballroom" constituted "only a degenerate relict, with at best but a very insignificant culture value, and too often stained with bad associations" (214). Similarly, Addams contrasted "the public dance halls filled with frivolous and irresponsible young people in a feverish search for pleasure" with "the old dances on the village green in which all of the older people of the village participated" (*Spirit of Youth* 13).

The Labor Museum participated in the same kind of longing for intergenerational recreation. Concerned about the omnipresence of commerce in young women's lives, "all that is gaudy and sensual, by the flippant street music, the highly colored theater posters, the trashy love stories, the feathered hats, the cheap heroics of the revolvers displayed in the pawn-shop windows," Addams wanted to recreate the self-sustaining relationships between parents and children (27). Moreover, while Addams sustained a fantasy of country life as harmonious, in contradistinction to the conflict-ridden family life of the city, she recognized the many examples of "family affection" and "family devotion" that sustained urban life, from the immigrant man who went without a coat in February so that he could afford to keep his son in school to the women who maintained clean and well-stocked homes even as they worked long hours in sweatshops (*Spirit of Youth* 34).

Unlike many of her peers, Addams did not doubt immigrant parents' commitment to their children's well-being. She testified to the "wonderful devotion to the child . . . in the midst of our stupid social and industrial relations, [and] all that keeps society human" (33). The family as a social unit "blends the experience of generations into a continuous story" (*Spirit of Youth* 34), and close communication and even friendship between generations was the key to preventing the ruin of young women and corruption of young men. Teenage girls in the work world, particularly vulnerable to the predations of the city, were also particularly uplifted by connections to their mothers. As she argued,

> The mothers who are of the most use to these . . . city working girls are the mothers who develop a sense of companionship with the changing experiences of their daughters. . . . Their vigorous family life allies itself by a dozen bonds to the educational, the industrial and the recreational organizations of the modern city. (*Spirit of Youth* 47)

But all the companionship in the world would be of no use if the daughters themselves were unable to see their mothers as peers but rather as primitives and sources of embarrassment. Addams devised the Labor Museum as a way not just to reconnect mothers and daughters but to make clear the links between handcraft—the old way that young women derogated—and factory work. The story Addams tells of her inspiration to establish the Museum embodies these issues and suggests a solution to them. Walking toward Hull-House one day, Addams saw "an old Italian woman, her distaff against her homesick face, patiently spinning a thread by the simple stick spindle so reminiscent of all Southern Europe" (172). This image of the persistence of traditional crafts in the face of immense cultural disruption and isolation dovetailed with Addams's concern that older immigrants "so often lost their hold upon their Americanized children," who felt contempt for the "greenness" of their parents' limited mastery of English and alienation from U.S. culture (HH 172).

Addams imagined the Labor Museum as a living history of handicrafts, tracing their development from the most basic techniques to their transformation by mechanization. In its exhibits, the Museum traced specific crafts such as spinning and put varieties of spindles "in historic sequence and order . . . to connect the whole with the present method of factory spinning" (173). By establishing a generic link between artisanal crafts and their industrialized equivalents, Addams hoped to show the factory-working children of immigrants that their labor was not so different from the work their parents participated in and they despised for its "greenness." By exposing her neighbors to the Museum, Addams also wanted to make possible interethnic harmony based in a belief in the commonality of human experience, since it "enabled even the most casual observer to see that . . . industry develops similarly and peacefully year by year among the workers of each nation, heedless of differences in language, religion, and political experiences" (HH 173).

Strongly affected by the pedagogical theories of John Dewey, particularly his declaration that "education is a process of living and not a preparation for future living" (78), Addams designed the Labor Museum as an experiential site of learning. Young women in the needle trades could actively relate the physical processes of their own work to the craftwork their mothers were exhibiting. As Addams argued, "If these young people could actually see that the complicated machinery of the factory had been evolved from simple tools, they might at least make a beginning toward that education which Dr. Dewey defines as 'a continuing reconstruction of experience'" (172). In addition, the Museum allowed immigrant parents, so often in the position of learning from their children about what it meant to be American, or using their children as intermediaries to interpret between them and the Anglo-American world, to reinvest in the parental role of teacher, guide, and transmitter of cultural knowledge (HH 174).

In Addams's narrative of intergenerational conflict, the teenage counterpart of the old woman at the distaff is "Angelina" who "did not wish to be too closely identified in the eyes of the rest of [her] cooking class [at Hull-House] with an Italian woman who wore a kerchief over her head, uncouth boots, and short petticoats" (HH 176). In a metaphor of generational distance that Addams must have found poignant, Angelina and her mother walked to Hull-House together, but entered through separate doors so that others would not know they were related. The Labor Museum changed all that, however.

> One evening [visiting the Museum], Angelina saw her mother surrounded by a group of visitors from the School of Education who much admired the spinning, and she concluded from their conversation that her mother was "the best stick-spindle spinner in America." When she inquired from me as to the truth of this deduction, I took occasion to describe the Italian village in which her mother had lived, something of her free life, and how, because of the opportunity she and the other women of the village had to drop their spindles over the edge of a precipice, they had developed a skill in spinning beyond that of the neighboring towns. I dilated somewhat on the freedom and beauty of that life—how hard it must be to exchange it all for a two-room tenement, and to give up a beautiful homespun kerchief for an ugly department store hat. I intimated it was most unfair to judge her by these things alone, and that while she must depend on her daughter to learn the new ways, she also had a right to expect her daughter to know something of the old ways. (HH 176)

The change in relationship between the two was immediate and tangible. Rather than rejecting her mother as a relic of the old world, Angelina "allowed her mother to pull out of the big box under the bed the beautiful homespun garments which had been previously hidden away as uncouth; and she openly came into the Labor Museum by the same door as did her mother, proud at least of the mastery of the craft which had been so much admired" (HH 177).

As is clear from Addams's story, the role of elites in reconciling immigrant mothers and their adolescent daughters is far from uncomplicated. Angelina values her mother because the visitors from the School of Education do. She reflects the values of the educated bourgeoisie in championing handcrafts over factory-made goods for the very reasons that Angelina herself might treasure the products of industrialization: mass-produced objects are uniform, cheaply made, inexpensive, disposable, ephemeral. Angelina is convinced of the worth of her mother's labor and the culture that she literally wears on her back because Jane Addams argues for the "beautiful homespun kerchief" over the "ugly department store hat" that was the staple of working girls.

Addams's defense of Angelina's mother has more than a touch of the imperialist aesthete, who "dilates" upon the "freedom and beauty" of primitive lives while maintaining the sophisticated superiority of her own cultural practices. But her goals in the Labor Museum went far beyond a sort of ethnic tourism or snobbery against the vulgarities of factory girls. Like the Arts and Crafts innovators for whom the Labor Museum was a touchstone, Addams believed in the "restorative power in the exercise of a genuine craft" (HH 260). Her critique of industrialization was not that the goods it produced were cheap and worthless, but that factory labor itself was depersonalizing and monotonous—that young women had been convinced that tedious industrial work was somehow more glamorous than the emotionally rewarding labor of their mothers. It's no surprise that Hilda Satt found Hull-House "an oasis in a desert of boredom and monotony" (97).

Indeed, the experience of intellectually tedious but physically exhausting labor was one of the things that united immigrant parents and their American-born children. Addams's goal in the Labor Museum was not to convince the parents that their ways were superannuated but to demonstrate to the children that work could be fulfilling in and of itself, not just as a means to gain spending power in a culture already drenched in commerce. Addams tells story after story of immigrants transformed by the opportunity to practice crafts or destroyed by the denial of that opportunity: the Bohemian goldsmith who succumbs to alcoholism and eventually suicide after working as a coal shoveler; the Russian women who, disappointed at missing a party at Hull-House, were shown the Labor Museum:

> [G]radually the thirty sodden, tired women were transformed. They knew how to use the spindles and were delighted to find the Russian spinning frame. Many of them had never seen the spinning wheel, which has not penetrated to certain parts of Russia, and they regarded it as a new and wonderful invention. They turned up their dresses to show their homespun petticoats; they tried the looms; they explained the difficulty of the old patterns; in short, from having been stupidly entertained, they themselves did the entertaining. (HH 174)

Even more significant for Addams was the re-establishment of the traditional role of community elders. In contrast to their usual helplessness in the face of a hostile foreign culture (whose hostility was often mirrored by their own children), the Russian spinners "were able for the moment to instruct their American hostesses in an old and honored craft, as was indeed becoming to their age and experience" (174). The Museum re-empowered immigrant parents, re-establishing them, as Addams herself pointed out, "into the position of teachers, and we imagine that it affords them a pleasant change from the tutelage in which all Americans, including their own children, are so apt to hold them" (HH 174).[7]

The Labor Museum raises disquieting questions, though. After all, as Barbara Kirshenblatt-Gimblett argues, even in the best of circumstances, "when efforts are made to the contrary, live exhibits tend to make people into artifacts because the ethnographic gaze objectifies" (415). How much could Addams control the responses of the mostly elite, mostly Anglo museum-goers, whose agendas were very different from the working girls whose mothers were the Museum's main exhibitors? This is particularly pressing given the timing of the Museum, which opened the same year in the same city as the Chicago World's Columbian Exposition, which has been widely discussed as a central site for the kind of objectifying ethnographic gaze Kirshenblatt-Gimblett describes.[8]

How much did the Labor Museum participate in what Svetlana Alpers has called "the museum effect—the tendency to isolate something from its world, to offer it up for attentive looking" (27)? How much did it "turn cultural materials into art objects" (Alpers 31), or transform immigrants into specimens? In some ways, the Labor Museum exemplifies what Kirshenblatt-Gimblett calls "in situ" ethnographic display, which is designed to "include more of what was left behind, even if only in replica, after the object was excised from its physical, social, and cultural settings" (389). In the Labor Museum, are immigrants themselves the objects, "confined to a pictorial, timeless ethnic space" (Haenni 511)? Undoubtedly, they have been removed from their original environments and cast into a new context.

At the same time, this analogy glosses over some significant differences between the Labor Museum and typical ethnographic display. Unlike the ethnographic exhibits of the World's Columbian Exposition, or the St. Louis World's Fair just over a decade later, the Museum made no effort to recreate an "authentic" "ethnic" environment. Addams consciously mixed and matched craftspeople of different national backgrounds practicing similar crafts to show the similarities between them, rather than showcasing the irreducibility of ethnic and "racial" identity.

Ethnographic display makes clear distinctions between observers and observed, encouraging spectators to see themselves as essentially different from those on display while at the same time assuring them that they are watching authentic "ethnic" activity, as though the exhibitors have no idea that they are there. Kirshenblatt-Gimblett argues that "live displays, whether recreations of daily activities or staged as formal performances . . . create the illusion that the activities one watches are being done rather than represented," itself a false image that allows viewers to believe that they are watching everyday life, rather than a performance (415). By contrast, the Labor Museum dissolved the line between audience and performers. On the one hand, the craftspeople in the Museum were represented as experts, and the work they did as separate from their everyday lives as factory workers, homemakers, pushcart peddlers and so on. At the same time, Addams's goal was to shrink the distance between immigrants and the American born, not calcify it. As Hilda Satt's experience shows, museum-goers were allowed to become craftspeople themselves, if only for the afternoon, and the immigrants' children were encouraged to see the links between their own factory labor and their parents' manual skills. Finally, the intended spectators of the Museum were the children of the "exhibits," not the separate class of viewers constructed by other kinds of ethnographic display. The educational process of the Labor Museum was not organized around a kind of Anglo-paternalism, but rather around the smoothing out of self-conscious difference between the women and men weaving, spinning, throwing pots, and so on, and the teenaged girls and boys who filed through the Museum, forming connections between their work and the previously degraded work of their parents.

Ironically, the Hull-House residents, mostly members of the same college-educated elite class as the bourgeois visitors to the Labor Museum, themselves constituted the primary ethnographic display on offer at the settlement.[9] As Shannon Jackson points out, "the daily living practices of the residents—the so-called private realms of experience—were perpetually on display" to anyone who visited (152). At Hull-House, most domestic activity typical of the American-born middle class was carried out in public spaces so that the cafeteria in which residents and guests all ate, and the public reception rooms that functioned as parlors for residents, turned downstairs life for residents into an ongoing *public* experiment. While the work of the spinners, weavers, potters, and the like was seen by Anglo observers as representative of larger cultural structures (for example, as Jackson observes, "the spinning of a neighborhood woman named Mrs. Brosnahan came to stand for 'Irish spinning'" [260]), the immigrant neighbors of Hull-House saw the day-to-day activities of house residents—the food they ate, the way they interacted with visitors, their leisure activities—as metonyms for the folkways of the native-born bourgeoisie.

The Labor Museum also existed as a peculiar inversion of the status of the fine art museums that came into existence after the Civil War: the Metropolitan Museum of Art in New York, the Philadelphia Museum of Art, the Boston Museum of Fine Arts, and the Art Institute of Chicago alone were founded between 1870 and 1874. As Alan Trachtenberg has demonstrated, the fine art museum "established as a physical fact the notion that culture filtered downward from a distant past, from overseas, from the sacred founts of wealth and private power" (144–45). The kind of art worthy of display in a museum—old, European, removed from (while idealizing through representation) common people—was institutionalized in opposition to the everyday world of crafts. The Labor Museum turned these assumptions inside out. The folkways the Museum exhibited *were* from the past and from overseas, but rather than being separated from their producer and their audience, the "works" (in both senses of the word) on display at the Labor Museum demonstrated the continuity between past and present, not the division implicit in fine art display.

However, like fine art museums and the various world's fairs, the Labor Museum made a clear distinction between industrial and preindustrial cultures. Moreover, Addams participated in an evolutionary discourse that represented immigrants and poor as occupying a lower sociobiological rung on the developmental ladder than their U.S.-born Anglo superiors. The Labor Museum "placed performances in sequence, one national performer after another, to document a developmental history," from the most "primitive" to the most "developed," although still preindustrial (Jackson 254). Addams constructed a transcultural narrative of handcrafts that informed the exhibits in the Museum: "It was possible to put these seven into historic sequence and order and to connect the whole with the present method of factory spinning. . . . Within one room a Syrian woman, a Greek, an Italian, a Russian, and an Irishwoman enabled [museum-goers] to see that there is no break in orderly evolution if we look at history from the industrial standpoint" (HH 173).

This is not the whole story, though. Rather than drawing an impassable line between artisanship and mass production, Addams folded all forms of production into the narrative of what she called "industrial history." Lectures at Hull-House and the Museum drew analogies between the evolution from spindle to wheel spinning with the development of the sewing machine and even heavy industrial machinery (HH 173). In addition, Addams argued that just as "George Eliot has made us love the belated weaver, Silas Marner," art and literature can illuminate to us the lives of industrial and sweatshop workers, reducing the gap between artisans and mechanics (173). Human history, she observed, is short, and "human progress is slow," so that the division between handloom and weaving machine is infinitesimal (HH 173). More importantly, the transgenerational reunion of mother and daughter was a microcosm of the historical pedagogy of the Labor Museum, itself a microcosm of Hull-House's agenda.

Perhaps the most difficult critique of the Labor Museum, and of Hull-House in general, is the charge that Addams was participating in a kind of genteel sensationalism, exploiting immigrants for the benefit of bourgeois settlement workers and other reformers, who could garner a sense of self-satisfaction by transforming immigrant poverty and "backwardness" into spectacle. Ruth Crocker's claim that *Twenty Years at Hull-House* "aestheticized the poor" and represented them in enough detail only "to teach the residents different lessons about life" (179) is a penetrating criticism of much late-nineteenth-century poverty relief, and Addams was certainly formed by the philanthropic conventions of her era. For many of her contemporaries, after all, the ghetto was a place to go slumming, "a liminal site of commercial entertainment . . . both potentially dangerous and safely classifiable within middle-class tourism" (Haenni 494).

I would argue, though, that Addams conceived of the Labor Museum *not* as a tourist attraction or a site of the objectification of "primitive" immigrant crafts. Indeed, looking back on her formative experiences with urban poverty in the East End of London, the mature Jane Addams felt deep ambivalence about what we might call the "tourism of degradation" that she witnessed as a young woman: "A small party of tourists were taken to the East End by a city missionary to witness the Saturday night sale of decaying vegetables and fruit" (HH 61). At the time, Addams was profoundly affected by this scene, and "while I was irresistibly drawn to the poorer quarters of each city [she visited on her two-year tour of Europe], nothing among the beggars of South Italy nor among the salt miners of Austria carried the same conviction of human wretchedness which was conveyed by this momentary glimpse of an East London street" (HH 62). On reflection, though, Addams recognized the manipulative and objectifying elements of her tour of the East End, which was "a most fragmentary and lurid view of the poverty of East London, and quite unfair," since it gave no sense of the reality of the lives of the inhabitants or the "gallantry" of poverty relief workers who lived side by side with East Enders. It is this very "fragmentary and lurid" representation of Hull-House's neighbors that the Labor Museum attempted to disrupt, in the eyes of both native-born spectators and the children of immigrant participants.

In her experiences with the Labor Museum, Addams attempted to grapple with several seemingly different but in fact interrelated problems. While poverty was almost overwhelming to immigrants, material needs were not their only concerns.[10] Many immigrant parents felt bewildered by the world into which they had brought their families and in which their children were flourishing, seemingly at the expense of the past. The knowledges they had brought with them were rendered irrelevant at best, and their American-born children repudiated them. In *Twenty Years at Hull-House,* Addams remembers even in her own childhood being "often distressed by the children of immigrant parents who were ashamed of the pit whence they were digged, and who counted themselves successful as they were able to ignore the past" (HH 42). For Addams, whose veneration of Abraham Lincoln was equaled only by her near-worship of her own father, the past was not to be rejected but mined for strategies for social interaction and coexistence.

Moreover, Addams was familiar with the groundbreaking work of Henry George, whose 1879 book *Progress and Poverty* argued that not only did industrial progress under free market capitalism not improve the lot of the poor, but in fact "the cause of increasing poverty [was] advancing wealth" (251). George's theories challenged the entrenched beliefs in laissez-faire economics and social Darwinism, and laid the groundwork for a more progressive approach to poverty relief. Jane Addams was clearly writing under his influence when she argued that "the present industrial system thwarts our ethical demands, not only for social righteousness, but for social order" (HH 166). But George's significance to Addams is philosophical as well: George's disarticulation of industrial advances from social progress gave her the imaginative space to reinvest the past, both her own and those of the immigrants with whom she worked, with positive value.[11] She recognized from the very beginning of her work at Hull-House that "in regard to entertaining immigrants [she needed to] preserve and keep whatever of value their past life contained" (HH 169).

Addams's investment in the past was not a form of genteel Luddism. Industrialization was not in and of itself destructive, but the alienation from the products of one's labor on the one hand and the commercialization of the culture on the other certainly were. The transformation of both work and leisure into commodities deeply disturbed Addams. In terms of labor, she insisted that even in factories, workers "must be connected with the entire product—must include fellowship as well as the pleasures arising from skilled workmanship and a cultivated imagination" (*Spirit of Youth* 127). The rationalization of industrial labor robbed workers of a sense of skill and a sense of self. But the commercialization of recreation was even more destructive to a democratic culture, since it captured not just a person's work hours but her imaginative life as well. The spending power of thousands of young new Americans constructed a new kind of city life in which adolescents had "only two possibilities, both of them commercial: first, a chance to utilize by day their new and tender labor power in its factories and shops, and then another chance in the evening to extract from them their petty wages by pandering to their love of pleasure" (8). Consumer capitalism gave and consumer capitalism took away; just as it created the conditions by which children of immigrants had money to burn, it provided plenty of opportunities to burn it.

The Labor Museum provided an alternative model of production and consumption. First of all, artisanal work could itself be recreational in the best sense of the word. Addams argued that "a long-established occupation may form the very foundations of the moral life" (HH 178), and cited examples of immigrants who staved off despair by participating in traditional crafts. In contrast to the enervation of factory work that "calls for an expenditure of nervous energy almost more than it demands muscular effort" (*Spirit of Youth* 108), craftwork engaged both body and mind.

Moreover, the Museum itself became a site of industrial production. In the wake of successful exhibits, the Museum "finally included a group of three or four women, Irish, Italian, and Danish, who have become a permanent working force in the textile department which has developed into a self-supporting industry" (HH 177). To this extent, then, the Labor Museum was more than a memorial of past skills or a monument to the "primitive." After all, most of the participants in the Museum's exhibits participated in the industrial world and the marketplace in one way or another—they were hardly cut off from modern modes of production and consumption. At the same time, the Museum could instruct the children of immigrants in the possibilities of labor beyond the experience of piecework:

> If a child goes into a sewing factory with a knowledge of the work she is doing in relation to the finished product; if she is informed concerning the material she is manipulating and the processes to which it is subjected; if she understands the design she is elaborating in its historic relation to art and decoration, her daily life is lifted from drudgery to one of self-conscious activity, and her pleasure and intelligence are registered in her product. (*Spirit of Youth* 122)

The Labor Museum was neither a nostalgic revisiting of the past nor a repudiation of modernity. Rather, it was a palimpsest of labor in which each tool illuminated all the others. The factory loom was not a corruption of a hand tool in and of itself, but instead the most recent development in the history of the work people do. The Labor Museum constructed a bridge between "old" and "new," existing alongside contemporary industrial methods and offering a model of participation in the cash economy that did not insist on alienation from one's labor.

Ultimately, the Labor Museum was designed and operated as a channel of communication between immigrants and their American-born children, using the vocabularies of labor as a common language. More than a "way to bond New World industry to Old World folk culture" (Dougherty 376), the Museum was an instrument of family reunification beyond the pieties and threats of the mainstream. Addams recognized the immense changes that were altering not just the fabric of American life but also the texture of that fabric: the years of adolescence were taking on new meaning, new associations, new sensations. Like her contemporaries, Addams saw the relations between immigrants and the dominant culture as metaphors for larger social structures, but she did not interpret this analogy through the language of primitivism or eugenics. From the conflicts and divided loyalties that defined the new bonds (and new separations) between immigrant women and their American-born children, U.S. culture could recognize its own new class of adolescents; in the reconciliation that the shared heritage of labor afforded, America could see its own solutions.

The reunion of mother and daughter was a microcosm of the historical pedagogy of the Labor Museum, itself a microcosm of Hull-House's agenda. And in Hull-House, Addams hoped to construct an alternate world for the immigrant poor in which conflict between classes and ethnicities was ameliorated by shared work and shared residence. In the final analysis, then, the Labor Museum offered a blueprint of how adults might truly connect with their teenage children, how those children might respect the past while participating fully in the present, and how industrial work might educate and nourish a labor force numbed by the blandishments of consumer capital. In a lesson that could inform us all, Addams designed the Museum to remind young first-generation Americans that their parents "might yield to our American life something very valuable," and remind immigrant parents that in adolescents they might again recognize "the value and charm of life" (*Spirit of Youth* 3); that is, for life and work to have some meaning, they must be infused with both (self-)respect and pleasure.

Notes

1. This theme is explicit, for example, in Anzia Yezierska's autobiographical novel, *Bread Givers* (1925), which is subtitled "a struggle between a father of the Old World and a daughter of the New."

2. In 1900, there were over 1.5 million native-born citizens of foreign parentage in Illinois (31% of the total population of the state), over 2.4 million in New York State (33% of the state's population), and over 1.4 million in Pennsylvania (almost 23% of the state population). Native-born white Americans between the ages of five and twenty constituted 29% of the population in Illinois, 25% in New York, and 29% in Pennsylvania.

3. All quotations from *Twenty Years at Hull-House* will be indicated by (HH) followed by the page number.

4. In the "sincere tribute of imitation," the young Jane tried to flatten her right thumb to make it more closely resemble that of her father, which was worn down by his work as a miller (HH 26). (See the account in James Salazar's chapter in this volume 259). Similarly, her feelings of awe toward him caused her (equally enjoyable?) paroxysms of shame at and pleasure of confession to her lies, since he so strongly disapproved of falsehood.

5. Of the two hundred girls De Koven Bowen surveyed, 173 lived at home. Of those 126 gave all their wages to their families. They made between $2.50 and $11 per week, mostly making between $4 and $8. The low pay often tied girls to their families, since De Koven Bowen estimated that a girl could not live on her own or even with roommates for less than $8 a week.

6. De Koven Bowen was particularly concerned by the intersection of capitalism and vice in the dance halls. She argued that "hundreds of young girls are annually started on the road to ruin, for the saloonkeepers and dance hall owners have only one end in view and that is profit" (*Public Dance Halls* 3). However, the young women were not blameless, since in the dance halls they could be seen to "sit on men's laps and allow them all kinds of indignities" (6).

7. That immigration to the United States reverses the power relations between parents and children is a truism of immigrant narratives. Writing as a young woman, Hilda Satt (later Polacheck) observed that "the idea that the mother knows less than the children very soon destroys respect" ("Old Woman" 5). Similarly, in her influential account of her own experience as an immigrant, Mary Antin noted that immigrant parents "must step down from their throne of parental authority, and take the law from their children's mouths," which led to the "sad process of disintegration of home life" (213).

8. For a sample of the analyses of the World's Columbian Exposition as objectifying ethnography par excellence, see Robert W. Rydell, *All the World's a Fair: Visions of Empire at American International Expositions, 1876–1916;* Julie K. Brown, *Contesting Images: Photography and the World's Columbian Exposition;* Benedict Burton, "Rituals of Representations: Ethnic Stereotypes and Colonized Peoples at World's Fairs"; Aram A. Yengoyan, "Culture, Ideology, and World's Fairs: Colonizer and Colonized in Comparative Perspectives"; and Micaela Di Leonardo, *Exotics at Home: Anthropologies, Others, American Modernity.*

9. In many ways, the female residents of Hull-House were a kind of exotic. Unlike most of their middle-class peers, these women were mostly unmarried and college educated; John P. Rousmaniere puts the number of women educated in colleges and female seminaries (both graduates and not) living in settlement houses at between 60% and 90% (47).

10. To illustrate that immigrants had needs beyond the material, Addams tells a story of a "Bohemian widow who supported herself and her two children by scrubbing," who, having heard a stirring lecture against materialism and nationalism "hastily sent her youngest child to purchase, with the twenty-five cents which was to have supplied them with food the next day, a bunch of red roses which she presented to the lecturer in appreciation of his testimony to the reality of the things of the spirit" (HH 172).

11. Addams's excavation of the past was personal as well as cultural and historical. Anticipating Freud, she ascribed to "the theory that our genuine impulses may be connected with our childish experiences, that one's bent may be tracked back to that 'No Man's Land' where character is formless but nevertheless settling into definite lines of future development" (HH 19).

Works Cited

Addams, Jane. *The Spirit of Youth and the City Streets.* New York: Macmillan, 1909.

———. *Twenty Years at Hull-House.* 1910. New York: Signet/NAL, 1981.

Alpers, Svetlana. "The Museum as a Way of Seeing." *Exhibiting Cultures: The Poetics and Politics of Museum Display.* Ed. Ivan Karp and Steven D. Lavine. Washington, D.C.: Smithsonian Institute Press, 1991. 27–42.

Antin, Mary. *The Promised Land.* 1912. New York: Penguin, 1997.

Brown, Julie K. *Contesting Images: Photography and the World's Columbian Exposition.* Tucson: U of Arizona P, 1994.

Burton, Benedict. "Rituals of Representations: Ethnic Stereotypes and Colonized Peoples at World's Fairs." *Fair Representations.* Ed. Robert W. Rydell and Nancy Guinn. Amsterdam: Amsterdam UP, 1994.

Crocker, Ruth. "Unsettling Perspectives: The Settlement Movement, the Rhetoric of Social History, and the Search for Synthesis." *Contesting the Master Narrative: Essays in Social History.* Ed. Jeffery Cox and Shelton Stromquist. Iowa City: U of Iowa P, 1998.

De Koven Bowen, Louise. *The Department Store Girl: Based on Interviews with 200 Girls.* Chicago: Juvenile Protective Association of Chicago, 1911.

———. *The Public Dance Halls of Chicago.* Rev. ed. Chicago: Juvenile Protective Association of Chicago, 1917.

Dewey, John. "My Pedagogic Creed." *School Journal* 54 (1897): 77–80.

Di Leonardo, Micaela. *Exotics at Home: Anthropologies, Others, American Modernity.* Chicago: U of Chicago P, 1998.

Dougherty, James. "Jane Addams: Culture and Imagination." *Yale Review* 71 (1982): 363–79.

George, Henry. *Progress and Poverty.* 1879. New York: Robert Schalkenbach Foundation, 1955.

Haenni, Sabine. "Visual and Theatrical Culture, Tenement Fiction, and the Immigrant Subject in Abraham Cahan's *Yekl.*" *American Literature* 71 (1999): 493–527.

Hall, G. Stanley. *Adolescence: Its Psychology and Its Relations to Physiology, Anthropology,*

Sociology, Sex, Crime, Religion, and Education. 1904. New York: Arno Press and the New York Times, 1969.

Hapke, Laura. *Tales of the Working Girl: Wage-Earning Women in American Literature, 1890–1925.* New York: Twayne Publishers, 1992.

Jackson, Shannon. *Lines of Activity: Performance, Historiography, and Hull-House Domesticity.* Ann Arbor: U of Michigan P, 2000.

Kirshenblatt-Gimblett, Barbara. "Objects of Ethnography." Alpers 386–443.

Peiss, Kathy. *Cheap Amusements: Working Women and Leisure in Turn-of-the-Century New York.* Philadelphia: Temple UP, 1986.

Perry, Elisabeth Israels. *Belle Moskowitz: Feminine Politics and the Exercise of Power in the Age of Alfred E. Smith.* New York: Oxford UP, 1987.

———. "'The General Motherhood of the Commonwealth': Dance Hall Reform in the Progressive Era." *American Quarterly* 37 (1985): 719–33.

Polacheck, Hilda Satt. *I Came a Stranger: The Story of a Hull-House Girl.* Ed. Dena J. Polacheck Epstein. Urbana and Chicago: U of Illinois P, 1989.

———. "The Old Woman and the New World." *The Butterfly* 3 (1909): 4–5.

Rosen, Ruth. *The Lost Sisterhood: Prostitution in America, 1900–1918.* Baltimore: Johns Hopkins UP, 1982.

Rousmaniere, John P. "Cultural Hybrid in the Slums: The College Woman and the Settlement House, 1889–1894." *American Quarterly* 22 (1970): 45–66.

Rydell, Robert W. *All the World's a Fair: Visions of Empire at American International Expositions, 1876–1916.* Chicago: Chicago UP, 1984.

Trachtenberg, Alan. *The Incorporation of America: Culture and Society in the Gilded Age.* New York: Farrar, Straus and Giroux, 1982.

Veblen, Thorstein. *The Theory of the Leisure Class.* 1899. New York: Augustus M. Kelley, 1975.

Yengoyan, Aram A. "Culture, Ideology, and World's Fairs: Colonizer and Colonized in Comparative Perspectives." *Fair Representations.* Ed. Robert W. Rydell and Nancy Guinn. Amsterdam: Amsterdam UP, 1994.

10

Character's Conduct

The Democratic Habits of Jane Addams's "Charitable Effort"

James Salazar

Introduction

In 1928, the organizers of the Chicago Association for Child Study and Parent Education, one of many emerging organizations dedicated to the new science of pedagogy and child rearing, decided to address their annual conference to one of the most important social reform projects in the nineteenth- and early-twentieth-century United States, the project of "Building Character." The Mid-West Conference on Character Development, as it was called, gathered together a diverse and esteemed group of clinical psychologists, primary and secondary school educators, doctors, social reformers, and university presidents and professors. Some were noted for their expertise in the scientific study of character development, others for their practical expertise in the "training of character" as a distinct method of "child rearing." The problems of character and "character building" were discussed from a number of different disciplinary and theoretical points of view, with paper sessions and roundtable discussions devoted to such an array of topics as Scientific Attitude toward Character Development, Standards for Character, Creative Expression and Character Development, The Use of Leisure Time for Character Development, Social Attitudes and Character, Religion and Character, Building Character through Unified Education, The Physical Basis of the Child's Emotional Health, How to Make or Break the Child, Creative Education and Character, Ideals and Character, and Discipline and Character (*Building Character* v–vi).

In assembling a panel on the topic of Social Attitudes and Character, the organizers turned to a person who not only was one of the nation's foremost social reformers, but who had also made the development of a "social ethic" the central aim of her reformist activities, the social reformer Jane Addams. As co-founder and leading theorist of the Hull-House Settlement, established in 1889 in the nineteenth ward of Chicago's West Side tenement district, Jane Addams had become by 1928 perhaps the most famous and influential voice for social justice, poverty relief, and child welfare in the United States.[1] Lauded (and occasionally reviled) as "the conscience of the nation" (McCarthy 109), Addams was ranked, "[i]n every early twentieth century public opinion poll before World War I . . . as the most admired American woman, often as the most admired American" (Katz 162). As a time in which explicit, external strategies of social regulation and control became the obsession of governmental agencies and liberal social thinkers alike, the Progressive Era had found a unique and often paradoxical advocate in Jane Addams. Addams envisioned Hull-House, the effective platform for her reform work, as a kind of "sociological laboratory" in which both the working-class, immigrant populations of the tenement district and the middle-class reformers who settled there were together and reciprocally "reformed" through a communal reworking and "readjustment" of the performed markers of class, ethnicity, and gender. More importantly for the conference organizers, Addams had, like many female reformers and charity workers before her, made the study of family and child development central to understanding and ameliorating the effects of urban industrialization on immigrant working classes.[2]

The brief paper that Addams presented at the conference, Social Attitudes and Character, took up a familiar theme in a familiar style for anyone acquainted either with her extensive writings or her well-publicized work at Hull-House. Her anecdotal narrative describes three cases in which she observed the effects of "social attitudes" on the children of working-class, immigrant families. Addams recounts in particular how the children of recent immigrants negotiate the complex demands of cultural assimilation, demands that often distance them from the "character-building" traditions of their parents. But what is perhaps most striking about Addams's account of the conflicting demands of these "social attitudes" is her deep reluctance to invoke the key concept of character in order to describe those demands. Eschewing the kinds of technical or prescriptive accounts of character formation typical of the conference, Addams rarely refers to character at all, making reference to it only at the very end of her essay. And what is most striking about her comments there is that they emphasize not a process of "building character" through the steady application of parenting or pedagogical methods but rather the emergence of character in situations of intense conflict between distinct cultural traditions.

Her discussion focuses specifically on the difficulties children born in the United States face in the conflict between the "attitudes" of their immigrant parents and the assimilative force of the "American attitudes" displayed, for example, in the mass media and "moving picture shows." After telling the story of three such children she's known, Addams recasts, almost as an afterthought, these stories in terms of a theory of character:

> [I]n many instances their character, I think, has been evolved out of this sense of conflict, if you please, between their background and the contemporaneous society and conditions in which they move. . . . To make a synthesis between the difference that confronts you in two given situations is certainly an opportunity for the development of character; that tendency of the emotional life which, instead of being oppressed by the old loyalties, insists that it shall encompass the new as well. ("Social Attitudes" 294–95)

Addams's remarks are interesting not only because of the reluctance with which they seem to offer such an offhand and glancing definition of the subject that everyone in her audience has come to hear her discuss but also because of the essentially intercultural concept of character to which she points. Addams's reluctance to invoke the concept of character seems to hinge on its inadequacy as an explanatory category for such scenes of intercultural conflict, scenes with which Addams's lifework was vitally concerned.

Why then was Addams so reluctant to evoke the concept of character at this conference explicitly devoted to the study of it? Does this suggest that the project of "character building" is perhaps an inadequate, even dangerous, response to the complex problems of class mobility and interethnic exchange to which Addams dedicated her life at Hull-House? Why does such a prominent social reformer, in an era in which social reform so insistently rallied around the "building of character," resist discussing such a concept in a paper ostensibly devoted to it? Might we understand such a reluctant evocation as itself a statement on the vexed value of the concept of character as an explanatory model for such scenes of cross-cultural contact, as a statement on its simultaneously promising yet perilous role as an object of social reform? How, in other words, is Addams redefining here the form and function of social reform by subtly yet insistently calling into question one of its most salient terms and potent strategies?

Taking this reluctance toward the notion of character as its prompt and clue, this essay examines how Jane Addams's successful and enormously influential model of poverty relief and social reform was founded less on a project of "building character" than on a wholesale reconceptualization of the character-building function of the traditional charity relation. For Addams, as for many other social reformers of her time, the "Friendly Visit" of an aid-dispensing, middle-class, and usually female charity worker to the homes of the poor and often immigrant working classes was the most important component of professional "poverty relief." While the social "contact" exercised through such a charity relation was very often the means through which monetary aid was distributed, it was more importantly the means through which the much more ameliorative coin of "character" was distributed through the palpable example of the charity worker's own exemplary middle-class character. In her account of such an economy of character emulation in *Democracy and Social Ethics* (1902) and *Twenty Years at Hull-House* (1910), however, Jane Addams critiques the radically disciplinary and ideological function of the charity relation by demonstrating how it articulates and reinforces the very class and cultural barriers that it presumes to overcome. The ingenuity and importance of Addams's argument, however, lie in its critique of the rhetoric of character on which charity work had traditionally relied and in its simultaneous recuperation of its uniquely "democratizing" social effects. In her theoretical works, as well as in her work at Hull-House, Addams remobilizes the reciprocally formative possibilities of cross-cultural identification contained in the traditional charity relation by extricating that relation from the emulatory function of character building and by challenging the gendered assumptions of women's work as philanthropic "stewards of character." By defining character as the complex, incomplete product of a continual and resolutely "social" engagement with scenes of class and cross-cultural contact—and by also continually realizing such scenes in the parlors, classrooms, workshops, and auditoriums of Hull-House—Addams demonstrates the power of a properly intercultural concept of character to the "Progressive" realization of a pluralist, democratic civic sphere.

Stewards of the Nation's Character

Charity work was, toward the end of the nineteenth century, essentially defined and motivated by the work of women. As Robyn Muncy has argued, however, the "female dominion in American reform" that emerged by the end of the nineteenth century was a dominion problematically characterized by "a combination of autonomy and circumscription" (xii). Charity organizations, often staffed, directed, and even funded by women were one of the few places that women could work outside of the home with relative autonomy and in a "professional" capacity. Charity work was thus one of the few professional arenas (along with teaching and nursing) in which women could pursue independent careers and exert an influence over public policy that was denied to them at the ballot box. This relative autonomy was dearly bought though, for it was predicated on an exclusion from most other professional fields and on a highly reductive concept of the essentially "benevolent" and morally sympathetic feminine character.

Women's circumscription within the profession of charity work was justified by their presumably "special" suitability for what was often identified as the most important "profession" of them all: the stewardship of the nation's character. As John Todd would so emphatically put it in his influential manual for young girls, *The Daughter at School,* "the profession of woman is that of being the educator of the human race, the former of human character" (208):

> [F]rom her very constitution and nature, from her peculiar sensibilities and tenderness, it seems to me that the great mission of woman is to take

> the world—the whole world—in its very infancy, when most pliable and most susceptible, and lay the foundations of human character. Human character, in all its interests and relations and destinies, is committed to woman, and she can make it, shape it, mould it, and stamp it just as she pleases. . . . I maintain that we are just what the ladies have made us to be. (207)

Thus while women's charity work was often justified in terms of their role, as Kathleen McCarthy has described it, as the nation's "civic stewards," this civic stewardship was more specifically conceived as a stewardship of the forming character of the nation through the stewardship of the "character" they were most immediately in contact with, that is, the character of their children, husbands, and brothers.

While the story of women's role as civic stewards is a familiar one, what has been left out of this story is an account of the theory of character on which it depends. Women's "professional" role as stewards of character underwrote their advancement into such professions as charity work, teaching, and nursing. As teachers and foreign missionaries, women brought their character-building influences to bear on children outside of their own homes, as well as on the "childlike" people they were charged with "civilizing." But it was in their capacity as charity workers, as many historians have argued, that women exercised their most pronounced influence over the public sphere. The diverse array of women's voluntary associations that emerged before the Civil War, and the more "scientific" charity organizations that developed after it, could rally their very significant influence over public opinion and government policy on such leading issues as abolition, education reform, and later child labor and factory reform because of their associations with the character-forming capacities of women.

The role of stewards of character that underwrote women's charity work, however, also generated its own unique dilemmas. Women could play an important and very public role in charity work largely because this work was not seen to be inherently "public" at all. Women were reliable guides for the formation and stewardship of character precisely because they were seen to be relatively free from the self-interested and prudential calculations characteristic of masculine agency in the public sphere. Thus the very social role that justified women's increasingly public influence as social reformers also legitimated and presupposed women's exclusion from the professions and enterprises of the public sphere. And by the decades of the 1880s and 1890s, an observation such as Todd's that "we are just what the ladies have made us to be" would also become a source of increasing anxiety as many sought to challenge this "feminization of American culture" with the formation of gender-specific character-building agencies. Organizations such as the Boy Scouts of America and the Young Men's Christian Association (YMCA), for example, sought to "preserve" the masculine elements of character in America's boys by replacing cross-gender character building with same-gender character imitation.[3] Similarly, while women were charged with building character in the youth of the nation (as well as with cultivating the character of their economically occupied husbands), it was often unclear whether women themselves were taken to "have" the attributes of character they were entrusted with instilling, since "having character" was invariably to evoke masculine-coded attributes associated with agency in the public sphere. The sacrificial and sympathetic benevolence that presumably qualified women as stewards of character, in other words, was often difficult to mimetically square with the self-reliant qualities that marked the possessor of true character itself.

Such a paradox vexed many of the antebellum feminist arguments for improving women's opportunities for education and self-culture, since such arguments relied on women's privileged position as formers, though not necessarily bearers, of public character. As Sarah Edgarton would formulate this paradoxical claim,

> The most she wants is not a character, a power and independence which erects "liberty poles," and shouts "freedom" from the forum; but the calm, still, holy consciousness of mental and moral power, the elevation and strength which is born of knowledge, of thought, and of self-reliance. (77)

Catharine Beecher's famous and influential argument for the establishment of women's colleges made more direct recourse to the domestic ideology of character formation and women's multiple positionalities within the traditional nuclear family:

> The success of democratic institutions, as is conceded by all, depends upon the intellectual and moral character of the mass of the people. . . . It is equally conceded, that the formation of the moral and intellectual character of the young is committed mainly to the female hand. The mother forms the character of the future man; the sister bends the fibres that are hereafter to be the forest tree; the wife sways the heart, whose energies may turn for good or for evil the destinies of a nation. Let the women of a country be made virtuous and intelligent, and the men will certainly be the same. The proper education of a man decides the welfare of an individual; but educate a woman, and the interests of a whole family are secured. (13)

Beecher's argument for enhancing and expanding women's access to higher education was typical in its emphasis on women's role as stewards of character. After the Civil War, such arguments were instrumental in the founding of the first women's colleges and the development of coeducational universities in the late 1860s and 1870s. The pursuit of such educational opportunities, however, in its emphasis on women's traditional role as stewards of character, produced by the Gilded Age an even greater frustration on the part of women with their increased access to higher education and yet a simultaneous lack of professional venues in which to put that education to work. If women were justified in pursuing such an education in order to enhance their capacities as stewards, such a stewardship all too often demanded that they take their place once again within the confines of the domestic scene.

The Snare of Character

In her semi-autobiographical work, *Twenty Years at Hull-House,* Jane Addams seems to trace the origins of the Hull-House Settlement back to just such a set of conflicting gender demands. In her reflections on college life at Rockford Seminary, Addams laments what she calls the "snare of preparation" in higher education. Higher education, she complains, "entangles" the practical energies of students with the "inactivity" of intellectual exercise "at the very period of life when they are longing to construct a world anew and to conform it to their own ideals" (Addams, *Twenty Years* 61). More precarious for young women, however, is that this protracted snare of preparation is relieved only by the equally frustrating snare of the "family claim," which demands that they sacrifice their training to the domestic stewardship of the traditional family. Thus after realizing that her extensive training in social theory, "mental and moral philosophy," literature, and history would find no immediate outlet outside of what she called "the family claim," Addams turns, like many of her contemporaries, to the otherwise scarce refuge offered by charity work. In describing her inspiration for what would become the Hull-House Settlement, Addams narrates a typical story of the unique appeal of charity work to the college-educated, middle-class woman:

> I gradually became convinced that it would be a good thing to rent a house in a part of the city where many primitive and actual needs are found, in which young women who had been given over too exclusively to study, might restore a balance of activity along traditional lines and learn of life from life itself; where they might try out some of the things they had been taught and put truth to "the ultimate test of the conduct it dictates or inspires." (61)

But while this famous and often recounted story of Addams's turn to charity work seems to be yet another example of nineteenth-century women sublimating their character-forming capacities into the legitimate domain of civic stewardship, Addams's full origin story for the founding of Hull-House shows that she was also keenly aware of the "snares" that such a conception of charity work also laid for women. Hence while Addams would set about founding a social settlement in order to give other women and herself a place to realize their ambitions to participate in the project of civic stewardship, she also founded the settlement in order to eliminate the conditions that put her in the position to need such a project in the first place.

Addams's autobiographical account of the origins of the Hull-House Settlement is somewhat typical in its derivation of the character of the institution from the autobiographical character of its primary founder. That story begins not with Addams's post-graduate crisis, but rather in the "Earliest Impressions" described at the beginning of *Twenty Years at Hull-House.* Virtually all of the "impressions" described in chapter one are, as Addams readily admits, impressions "directly concerned with my father, although of course I recall many experiences apart from him" (7). As Allen Davis has argued, such a genealogy of Hull-House reiterates familiar patterns in nineteenth-century women's autobiographical writing. The tropes of an "impressive young woman" and the idealized "affection between a tender daughter and a solicitous father," along with tales of overcoming handicaps and childhood plans are, Davis argues, elements that are also "quite common in the autobiographies and the legends of the famous as an explanation for their later acts and deeds of glory" (Davis, *American Heroine* 160; 162). Most readers of *Twenty Years at Hull-House* just as predictably read these opening pages for the information they provide on the "influence" of this public-spirited and kindhearted father over his daughter's development as a social reformer.[4] Davis's argument that "Jane Addams was probably not consciously aware that she was patterning her first chapter after the fictions of her day or that she was using a genteel shorthand for a special relationship between father and daughter" (Davis 161) belies the ways that Addams makes questioning these autobiographical conventions the very point of the chapter.

Addams's use of the autobiographical mode is distinctive in that it doesn't just serve to delineate the formative influences on her young character and hence on the institution of Hull-House itself, but rather to call into question the autobiographical assumptions about character formation on which such an institutional genealogy relies. Addams is careful to reiterate, in the opening lines and first chapter of *Twenty Years at Hull-House,* the theoretical presumptions behind such an autobiographical narrative opening:

> On the theory that our genuine impulses may be connected with our childish experiences, that one's bent may be tracked back to that "No-Man's Land" where character is formless but nevertheless settling into definite lines of future development, I begin this record with some impressions of my childhood. (7)

But while this opening sentence anticipates the autobiographical expectations of her readers, she proceeds through the rest of the chapter to critically test such expectations through the account of her relationship to her father.

Jane Addams's father, John H. Addams, was known as a prototypical "self-made man" who had made his mark first as the founder of flour and timber mills and other businesses in and around Cedarville, Illinois, and who later became a successful railroad speculator and eventually a prominent Illinois state legislator. Chapter one describes the young Jane Addams's close and adulatory relationship with her father in the years between her mother's death when she was two and a half and her father's second marriage when she was eight years old. In the account of what she calls her "doglike affection" for her father, Addams details how that affection expressed itself as a strong desire to imitate and remake her body in the image of his own. Addams's account initially describes this imitative desire as a feature of the character-forming influences usually directed toward a mother: "I centered on him all that careful imitation which a little girl ordinarily gives to her mother's ways and habits" (12). Her redirection of this imitative desire to her father, however, also transforms its expressive form:

> I had a consuming ambition to possess a miller's thumb, and would sit contentedly for a long time rubbing between my thumb and fingers the ground wheat as it fell from between the millstones. . . . I believe I have never since wanted anything more desperately than I wanted my right thumb to be flattened, as my father's had become, during his earlier years of a miller's life. Somewhat discouraged by the slow process of structural modification, I also took measures to secure on the backs of my hands the tiny purple and red spots which are always found on the hands of the miller who dresses millstones . . . [by] spread[ing] out my hands near the millstones in the hope that the little hard flints flying from the miller's chisel would light upon their backs and make the longed-for marks. (14)

What is striking about her story is that, rather than trying to *imitate* the professional activities, "habits," or persona of her father, the young Addams tries to *inscribe* the traces of that professional identity onto her own body. Unlike the "imitation" of a "mother's ways and habits," Addams replaces imitation with inscription and recordation through an odd kind of corporeal literalization of his professional habits and in particular their body-modifying effects. She doesn't cultivate his habits, in other words, but rather tries to inscribe the residual traces of those habits onto, or as the shape of, her own body.

While Addams initially wonders aloud that "[i]t is hard to account for the manifestations of a child's adoring affection, so emotional, so irrational, so tangled with the affairs of the imagination" (11), by the end of her narration she *is* able to account for these "grotesque attempts to express . . . [her] doglike affection" (12):

> This sincere tribute of imitation, which affection offers to its adored object, had later, I hope, subtler manifestations, but certainly these first ones were altogether genuine. In this case, too, I doubtless contributed my share to that stream of admiration which our generation so generously poured forth for the self-made man. (14)

Addams reproduces the professional marks of her father's body not, according to her own retrospective reading, out of a desire to become her father—to follow in his footsteps as an exemplary model of character—but in order to signify and to pay "tribute" to the "adored object" with the gift of imitation. Addams responds to her own feelings for him by wanting to give back to him an image of himself, an image of himself *as* a "self-made man." What is most important about this scene is, for Addams, how it is part of the broader "stream of admiration which our generation so generously poured forth for the self-made man." Addams tells this story not simply to describe the features of character that will influence her later work as a social reformer but rather in order to retroactively indict the rhetoric of character that gave shape and expression to her love for her father, and to extricate her intensely personal bond with him from the logic of reflective identification. The story's import is thus not as a report on the fatherly influences on her formless character but as an autobiographical diagnosis of the cultural elements participating in and governing that formation.

In the subsequent chapter, titled the "Influence of Lincoln," Addams extends this autobiographical critique of childhood "influences" to more explicitly call into question the cultural iconography and "hero worship" of "the self-made man" by analyzing the distinctly cultural dimensions of her own "childish admiration for Lincoln" (24). Like the story of her own father, the purpose of Addams's account of Abraham Lincoln, whom her father had known as a young man and had remained friends and correspondent with throughout his life, is to extricate the real respect and fascination she had for "that remarkable personality" from the "hero worship" of the self-made man (26). What she claims to learn in the chapter is that the "greatness" of such a man as Lincoln derives not from his self-constituted power of character, but rather from his ability to "draw" on the "capital fund" of "the people themselves" (29). To mistake that distributed source of political power, she observes, for a feature simply of Lincoln himself, would be to fall into the fetishizing trap of "hero worship." What she learns through the example of Lincoln, a lesson she'll make the cornerstone of Hull-House, is that the rhetoric of character subverts the capacity to recognize and coordinate the collective powers of a constituency, a power all too often misrecognized as the sui generis power of the self-made character. It is thus when she witnesses the democratic possibilities of collective action at the "Old Settler's Day" that she realizes the distorting effects of the rhetoric of self-made character:

> I remember that I was at that time reading with great enthusiasm Carlyle's "Heroes and Hero Worship," but on the evening of "Old Settlers' Day," to my surprise, I found it difficult to go on. Its sonorous sentences and exaltation of the man who "can" suddenly ceased to be convincing. (29)

In her delineation of the events that inspired her to found, with Ellen Gates Starr, the Hull-House Settlement, Addams thus turns the expectations of the autobiographical mode against themselves. Her narrative tells a story not of the "influences" of "great men" over her still-forming character but of her overcoming such an ideology of influence and emulation, and of how she came to realize her most basic principles of social reform precisely through that overcoming.

Charity's Therapy

While *Twenty Years at Hull-House* is perhaps the most widely read of Jane Addams's writings today, her earlier work *Democracy and Social Ethics* provides her most theoretical—and widely read in her own day—

account of the "mission" to which Hull-House was dedicated, the mission, as she terms it at the end of *Twenty Years,* to "socialize democracy":

> The educational activities of a Settlement, as well as its philanthropic, civic, and social undertakings, are but differing manifestations of the attempt to socialize democracy, as is the very existence of the Settlement itself. (290)

Her discussion in *Democracy and Social Ethics* collects together the criticisms of the "individualist ethic" scattered throughout *Twenty Years at Hull-House* and develops them into a sustained theoretical critique of the reflective epistemology of character emulation and its role in producing, rather than resolving, the "maladjustments" of Gilded Age society. The notion of "maladjustment" had emerged by the Gilded Age as a kind of metonymic shorthand for the systemic and radically dislocating transformations of urban industrialization, mass migration, and commodity culture. Social reform was thus often conceived in the last decades of the nineteenth century and first decades of the twentieth as a technical process of restoring a proper "adjustment" between individuals and their "institutional," usually "industrial" environment. Scott Nearing, for example, in his 1910 study, *Social Adjustment,* argues "[t]hat maladjustment exists in numerous virulent forms, in many parts of the United States [. . . and that] maladjustment is (1) due to economic causes, (2) involving social cost, and (3) remediable through social action" (vii).

In *Democracy and Social Ethics,* Jane Addams takes up this common trope of "maladjustment" as she also diagnoses the social dislocations brought about by the manifold transformations of Gilded Age society. The ethnographically detailed opening pages of the introduction seem to evoke the terms of a commonly described scene of working-class discontent:

> All about us are men and women who have become unhappy in regard to their attitude toward the social order itself; toward the dreary round of uninteresting work, the pleasures narrowed down to those of appetite, the declining consciousness of brain power, and the lack of mental food which characterizes the lot of the large proportion of their fellow-

> citizens. These men and women have caught a moral challenge raised by the exigencies of contemporaneous life; some are bewildered, others who are denied the relief which sturdy action brings are even seeking an escape, but all are increasingly anxious concerning their actual relations to the basic organization of society. (6)

The men and women "unhappy in regard to their attitude toward the social order itself," it would seem, are unhappy because this "social order" so relentlessly "declines" and impoverishes their lives with its "dreary round[s]" of work and "narrowed" pleasures. Addams's account at first glance seems to evoke in familiar terms the "dehumanizing" effects of industrial labor on the working classes. But as the passage develops, what becomes clear is that these "unhappy" men and women are *not* the ones who are experiencing these dehumanizing effects of "the social order." Toward the end of the passage the unhappy people are shown to be, oddly enough, not unhappy because of their own mind-numbing labor, but because they are on the contrary "denied the relief which sturdy action brings." What these people are unhappy about, the passage seems to suggest, is that *someone else* is suffering from such conditions. The unhappy people are unhappy, we realize in returning to the first line, not because of their position within the social order itself, nor in "their attitude *toward*" that social order, but rather "in regard to" that attitude, *because of* that attitude, an attitude apparently unhappily burdened by its awareness of the punishing effects of this social order *on others.* What Addams emphasizes, in other words, in this curious transposition of working-class dehumanization and middle-class "anxiety," is that the most damaging, "maladjusting" effects of Gilded Age industrialization are not those imposed on the working classes but rather those produced within a middle class anxiously aware of such an imposition and thereby "caught in [its] moral challenge."

Addams evokes the vernacular of "maladjustment" commonly used to describe the rapid and dislocating transformations in the social, economic, demographic, and urban order of Gilded Age society, yet does so in order to apply such a concept to the mental and moral travails of those who stand witness to, rather than directly undergo, such transformations. The "maladjustment" of greatest concern, she goes on to explain, is the "mental attitude of maladjustment" (6) or "nervousness" produced by these dislocations in the minds of the middle class. Catharine Beecher would as early as 1841 make such an argument when she portended the "difficulties" posed, particularly to "American women," to the nervous system by the "overstimulation" of the nation's quickening "high commercial, political, and religious stimulus" (20). But it wouldn't be until the Gilded Age that "American Nervousness" would appear as a distinct vernacular of national self-analysis. George M. Beard's 1881 study, *American Nervousness: Its Causes and Consequences,* established "nervousness" as the iconic symptom of modern "civilization." But unlike this common association of American Nervousness with modernization and urban industrialization, Addams makes the subtle, but for her crucial, shift of attention from the maladjustments of such an industrial order to the maladjustment produced by an *awareness of* its most pernicious effects. Thus as her argument progresses, it becomes clear that the "dreary round of uninteresting work," narrowed pleasures, and declining consciousness of the "unhappy" people also describes a middle class becoming all-too-painfully aware of, in the terms of Jacob Riis, "how the other half lives."[5]

Addams describes this maladjustment as a discrepancy between the recognition of a new social ethic and one's ability to apply that ethic to their own lives; a maladjustment, in short, between the consciousness of poverty and the "conduct" that awareness demands:

> The test they would apply to their conduct is a social test. They fail to be content with the fulfillment of their family and personal obligations, and find themselves striving to respond to a new demand involving a social obligation; they have become conscious of another requirement, and the contribution they would make is toward a code of social ethics. The conception of life which they hold has not yet expressed itself in social changes or legal enactment, but rather in a mental attitude of maladjustment, and in a sense of divergence between their consciences and their conduct. (6)

The "social ethic," in Addams's analysis, therefore emerges not from a set of philanthropic imperatives or dicta, but rather from the sensibility that she sees emerging in middle-class society and which seeks to find expression in the "conduct" of philanthropic enterprise. A philanthropic sensibility, in other words, is the inexorable and unnerving "maladjustment" of the Gilded Age. This definitive theoretical text by one of America's foremost social reformers makes the quite surprising case that a philanthropic sense of "social obligation" is not simply a reformist "solution" to the "maladjustments" of Gilded Age America but is also in a fundamental way the most pernicious "maladjustment" of all.

Since this consciousness "had not yet expressed itself in social changes or legal enactment" but only "in a mental attitude of maladjustment," however, the charity work that seeks such social changes and legal enactments is what will conveniently provide ready therapy for this anxious state of maladjustment. This admission of the narcissistically therapeutic effects of charity work has been cited by many as one of the most compromising aspects of Addams's own reformist work, and of nineteenth-century women's charity work more broadly. Jill Conway, for example, argues that "[t]he initial impulse for this kind of feminine migration to the slums was not identification with the working class, as in the European settlement movement, but the recognition that there was a social cure for the neurotic ills of privileged young women in America because their ailments were socially induced" (170–71). Addams's writings of course provide ample evidence for such a view, since she openly ascribes such motives to the development of Hull-House and of social reform in general. She not only describes the founding vision of Hull-House as conditioned by her own personal "nadir of . . . nervous depression and sense of maladjustment" (Addams, *Twenty Years* 55) but also the figure of the "anxious," college-educated woman plays a central role in such key essays as "Subjective Necessity for Social Settlements" and "Filial Relations."[6]

But it would be a mistake to take such a story of the "subjective necessity" of the social settlement as also the final statement of its "objective value."[7] Addams's rhetorical grafting of the challenges facing middle-class women onto the travails of working-class poverty is a vexed one, but a thereby no less important one. Addams's situating of the problem of charity work squarely within the psychological dilemmas imposed in particular on middle-class women doesn't simply reduce "poverty relief" to a therapeutic hobby of middle-class women. Rather it demonstrates how the "social ethic" is first experienced by women not because of their "innate" moral sensibility or "benevolent" orientation, but rather as a product of the restrictive gender roles they must negotiate.

Addams is thus able to show in her subtle transposition how a prototypically feminist challenge, rather than a circumscribing feminine sensibility, is the vehicle for a new kind of philanthropically disposed desire for "contact with the moral experiences of the many":

> They desire both a clearer definition of the code of morality adapted to present day demands and a part in its fulfillment, both a creed and a practice of social morality. In the perplexity of this intricate situation at least one thing is becoming clear: if the latter day moral ideal is in reality that of a social morality, it is inevitable that those who desire it must be brought in contact with the moral experiences of the many in order to procure an adequate social motive. (6)

Addams situates the work of women to realize the "social ethic" as a final stage of America's developing "democracy," for it compels the realization of that democracy not as abstract principles or legal rights (rights that were failing to secure "social" equality in the segregated South and also across the United States) but rather as a transformative, engaged, and deeply personal interaction with ethnic, class, and gender alterity:

> We are thus brought to a conception of Democracy not merely as a sentiment which desires the well-being of all men, nor yet as a creed which believes in the essential dignity and equality of all men, but as that which affords a rule of living as well as a test of faith.
>
> We are learning that a standard of social ethics is not attained by traveling a sequestered byway, but by mixing on the thronged and common road where all must turn out for one another, and at least see the size of one another's burdens. To follow the path of social morality results perforce in the temper if not the practice of the democratic spirit, for it implies that diversified human experience and resultant sympathy which are the foundation and guarantee of Democracy . . .
>
> We realize, too, that social perspective and sanity of judgment come only from contact with social experience; that such contact is the surest

> corrective of opinions concerning the social order, and concerning efforts, however humble, for its improvement. (7)

In relatively straightforward fashion, Addams's argument for the "mixing on the thronged and common road" seeks to establish the grounds for giving democracy a final, "social" expression. And it was in providing such an arena for engaged, culturally diverse social interactions that Hull-House became such an innovative and extraordinarily influential institution of social reform. But what Addams is not altogether clear about is, in what does such an "identification with the common lot" (9) consist? How does such a proximity to differences of ethnicity, class, and gender produce an "identification" that ameliorates "maladjustment," and is that adjustment secured only through an erasure of those differences? What do such contacts "adjust" and how does that adjustment transform individuals into democratic subjects? And how, finally, is such a scene of interethnic and interclass identification a vision of a fully realized democracy and also a powerful tool of social reform?

Character's Coins

Addams elaborates her vision of such a democratized social sphere through an account of one of the most important, and yet one of the most "maladjusted," of social relations, the charity relation. As her description of the "Charitable Effort" in chapter one insists, one of the most transformative and potentially productive scenes of social "contact" was the relationship between the charity worker and the charity recipient:

> Probably there is no relation in life which our democracy is changing more rapidly than the charitable relation—that relation which obtains between benefactor and beneficiary; at the same time there is no point of contact in our modern experience which reveals so clearly the lack of that equality which democracy implies. We have reached the moment when democracy has made such inroads upon this relationship, that the complacency of the old-fashioned charitable man is gone forever; while, at the same time, the very need and existence of charity, denies us the consolation and freedom which democracy will at last give. (11)

The Friendly Visit of a charity worker to the home of a "needy" family had long been the bedrock of charity work in the United States. Rooted in the traditional Protestant duty to visit the poor and less fortunate among one's neighbors, Friendly Visiting was an activity premised on women's role as stewards of character and hence was the central means through which many antebellum benevolence societies distributed aid to the poor. By the 1870s and 1880s, however, the informal and aid-dispensing practices of antebellum Friendly Visiting took on a central role in the rise of the "scientific charity" of the "the charity organization movement."

But in so doing, Friendly Visiting also dramatically changed in its function. In their efforts to bring organizational efficiency and broad social scope to the problem of poverty relief, the "organizers" of scientific charity de-emphasized the aid-dispensing function of the Friendly Visit in order to make it into more of a scientific tool of information-gathering and of cross-class emulation and "uplift." As a practical matter, the Friendly Visit was a means of scrutinizing and assessing the poor. Visitors attempted to distinguish the truly "needy" from the "undeserving" and self-destructive "failures," and also made a determination as to how best to enable a family or individual to "help themselves" (Bremner, *American Philanthropy* 95). Charity organizations of the Gilded Age also operated under the assumption that poverty needed to be understood in terms of social factors beyond the individual's control. Hence the charity worker attempted in her visit to determine how best to financially support a family not by simply meeting their short-term needs but by making a "structural" change so that they were no longer dependent on charity aid. Often this meant referring the "worthy case" to an aid-dispensing agency suited to administer to their specific need by "providing such services as penny saving banks, coal-saving funds, provident wood-yards, day nurseries for the children of working mothers, and workrooms where women could be trained to become nursemaids, laundresses, or seamstresses" (Bremner, *American Philanthropy* 95). Thus one of the driving goals of "scientific charity" was, through the study of the conditions of poverty and the scientific application of structural reform, to make charity itself obsolete. As Frank Dekker Watson would put it in his early review of the movement, "In this sense it is the purpose of every charity organization society to work for its own extinction" (101).

In addition to scientifically assessing the recipient's needs while cognizant of the "environmental" factors leading to poverty, the Friendly Visitor also made character reform a central tool of poverty relief.[8] On the one hand, the visitor needed to be a skilled reader of character in order to assess whether the family or its breadwinners had the traits of character that would enable them to eventually triumph over the economic, legal, and social obstacles arrayed against them. The poor were often quite aware of this surveillance function, as Addams points out:

> In moments of indignation the poor have been known to say: "What do you want, anyway? If you have nothing to give us, why not let us alone and stop your questionings and investigations?" "They investigated me for three weeks, and in the end gave me nothing but a black character," a little woman has been heard to assert. (*Democracy* 15)

On the other hand, the Friendly Visitor also mobilized their presumed skills as stewards of character in order to "uplift" the individual by building up their capacities for self-determining action. The Friendly Visit did not just serve to distribute aid and gather information; it also functioned to uplift and alleviate the sufferings of the poor through the ameliorative effects of class contact. The "aid" the Friendly Visitor provided was the example of her own "successful" middle-class character, a character through which the poor, in aspiring to it, would learn what it means to "help themselves."

The "friendliness" of the Friendly Visit was therefore also a key instrument of poverty relief. By establishing a "friendly relation" with the poor, the visitors opened up a "sympathetic" channel for information gathering and also made their own "superior" and "successful" character an ameliorative force in the lives of the poor. Charity workers often emphasized the *social* importance of the Friendly Visit as a means of putting the classes in a sympathetic relation to one another, a relation wherein the "silent example" of the visitor could exert its greatest influence. But while workers continually emphasized the "friendliness" of the Friendly Visit, that is, the treating of the poor simply as part of their extended circle of friends and social contacts, they were also well aware that to function as "examples" they needed to constantly distinguish themselves from the poor by exemplifying the traits of their superior class character. The Associated Charities, for example, in a leaflet they issued on "The Friendly Visitor," at first disavows the reformist instrumentalization of friendship, only to explain that the visitor should *appear* as a friend only in order to exert more effectively the "silent influence" of a social better:

> We are friendly visitors when we call upon our immediate neighbors. . . . We are not to burst upon those of our acquaintance who happen to be poor with advice, moralizing, inquisitiveness or gratuities. When we first meet them we are strangers, and must show the respect due to persons upon whom we have no claim. . . . In any case let us remember that, as nothing springs from nothing, we must ourselves be frank, courteous, patient, sensible, and really friendly, if we are to inspire like qualities in those we seek to influence. Example will do much more than preaching. What we are, and not what we do, counts most. (qtd. in Watson 150)

The "example" had long been preferred to exhortation in the building of character because it enabled the individual to form a "self-made" character through interpretive emulation rather than by simply having a derivative character "stamped" onto them through the pedagogical application of rules of conduct and moral injunctions. The friendliness of the Friendly Visit was thus often modeled on the patronizing solicitude of the parent-child relation. As Mrs. E. E. Kellogg argues in her child-raising guide, *Studies in Character Building,* "example counts far more than precept" (112):

> A constant discipline of self on the part of parents is a necessary requisite for effective work in character shaping. They must learn to become good models, for what they *are,* will teach the child far more than what they *say.* What they would build into the child's character they must themselves possess. (23)

The primary goal of the Friendly Visitor was thus not to advise the poor but rather to offer the better advice in the presentation they made of their own character. The hope of such an ennobling influence was that the poor would inculcate the traits of thrift, self-restraint, and enterprise that were taken to be the vehicles to "success." The beneficiary of such a charitable gift of character, however, was put in the position of having to deduce those traits from the manner and conduct of the charity visitor. The decorum of the Friendly Visitor—the cleanliness of her clothes, correctness of speech, deliberateness in conversation, and buoyancy of spirit—had to function as the ambiguous indicators of an otherwise invisible character. How the beneficiary was to deduce from the mannered performances of the visitor the practical traits of character that would uplift them was, of course, left as an uncertain but by no means less necessary feat of interpretation.

The purpose of the Friendly Visit was to provide a positive example of successful, middle-class character in order if not to lift them out of their condition at least to assign them responsibility for that condition, and not to dictate the terms of character and success that would lift the poor out of their impoverished condition.[9] Jane Addams's innovations as a reformer and social theorist, however, derive from her ability to appropriate the power of emulation in class contact and to extricate it from the "individualist" rhetoric of "self-making" and character formation. Addams and Ellen Gates Starr opened Hull-House fully prepared to display the ennobling trappings of their class. When they moved into the mansion originally built by Charles J. Hull but later surrounded by the encroaching tenements of a growing Chicago, they sought to restore the house as an emblem of their own class character:

> We furnished the house as we would have furnished it were it in another part of the city, with the photographs and other impedimenta we had collected in Europe. . . . While all the new furniture which was bought was enduring in quality, we were careful to keep it in character with the fine old residence. . . . We believed that the Settlement may logically bring to its aid all those adjuncts which the cultivated man regards as good and suggestive of the best life of the past. (Addams, *Twenty Years* 66)

But while Addams avowed her missionary role as representative of "cultivated man," she also did so by remobilizing the possibilities of reciprocal exchange over the top-down transmission of culture possible in the performances of class character: "Hull-House was soberly opened on the theory that the dependence of classes on each other is reciprocal; and that the social relation is essentially a reciprocal relation, it gives a form of expression that has peculiar value" (Addams, *Twenty Years* 64).

In the chapter "Charitable Effort" of *Democracy and Social Ethics*, Addams works through what recognition of such a "reciprocal" relation of class contact would mean through a detailed analysis of the Friendly Visit. Addams's account of the corrosive effects of the Friendly Visit on the poor it presumably serves, unlike more contemporary critiques of social welfare, indicts rather than affirms the rhetoric of character that operates through it. For while Addams seizes on the character-forming function of the Friendly Visit, she also seeks to transform it from an instrument of class and ethnic domination into one of reciprocal recognition. In "Charitable Effort," Addams describes a scene in which the character-building effects of class emulation have gone very much awry. Unlike the hero-worship she herself showed to the class position of her father as a child, what confounds the emulatory function of the Friendly Visit is not only a failure of the beneficiary to imitate and reflect the character of the charity worker, but more drastically the charity worker finds that she is as well a bankrupt spokesperson for the virtues of character she presumably represents:

> The daintily clad charitable visitor who steps into the little house made untidy by the vigorous efforts of her hostess, the washerwoman, is no longer sure of her superiority to the latter; she recognizes that her hostess after all represents social value and industrial use, as over against her parasitic cleanliness and a social standing attained only through status. (12)

Echoing Thorstein Veblen's critique of the empty signs of "leisure class" character, Addams details the ways that emulation breaks down as a mode of poverty relief. The daintily clad "young college woman, well-bred and open-minded" (12), who visits the poor family certainly signifies the characteristics of her class, but what thwarts the emulatory function is the emptiness of her signifiers of character as practical guides for the family she visits. The "messages" the charity worker is to send through the example of her own character are the "industrial virtues" that the modern class distinction between "people who work with their hands and those who do not" prevents her from having: "As she daily holds up these standards, it occurs to the mind of the sensitive visitor . . . that she has no right to say these things; that her untrained hands are no more fitted to cope with actual conditions than those of her broken-down family" (13).

Not only is the Friendly Visitor unable to exemplify the "industrial virtues" that would help the family advance to a more secure economic position; she also fails to exemplify the "successful" character of her own middle-class background. Indeed, what Addams shows is that the emulatory function is fundamentally undercut by the very gesture of charity itself, for the visitor's charity is not representative of the self-interest characteristic of her class: "Success does not ordinarily go, in the minds of the poor, with charity and kind-heartedness, but rather with the opposite qualities. The rich landlord is he who collects with sternness, who accepts no excuse, and will have his own" (15). The charity worker is thus stuck in a bind of sympathetic identification while also maintaining her role as recriminatory class exemplar. She is drawn into the no man's land of a failed identification with the poor and a failed identification with her own class, a failure signaled by the lack of emulatory "respect":

> The charity visitor, just because she is a person who concerns herself with the poor, receives a certain amount of this good-natured and kindly contempt, sometimes real affection, but little genuine respect. The poor are accustomed to help each other and to respond accordingly to their kindliness; but when it comes to worldly judgment, they use industrial success as the sole standard. In the case of the charity visitor who has neither natural kindness nor dazzling riches, they are deprived of both standards, and they find it of course utterly impossible to judge of the motive of organized charity. (16)

More ominous still, the breakdown of class emulation in the Friendly Visit transforms it from a vehicle of poverty relief into an instrument of impoverishment. The Friendly Visitor asserts "industrial virtues" she herself does not represent, and these "virtues" of "industry and "self-denial" serve to embed her recipients in the conditions of poverty they seek to relieve. The visitor "feels the sordidness of constantly being obliged to urge the industrial view of life" (18) because such a view seeks to reconcile and "adjust" the working classes to their industrial lives rather than transforming the "wearing and brutalizing" conditions of their "unceasing bodily toil" (12). The charity relation thus functions, in its demand for a class mobility its system of character stewardship actively undermines, as a kind of disciplining technology for maintaining and policing the working classes in their poverty under the pretense of "bettering" them. As Addams says of the "bruised and battered" man "chilled" by his encounter with the Friendly Visitor: "He does not recognize the disciplinary aspect of the situation" (16).

Addams's attack on the disciplining aspects of character building that operate through the Friendly Visit should not be taken, however, as a wholesale rejection of the democratic possibilities of class emulation. Addams's goal in charting the failings of the charity relation as a method of poverty relief is to put its system of class emulation back on a securely democratic footing. As she makes clear in *Twenty Years at Hull-House,* the social exchanges that transpire through character emulation are vital to a democratic society:

> Morality certainly develops far earlier in the form of moral fact than in the form of moral ideas, and it is obvious that ideas only operate upon the popular mind through will and character, and must be dramatized before they reach the mass of men. . . . Ethics as well as political opinions may be discussed and disseminated among the sophisticated by lectures and printed pages, but to the common people they can only come through example—through a personality which seizes the popular imagination. . . . The personal example promptly rouses to emulation. (100–101)

What derails the democratizing power of character emulation, however, is when it is throttled by the specular logic of self-reflection and self-making. What derails the class contact of the charity relation, in other words, is the expectation by the Friendly Visitor that in order to steward character she needs to see herself reflected in the poor that she serves. As the young Addams very quickly learned, such "tributes" are exactly what thwart a social engagement with the other *as such.* Only in situations of contact with one's social others who do not demand of them that they reflect or emulate one's own character, does emulation have the power to fully democratize the civic sphere. Such a "democracy" depends, Addams contends, on the recognition that character is a medium of social exchange rather than a measure of social merit. Such a democracy depends on the renunciation of character itself:

> When the entire moral energy of an individual goes into the cultivation of personal integrity, we all know how unlovely the result may become; the character is upright, of course, but too coated over with the result of its own endeavor to be attractive. In this effort toward a higher morality in our social relations, we must demand that the individual shall be willing to lose the sense of personal achievement, and shall be content to realize his activity only in connection with the activity of the many. (Addams, *Twenty Years* 120)

Words as Deeds

Jane Addams forged a distinctively new role for women's charity work and for social reform more broadly. Addams saw in the charity relation an opportunity to "relieve" poverty and also an opportunity to realize the radically democratic potentials of its cross-cultural exchanges. She parlayed women's constricted role as stewards of character into a sustained critique of Gilded Age notions of character and a critical practice of social reform of unparalleled scope, efficacy, and impact. And she did all of this by simply creating a unique and indeterminate space for social contact between individuals from a wide variety of ideological backgrounds, cultural traditions, classes, professions, genders, and sexualities. In theorizing this scene of pluralist contact, however, Addams was admittedly and often frustratingly vague as to how it produced the spectacular results that it did, and in particular, what exactly it meant for an individual to engage with it.

Addams does make one important and very telling statement about how such a social ethic was realized, a statement that also articulates the interconnections between her work as a social theorist and her work as a social reformer. In *Democracy and Social Ethics,* Addams offers an easily overlooked yet informative example of the development of the social ethic. In the introduction, Addams gives two examples of cultural locations where the social ethic was currently being fostered. The first example is the "Newspaper" that, with its "frank reflection of popular demand" and "omnivorous curiosity equally insistent upon the trivial and the important," makes way in a populist form for "the first dawn of social consciousness" (8). The second example she cites is "Literature." Literature (or more specifically the "novel") is a vehicle of the social ethic because its presentation of a "wide reading of human life" is "a preparation for better social adjustment—for the remedying of social ills" (8). Literature, she argues, breaks the "insensibility and hardness" of the individualist ethic, an ethic that "is due to the lack of imagination which prevents a realization of the experiences of other people" (8). Literature's staging of scenes of social contact and its evocation of literary character thus make it an "imaginative" realm generative of the social ethic.

Addams's use of the term "imagination" as the key faculty for apprehending cultural diversity echoes, in a very telling way, with another crucial and previously discussed moment of the introduction. When Addams opens the introduction with an account of the "maladjusted" and "unhappy" "men and women," her delineation of what plagues "them" and of what "they" desire from the social ethic takes place from the comfortable distance of the third-person narrative perspective. She thus unfolds the tale of "their" unhappiness from a distant, observing, analytical perspective, noting the causes and conditions of their unhappiness with detachment and professional acumen. She records the facts but, following the common narrative convention, makes herself invisible as a narrating character. All of this changes, however, at the moment when she "imagines" how these men and women might express "their" own sense of the social ethic:

> These men and women have realized this [the value of "contact with the moral experiences of the many"] and have disclosed the fact in their eagerness for a wider acquaintance with and participation in the life about them. They believe that experience gives the easy and trustworthy impulse toward right action in the broad as well as in the narrow relations. We may indeed imagine many of them saying: "Cast our experiences in a larger mold if our lives are to be animated by the larger so-

> cial aims. We have met the obligations of family life . . . and we see no other way in which to prepare ourselves for the larger social duties." Such a demand is reasonable, for by our daily experiences we have discovered that we cannot mechanically hold up a moral standard. . . . We are thus brought to a conception of Democracy not merely as a sentiment which desires the well-being of all men, nor yet as a creed which believes in the essential dignity and equality of all men, but as that which affords a rule for living as well as a test of faith. (6–7)

In the overall trajectory of her argument this moment is a crucial one, as Addams moves from a diagnosis of the concept of "maladjustment" to the thesis on its resolution through a democratizing social ethic. More importantly, this moment is also marked by a definitive transition in narrative perspective, as the third-person perspective of her description of "these men and women" and their pursuit of a diverse and broad range of social experiences shifts by the end of the paragraph to the first person (plural) perspective of a narrating "we." It is a "we," moreover, that remains both the subject as well as the source of narration for the rest of the introduction.

The introduction of this "we" thus complicates the argument by implicating Addams herself in the actions and realizations of the "men and women" she's describing, and also by the same gesture extending that process to include the reader as well. And just in case this shift is mistaken for an arbitrary rhetorical flourish, Addams's brief "Prefatory Note" is clear to underscore the stakes of this narrative shift. After explaining in the "Prefatory Note" that the chapters of *Democracy and Social Ethics* had originally been given as a series of lectures, Addams goes on to note that

> [i]n putting them [the lectures] into the form of a book, no attempt has been made to change the somewhat informal style used in speaking. The "we" and "us" which originally referred to the speaker and her audience are merely extended to possible readers. (3)

It is a strange offer, this "extended" offer of the "we," an offer virtually no author *explicitly* gives and yet reading so often assumes. In extending this "we" explicitly to a reader who may or may not feel the interpellative force of the narrative perspective, Addams asserts a kind of textual community with "these men and women," herself, and her "possible readers," modeled on the speech scene of the spoken lecture.

While this assertion and hailing of the reading subject could be explained as the act of a "pragmatist" writer concerned that her texts and ideas find their mark in the shared concerns of a "real" audience, Addams's shift does more than simply exemplify pragmatist writing practices. Her shift exemplifies the kind of complex scene of alterity and imagination required of the social ethic, and does so in two ways. First, Addams's shift from a discussion of "they" to a discussion of "we" demonstrates how the collectivity of such a "we" depends on a retention of the distinctiveness of its members even as they are subsumed by a collective speaking voice. A collective and self-announcing "we," Addams's narrative suggests, finds expression only by "imagining" what "they" might be "saying" ("We may indeed imagine many of them saying: '. . .' "). The narrator who speaks of "them," furthermore, can invoke the "we" only through an imaginative act in which "they" are no longer narratively represented but "imagined" to speak in their own voice. And yet "they," one might be inclined to argue, do not *really* speak, for their speech is being "imagined" by the "we." Yet because "they," in being imagined, thereby become members of the "we," "they" too are "imagining" what "they" are saying, that is, they are "really" speaking. "They" authentically come to speech, in other words, through the collective voice of the "we" but only if they are simultaneously "imagined" as speakers distinct from that "we."

Second, Addams asserts a vision of collectivity comprised of a complex amalgam of "real" and "textual" characters. Her "men and women" are textual characters who enable the speaker, Jane Addams, to invoke a "we" in relation to herself and her presumably "real" though no more easily locatable "possible readers." More importantly, in order to legitimate the collective assertion of the book's central claims, Addams must take up a position within the text as a textual character defined in relation to the thoughts and feelings of the text's own "men and women." The "we" that dominates and narrates the rest of the introduction ("We are learning . . ." "We have come . . ." "We do not believe . . ." We realize, too . . .") can assert the central theses of the book ("We are thus brought to a conception of Democracy . . .") only by making itself but not only itself the object of that narration. Addams can, in other words, assert her textual claims only by herself becoming, in a sense, a textual character who both describes and is being described by the text. Addams thus presents through the narrative development of her "theory" a model of social contact and its complex reorganization of the boundaries and identifications of character. For a theorist whose deeds at Hull-House and as a social reformer have garnered vastly more attention than her theoretical writings, such a presentation is an important reminder that words are not simply servants to the deeds of social reform but rather are the necessary social bodies through which such deeds can themselves transpire.

Notes

1. It is difficult here to summarize Jane Addams's diverse and far-reaching accomplishments as a social reformer, policy maker, community organizer, government inspector, informal presidential advisor, and coalition builder. For a comprehensive but relatively concise overview of Addams's diverse body of work as a social reformer, see Robyn Muncy, *Creating a Female Dominion in American Reform, 1890–1935*, 3–37. The most recent book-length study of Addams's unique brand of social reform is Jean Bethke Elshtain, *Jane Addams and the Dream of American Democracy: A Life.* For an excellent historiographical account of Addams's use of interpersonal and communal performance within the complex civic and domestic geography of Hull-House, see Shannon Jackson, *Lines of Activity: Performance, Historiography, Hull-House Domesticity.*

2. For a more detailed account of Addams's impact specifically on "women's and children's issues," see Ladd-Taylor (110–26).

3. For an excellent account of the role of gender and sexuality in the founding of "character-building agencies," see David I. Macleod, *Building Character in the American Boy: The Boy Scouts, YMCA, and Their Forerunners, 1870–1920*, 44–59. See also Gail Bederman, *Manliness and Civilization: A Cultural History of Gender and Race in the United States, 1880–1917*.

4. Jean Bethke Elshtain, for example, begins her account of Addams's life and work with just such an autobiographical reiteration: "John Addams's deep civic involvement clearly influenced his daughter's development. . . . To his precocious, civic-minded daughter, he was a figure to admire and to emulate" (2).

5. For a full account of such jarring "discoveries" of poverty, see Robert H. Bremner, *From the Depths: The Discovery of Poverty in the United States.*

6. "Subjective Necessity for Social Settlements" was a lecture republished as chapter six in *Twenty Years at Hull-House*, and "Filial Relations" appears as chapter two in *Democracy and Social Ethics*.

7. See Jane Addams, "The Objective Value of a Social Settlement," originally published with "Subjective Necessity" in Henry C. Adams, ed., *Philanthropy and Social Progress*.

8. The Friendly Visit, in other words, targeted what Lori Merish in her essay in this volume, citing Mary Poovey, describes as the "poverty" *and* the "pauperism" of the poor.

9. Toynbee Hall, the settlement in England that provided the original model for the Hull-House Settlement, was much more explicitly founded on the aesthetic and civilizing promise of class contact. The group of middle-class men who decided to live among the poor in London's East End made it their mission to expose "the poor" to the art, literature, and philosophy presumably denied to them by their class position: "The poor need more than food; they need also the knowledge, the character, the happiness which are the gifts of God to this Age." Samuel Barnett, "Twenty-One Years of University Settlements," *Practicable Socialism*, London, 1915, 165. Qtd. in Allen F. Davis, *Spearheads for Reform: The Social Settlements and the Progressive Movement, 1890–1914*, 7. For a more thorough account of such a "cultural philanthropy" in the United States, see Helen Lefkowitz Horowitz, *Culture and the City: Cultural Philanthropy in Chicago from the 1880s to 1917*.

Works Cited

Addams, Jane. *Democracy and Social Ethics*. 1902. Urbana: U of Illinois P, 2002.

———. "The Objective Value of a Social Settlement." *Philanthropy and Social Progress, Seven Essays by Miss Jane Addams, Robert A. Woods, Father J. O. S. Huntington, Professor Franklin H. Giddings and Bernard Bosanquet*. 1893. *The Jane Addams Reader*. Ed. Jean Bethke Elshtain. New York: Basic Books, 2002. 29–45.

———. "Social Attitudes and Character." *Building Character: Proceedings of the Mid-West Conference on Character Development, February, 1928*. 291–95.

———. *Twenty Years at Hull-House*. 1910. New York: Penguin, 1998.

Beard, George M. *American Nervousness: Its Causes and Consequences*. New York, 1881.

Bederman, Gail. *Manliness and Civilization: A Cultural History of Gender and Race in the United States, 1880–1917*. Chicago: U of Chicago P, 1995.

Beecher, Catharine. *A Treatise on Domestic Economy*. 1841. New York: Schocken Books, 1977.

Bremner, Robert H. *American Philanthropy*. 2nd ed. Chicago: U of Chicago P, 1988.

———. *From the Depths: The Discovery of Poverty in the United States*. New York: New York UP, 1956.

Chicago Association for Child Study and Parent Education. *Building Character: Proceedings of the Mid-West Conference on Character Development, February, 1928*. Chicago: U of Chicago P, 1928.

Conway, Jill. "Women Reformers and American Culture, 1870–1930." *Journal of Social History* 5.2 (Winter 1971–72): 164–77.

Davis, Allen F. *American Heroine: The Life and Legend of Jane Addams.* Chicago: Ivan R. Dee, 2000.

———. *Spearheads for Reform: The Social Settlements and the Progressive Movement, 1890–1914.* New York: Oxford UP, 1967.

Edgarton, Sarah C. "Female Culture." *Mother's Assistant, vol. 3.* 1843. *Antebellum American Culture.* Ed. David Brion Davis. University Park: Pennsylvania State UP, 1979. 76–77.

Elshtain, Jean Bethke. *Jane Addams and the Dream of American Democracy: A Life.* New York: Basic Books, 2002.

Horowitz, Helen Lefkowitz. *Culture and the City: Cultural Philanthropy in Chicago from the 1880s to 1917.* Lexington: UP of Kentucky, 1976.

Jackson, Shannon. *Lines of Activity: Performance, Historiography, Hull-House Domesticity.* Ann Arbor: U of Michigan P, 2000.

Katz, Michael B. *In the Shadow of the Poorhouse: A Social History of Welfare in America.* New York: Basic Books, 1986.

Kellogg, Mrs. E. E. *Studies in Character Building: A Book for Parents.* Battle Creek: Good Health Publishing, 1905.

Ladd-Taylor, Molly. "Hull House Goes to Washington: Women and the Children's Bureau." *Gender, Class, Race, and Reform in the Progressive Era.* Ed. Noralee Frankel and Nancy S. Dye. Lexington: UP of Kentucky, 1991. 110–26.

Macleod, David I. *Building Character in the American Boy: The Boy Scouts, YMCA, and Their Forerunners, 1870–1920.* Madison: U of Wisconsin P, 1983.

McCarthy, Kathleen D. *Noblesse Oblige: Charity and Cultural Philanthropy in Chicago, 1849–1929.* Chicago: U of Chicago P, 1982.

Muncy, Robyn. *Creating a Female Dominion in American Reform, 1890–1935.* New York: Oxford UP, 1991.

Nearing, Scott. *Social Adjustment.* New York: Macmillan, 1910.

Riis, Jacob A. *How the Other Half Lives: Studies among the Tenements of New York.* 1890. New York: Dover Publications, 1971.

Todd, John. *The Daughter at School.* Northampton: Hopkins, Bridgman, and Company, 1854.

Watson, Frank Dekker. *The Charity Organization Movement in the United States: A Study in American Philanthropy.* New York: Macmillan, 1922.

Selected Bibliography

Addams, Jane. *Democracy and Social Ethics.* 1902. Urbana: U of Illinois P, 2002.

———. *The Spirit of Youth and the City Streets.* New York: Macmillan, 1909.

———. *Twenty Years at Hull-House.* 1910. New York: Penguin, 1998.

Anstruther, Eva. "Ebb and Flow." *Harper's New Monthly Magazine* 89.530 (July 1894): 219–21.

Arthur, T[imothy]. S[hea]. *The Seamstress. A Tale of the Times.* Philadelphia: R. G. Berford, 1843.

Bercovici, Konrad. *Crimes of Charity.* New York: Knopf, 1917.

Boydston, Jeanne. *Home and Work: Housework, Wages, and the Ideology of Labor in the Early Republic.* New York: Oxford UP, 1990.

Brackney, William H. *Christian Volunteerism in Britain and North America.* Westport: Greenwood Press, 1995.

"Bread upon the Waters: A Sketch from Life." *Ladies' Repository* 27.8 (August 1867): 462–64.

Bremner, Robert H. *American Philanthropy.* 2nd ed. Chicago: U of Chicago P, 1988.

———. *From the Depths: The Discovery of Poverty in the United States.* New York: New York UP, 1956.

Brownson, Orestes. *Defense of the Article on the Laboring Classes.* Boston: William H. Greene, 1840.

———. *The Laboring Classes.* New York: Elton's, 1840.

Carey, Mathew. *Letters on the Condition of the Poor.* Philadelphia: Haswell and Barrington, 1835.

———. *Miscellaneous Essays.* Philadelphia: Carey and Hart, 1830.

———. "A Plea for the Poor." *The Jacksonians on the Poor: Collected Pamphlets.* New York: Arno Press, 1971.

Carlin, Deborah. "'What Methods Have Brought Blessing': Discourses of Reform in Philanthropic Literature." *The (Other) American Traditions: Nineteenth-Century Women Writers.* Ed. Joyce W. Warren. New Brunswick: Rutgers UP, 1993. 203–25.

Channing, Walter. "An Address on the Prevention of Pauperism." *The Jacksonians on the Poor: Collected Pamphlets.* New York: Arno Press, 1971.

Cheal, David. *The Gift Economy.* New York: Routledge, 1988.

Conway, Jill. "Women Reformers and American Culture, 1870–1930." *Journal of Social History* 5.2 (Winter 1971–72): 164–77.

Crocker, Ruth. "Unsettling Perspectives: The Settlement Movement, the Rhetoric of Social History, and the Search for Synthesis." *Contesting the Master Narrative: Essays in Social History.* Ed. Jeffery Cox and Shelton Stromquist. Iowa City: U of Iowa P, 1998.

Davis, Allen F. *Spearheads for Reform: The Social Settlements and the Progressive Movement, 1890–1914.* New York: Oxford UP, 1967.

Davis, Rebecca Harding. "Life in the Iron Mills." 1861. New York: Feminist Press, 1982.

———. *Margret Howth: A Story of To-Day.* 1861–62. New York: Feminist Press, 1990.

De Koven Bowen, Louise. *The Department Store Girl: Based on Interviews with 200 Girls.* Chicago: Juvenile Protective Association of Chicago, 1911.

Dodge, Mary Mapes. "Sunday Afternoon in a Poor-House." 1876. *Nineteenth-Century American Women Writers: An Anthology.* Ed. Karen L. Kilcup. Cambridge: Blackwell, 1997. 243–46.

Donovan, Josephine. *New England Local Color Literature: A Woman's Tradition.* New York: Ungar, 1983.

Eiselein, Gregory. *Literature and Humanitarian Reform in the Civil War Era.* Bloomington: Indiana UP, 1996.

Fern, Fanny [Sara Parton]. "A Bit of Injustice." *Ruth Hall and Other Writings.* Ed. Joyce W. Warren. New Brunswick: Rutgers UP, 1990. 318.

———. *Ruth Hall and Other Writings.* Ed. Joyce W. Warren. New Brunswick: Rutgers UP, 1990

Fetterley, Judith, and Marjorie Pryse. *Writing out of Place: Regionalism, Women, and American Literary Culture.* Urbana: U of Illinois P, 2003.

Field, Mrs. H. M. "A Queer Mistake." *Overland Monthly and Out West Magazine* 14.5 (May 1875): 407–18.

Follen, Eliza Lee Cabot. *Sketches of Married Life.* 1838. Rev. ed. Boston: William Crosby and H. P. Nichols, 1847.

Foner, Philip S. *Women and the American Labor Movement: From the First Trade Unions to the Present.* New York: The Free Press, 1982.

Freeman, Mary E. Wilkins. *The Best Stories of Mary E. Wilkins.* Ed. Henry Wysham Lanier. New York: Harper, 1927.

———. "A Gentle Ghost." *Harpers New Monthly Magazine* 79.471 (August 1889): 366–73.

———. *A Humble Romance and Other Stories.* New York: Harper, 1887.

———. *Mary E. Wilkins Freeman: A New England Nun and Other Stories.* Ed. Sandra Zagarell. New York: Penguin, 2000.

———. *Pembroke.* 1894. New Haven: College and University P, 1971.

——. *Selected Stories of Mary E. Wilkins Freeman.* Ed. Marjorie Pryse. New York: Norton, 1983.

Gandal, Keith. *The Virtues of the Vicious: Jacob Riis, Stephen Crane, and the Spectacle of the Slum.* New York: Oxford UP, 1997.

Gaskell, Elizabeth. *North and South.* 1854–55. London: Penguin, 1986.

George, Henry. *Progress and Poverty.* 1879. New York: Robert Schalkenbach Foundation, 1955.

Ginzberg, Lori D. *Women and the Work of Benevolence: Morality, Politics, and Class in the Nineteenth-Century United States.* New Haven: Yale UP, 1990.

Glasser, Leah Blatt. *In a Closet Hidden: The Life and Work of Mary E. Wilkins Freeman.* Amherst: U of Massachusetts P, 1996.

Gurteen, Humphreys. *A Handbook of Charity Organizations.* Buffalo: Published by the Author, 1882.

Hapke, Laura. *Tales of the Working Girl: Wage-Earning Women in American Literature, 1890–1925.* New York: Twayne Publishers, 1992.

Harper, Frances E. W. *Iola Leroy, or Shadows Uplifted.* 1892. New York: Oxford UP, 1988.

Harris, Sharon M. *Rebecca Harding Davis and American Realism.* Philadelphia: U of Pennsylvania P, 1991.

Harvey, David. *The Urban Experience.* Baltimore: Johns Hopkins UP, 1989.

Herbert, Miss M. J. "Poor-House Jan." *Ladies' Repository* 9.4 (April 1872): 248–52.

Hobson, Barbara. *Uneasy Virtue: The Politics of Prostitution and the American Reform Tradition.* New York: Basic Books, 1987.

Hofstadter, Richard. *Social Darwinism in American Thought.* Boston: Beacon, 1944.

Hopkinson, Corinne Aldrich. "The Three Marys of Sharpsville." *Atlantic Monthly* 31.188 (June 1873): 663–69.

Horowitz, Helen Lefkowitz. *Culture and the City: Cultural Philanthropy in Chicago from the 1880s to 1917.* Lexington: UP of Kentucky, 1976.

Jewett, Sarah Orne. *"The Country of the Pointed Firs" and Other Stories.* New York: Doubleday, 1989.

——. *The Uncollected Short Stories of Sarah Orne Jewett.* Ed. and Intro. Richard Cary. Waterville: Colby College P, 1971.

Katz, Michael B. *In the Shadow of the Poorhouse: A Social History of Welfare in America.* New York: Basic Books, 1986.

——. *Poverty and Policy in American History.* New York: Academic Press, 1983.

Lasseter, Janice Milner, and Sharon M. Harris, eds. *Rebecca Harding Davis: Writing Cultural Autobiography.* Nashville: Vanderbilt UP, 2001.

Laurie, Bruce. *Working People of Philadelphia, 1800–1850.* Philadelphia: Temple UP, 1980.

Lee, Hannah Farnham Sawyer. *Elinor Fulton.* Boston: Whipple and Damrell, 1837.

——. *Rosanna, or Scenes in Boston.* Cambridge: John Owen, 1839.

——. *Three Experiments of Living.* Boston: Wm. S. Damrell, 1837.

Long, Lisa A. "Imprisoned in/at Home: Criminal Culture in Rebecca Harding Davis' *Margret Howth: A Story of To-day.*" *Arizona Quarterly* 54.2 (1998): 65–98.

——. "The Postbellum Reform Writings of Rebecca Harding Davis and Elizabeth

Stuart Phelps." *The Cambridge Companion to Nineteenth-Century American Women's Writing.* Ed. Dale M. Bauer and Philip Gould. Cambridge: Cambridge UP, 2001. 262–83.

Loughead, Flora Haines. "Sealskin Annie." *Overland Monthly and Out West Magazine* 16.91 (July 1890): 44–49.

Lowell, Josephine Shaw. *Public Relief and Private Charity.* 1884. New York: Arno Press, 1971.

Lynn, Lizzie. "Dependence: Or What Made One Woman Meanly Penurious." *The Una: A Paper Devoted to the Elevation of Women* 1.3 (April 1, 1853): 33–34.

Martin, George Madden. "Rights of Man." *Harper's Monthly Magazine* 106.633 (February 1903): 416–33.

McCarthy, Kathleen D. *Noblesse Oblige: Charity and Cultural Philanthropy in Chicago, 1849–1929.* Chicago: U of Chicago P, 1982.

Montgomery, David. "Wage Labor, Bondage, and Citizenship in Nineteenth-Century America." *International Labor and Working-Class History* 48.6 (Fall 1995): 6–27.

Muncy, Robyn. *Creating a Female Dominion in American Reform, 1890–1935.* New York: Oxford UP, 1991.

Parker, Pamela Corpron. "Fictional Philanthropy in Elizabeth Gaskell's *Mary Barton* and *North and South.*" *Victorian Literature and Culture* 25 (1997): 321–31.

Peiss, Kathy. *Cheap Amusements: Working Women and Leisure in Turn-of-the-Century New York.* Philadelphia: Temple UP, 1986.

Pfaelzer, Jean. *Parlor Radical: Rebecca Harding Davis and the Origins of American Social Realism.* Pittsburgh: U of Pittsburgh P, 1996.

Phelps, Elizabeth Stuart. *Chapters from a Life.* Boston: Houghton, Mifflin, 1900.

———. *Hedged In.* Boston: Fields, Osgood, and Co., 1870.

———. "The Tenth of January." 1868. *The Silent Partner and "The Tenth of January."* New York: Feminist Press, 1983. 305–51.

Polacheck, Hilda Satt. *I Came a Stranger: The Story of a Hull-House Girl.* Ed. Dena J. Polacheck Epstein. Urbana and Chicago: U of Illinois P, 1989.

Pumphrey, Ralph E., and Muriel, W., eds. *The History of American Social Work: Readings in Its Philosophical and Institutional Development.* New York: Columbia UP, 1961.

Richmond, Mary E. *Friendly Visiting among the Poor: A Handbook for Charity Workers.* 1899. Montclair: Patterson Smith, 1969.

Riis, Jacob A. *How the Other Half Lives: Studies among the Tenements of New York.* 1890. New York: Dover Publications, 1971.

Rosen, Ruth. *The Lost Sisterhood: Prostitution in America, 1900–1918.* Baltimore: Johns Hopkins UP, 1982.

Rothman, David J. *The Discovery of the Asylum: Social Order and Disorder in the New Republic.* Boston: Little, Brown, 1971.

Rousmaniere, John P. "Cultural Hybrid in the Slums: The College Woman and the Settlement House, 1889–1894." *American Quarterly* 22 (1970): 45–66.

Ryan, Susan M. *The Grammar of Good Intentions: Race and the Antebellum Culture of Benevolence.* Ithaca: Cornell UP, 2003.

———. "Misgivings: Melville, Race, and the Ambiguities of Benevolence." *American Literary History* 12.4 (Winter 2000): 685–712.

Sáez, Barbara J. "The Discourse of Philanthropy in Nineteenth-Century America." *American Transcendental Quarterly* 11.3 (September 1997): 163–70.

Sander, Kathleen Waters. *The Business of Charity: The Woman's Exchange Movement, 1832–1900*. Urbana: U of Illinois P, 1998.

Scott, Anne Firor. *Natural Allies: Women's Associations in American History.* Urbana: U of Illinois P, 1993.

Searing, Annie E. P. "Mandy's Baby." *New England Magazine* 20.1 (March 1896): 15–21.

Sedgwick, Catharine Maria. *The Poor Rich Man, and The Rich Poor Man.* 1836. New York: Harper and Bros., 1868.

Spofford, Harriet Prescott. "Miss Moggaridge's Provider." *Atlantic Monthly* 27.159 (January 1871): 17–27.

Stansell, Christine. *City of Women: Sex and Class in New York, 1789–1860*. Urbana: U of Illinois P, 1987.

Stray Leaves from a Seamstress. The Una: A Paper Devoted to the Elevation of Women 1.4 (May 2, 1853); 2.3 (March 1854).

Sumner, William Graham. *What Social Classes Owe to Each Other.* 1883. Caldwell: Caxton, 1989.

Thanet, Octave. "The Indoor Pauper: A Study." *Atlantic Monthly* 47.284 (June 1881): 749–64.

———. "The Indoor Pauper: A Study, II." *Atlantic Monthly* 48.286 (August 1881): 241–52.

Thomson, Rosemarie Garland. "Benevolent Maternalism and Physically Disabled Figures: Dilemmas and Female Embodiment in Stowe, Davis, and Phelps." *American Literature* 68 (1996): 555–86.

Tice, Karen W. *Tales of Wayward Girls and Immoral Women: Case Records and the Professionalization of Social Work.* Urbana: U of Illinois P, 1998.

Treudley, Mary Bosworth. "The 'Benevolent Fair': A Study of Charitable Organization among American Women in the First Third of the Nineteenth Century." *Compassion and Responsibility: Readings in the History of Social Welfare Policy in the United States.* Ed. Frank R. Breul and Steven J. Diner. Chicago: U of Chicago P, 1980. 132–45.

Trattner, Walter I. *From Poor Law to Welfare State: A History of Social Welfare in America.* New York: The Free Press, 1994.

Van Etten, Ida M. "Working Women." *North American Review* 144.364 (March 1887): 312–16.

A Working Girl. "Among the Rose Roots." *Harper's New Monthly Magazine* 66.391 (December 1882): 105–11.

Warner, Amos G. *American Charities: A Study in Philanthropy and Economics.* New Brunswick: Transaction, 1989.

Warren, Joyce W. "Fracturing Gender: Woman's Economic Independence." *Nineteenth-Century American Women Writers: A Critical Reader.* Ed. Karen L. Kilcup. Malden, Mass.: Blackwell, 1998. 146–63.

Watson, Frank Dekker. *The Charity Organization Movement in the United States: A Study in American Philanthropy.* New York: Macmillan, 1922.

Wenocur, Stanley, and Michael Reisch. *From Charity to Enterprise: The Development of American Social Work in a Market Economy.* Urbana: U of Illinois P, 1989.

Woodroofe, Kathleen. *From Charity to Social Work in England and the United States.* London: Routledge and Kegan Paul, 1968.

Wright, Conrad Edick. *The Transformation of Charity in Postrevolutionary New England.* Boston: Northeastern UP, 1992.

Contributors

Jill Bergman is an associate professor of English at the University of Montana. She has published on William Faulkner, Charlotte Perkins Gilman, and Pauline Hopkins, and is currently at work on a book on motherhood and nationalism in the work of Pauline Hopkins.

Debra Bernardi is an associate professor in the Department of Languages and Literature at Carroll College in Helena, Montana. Her work on domestic and gothic fiction by American women has appeared in several publications, including *Separate Spheres No More,* edited by Monika Elbert, and the journal *Legacy.* She also writes movie and television reviews for the Helena paper *Queen City News.*

Sarah E. Chinn teaches American literature at Hunter College, CUNY. This essay is adapted from her book in progress, *New Americans, New Identities: The Children of Immigrants and the Redefinition of Adolescence, 1890–1925.* She is also the author of *Technology and the Logic of American Racism: A Cultural History of the Body as Evidence* (2000).

Monika Elbert, Associate Editor of the *Nathaniel Hawthorne Review,* is Professor of English at Montclair State University. She has published widely on Hawthorne as well as on other nineteenth-century American writers. Her recent work includes essays on Hawthorne and the feminization of history and on Catharine Beecher's influence on Charlotte Perkins Gilman.

Lori Merish teaches in the English Department at Georgetown University. The author of *Sentimental Materialism: Gender, Commodity Culture, and 19th-Century American Literature* (Duke UP, 2000), she is completing a book titled *Laboring Women and the Languages of Class: Sex, Race, and U.S. Working-class Women's Cultures, 1830–1860*.

Terry D. Novak is an associate professor of English at Johnson and Wales University in Providence, Rhode Island. Her research focuses on race and gender issues in the writings of nineteenth-century American women writers.

James Salazar is an assistant professor of English at Temple University. He has published in *American Quarterly* and has a forthcoming essay in *Leviathan: A Journal of Melville Studies*. He is currently completing a book manuscript titled *Bodies of Reform: The Rhetoric of Character in Gilded-Age America*.

Mary Templin teaches in the University Honors Program at the University of Toledo. She is currently working on a book about women's antebellum panic fiction and has published essays in *Legacy* and *Centennial Review*.

Karen Tracey is an associate professor of English and Coordinator of Writing Programs at the University of Northern Iowa. She is the author of *Plots and Proposals: American Women's Fiction, 1850–1890*, and a co-author of *The Craft of Argument with Readings*.

Whitney A. Womack is an assistant professor of English and an affiliate in Women's Studies and Black World Studies at Miami University, Hamilton campus. She has published articles and biographical entries on nineteenth-century British and American women writers, including Harriet Beecher Stowe, Elizabeth Gaskell, Elizabeth Siddal, and Margaret Sackville.

Index